BABA OF KARO

BABA OF KARO IN 1949

BABA OF KARO

A Woman of the Muslim Hausa

MARY F. SMITH

Introduction and Notes by
M. G. SMITH

Foreword by
HILDA KUPER

91 - 1972

NEW HAVEN AND LONDON
YALE UNIVERSITY PRESS

First published 1954 in the United
Kingdom by Faber & Faber Ltd., London.
First published 1964 in the United States of
America by Praeger Publishers, New York.

Printed in the United States of America

Library of Congress Cataloging in Publication Data

Baba, of Karo, 1877–1951.
  Baba of Karo, a woman of the Muslim Hausa.

  Originally published: New York: Praeger, 1964.
With new introd.
  Includes index.
  1. Baba, of Karo, 1877–1951. 2. Hausas—Social
life and customs. 3. Hausas—Biography. I. Smith,
Mary Felice, 1924–   II. Title.
DT515.45.H38B323   1981   966.9 [B]   81-40433
ISBN 0-300-02734-6   AACR2
ISBN 0-300-02741-9 (pbk.)

10 9 8 7 6 5 4 3

CONTENTS

ILLUSTRATIONS

FOREWORD

I feel privileged to have been asked to write a foreword to *Baba of Karo* which I initially enjoyed reading soon after its publication in 1954. Few books withstand the test of time, particularly in this era of artificially induced production, and even then a second reading is often tedious—events lose their novelty and characters their spontaneity. Mary Smith's *Baba* is an exception: it is an original of enduring quality.

Baba of Karo does not fall within the narrow confines of any single discipline, nor does it conform to a conventional academic or literary genre. It is not a historical reconstruction of a dead past, or a comprehensive ethnography, or a political treatise, or a feminist protest, or a book on race, colour, or creed; it is not even a straightforward autobiography. Yet it contains material and insights relevant to each of these interests and issues.

In 1949 when Mary Smith began the interviews on which this book is based, many reputable historians were contemptuous of "oral tradition"; social scientists focussed in general on the analysis of groups, deliberately ignoring, and thereby dehumanising, the individual; women's studies and other specialised studies by members of increasingly aware and critical minority status groups were not yet admitted into the academic arena. For fieldworkers, it could be described as the era P. T. (pre-tape-recording)—the notebook was the record.

Mary Smith had come to Northern Nigeria with her husband, Michael G. Smith, at the beginning of his anthropological career. The couple worked together closely, complementing each other in their interests and skills. Both became fluent in Hausa, and while he collected material from the men for his subsequent classical analysis of the histories and social systems of Northern Nigerian Emirates, Mary gathered less accessible but equally illuminating information from women in their more secluded domestic domain. Baba, an elderly and wise Hausa woman, became one of her friends and willingly responded to a request to tell the story of her life and speak of things she knew.

7

FOREWORD

Baba had the gifts of the universal storyteller—a graphic style, a feel for drama, the skill to embellish with song and verse, and an appreciation of an audience. She also had a wide range of experience, a remarkable memory, and a sense of history. In the end, Mary remained with the difficult and challenging task of translating and editing a corpus of rich material for a new public. Each stage in this process is loaded with questions: How literal should translation be? How can one best express the idiom of a culture in a foreign language? What words for which there is no conceptual equivalent must be retained without overburdening the reader? What is meaningful, and for whom? Happily, Mary Smith chose an easy conversational style and the minimum of foreign words to communicate and interpret Baba's text to others.

The story begins with a period prior to British control and carries through to after World War II. Baba died in 1951. Major political and economic changes are mirrored in her personal chronology as she moves from childhood through marriages to old age. Slavery and internecine wars and raids are part of her early life. There is a compelling authenticity in her accounts of cases of kidnapping, the taking of hostages, the giving of ransom, the exodus in face of danger, the establishment of new homes, and the essential adaptations for survival in economic and political crises. The accuracy of Baba's memory is confirmed by the material in Michael Smith's more formal introduction and by the scholarly notes on critical points in each chapter.

Baba's story is one of the most convincing validations of the value of oral history as a resource of social historians. But of course it may be difficult to find or recognise a Baba. It is in some ways easier for the anthropologist living with the people, who is immersed in the culture and for whom the spoken text based on knowledge of the language has long been recognised as an essential tool in the field situation. Individuals stand out, personal relationships develop, and the reliability of individual informants can be tested. The life story of a particular adult, responding as a willing informant, produces not only a wealth of material on customs, but adds a historical dimension to the interpretation by forcing the realisation of a time perspective beyond the ethnographic present. History and anthropology come together. The material is also distinct from the impersonal norms derived from analysis of rites of passage or abstracted as developmental cycles.

8

FOREWORD

While a conventional ethnography may present models and paradigms, the life of an individual reveals the unexpected events, the quicksands of relationships, the shifting options. Baba, who did not idealise her life, nor meekly accept and resign herself, confronts the human condition, the existential reality.

Baba's experiences and attitudes as a Muslim Hausa run counter to a number of commonly held stereotypes. African women are frequently described as downtrodden, oppressed, subservient creatures exploited for their labour and biological potential; Muslim women are often described as pitiable or contemptible, mysterious or unimportant, excluded from "real life" by Islamic law which also legitimises the double standard implicit in polygamy. But Baba speaks with pride of her Hausa forefathers, her cultural heritage, and the training she received in dealing with people and in the handling of her affairs. She is at ease in a world which Westerners might condemn or dismiss, but it is a world of personal relations with men and women of different ages, skills, and social positions, involving her in complex sets of rights and obligations. These she takes, or appears to take, for granted. In some situations she is more free, in others less free, than "liberated" women in Western societies; but "freedom" and "liberation" are subjective interpretations, not easy for outsiders to measure or evaluate.

However, marriage is often used as a testing ground of the degree of autonomy of women within the constraints of custom, and here again Mary Smith's book provides fascinating material. Among the Muslim Hausa, marriage, an essential qualification for admission into adult life, took different forms, and the status of women was further complicated by the availability of slaves, male and female, and the laws regulating inheritance. Divorce was relatively easy for either party and carried no stigma; a divorcée was expected to remarry and bear children. Baba married four times—slightly more than the average. But Baba was barren. This misfortune caused her deep sorrow and had repercussions on close relationships throughout her adult life. But Baba was not rejected or despised, and the public reactions to her reflect a range of cultural resources available to meet a widely recognised affliction: she adopted children, arranged marriages, organised rituals, and in old age acted as honorary midwife for an extensive circle of kin—a highly rated and symbolic role. Baba

FOREWORD

does not idealise or romanticise her life, but it is clear that she was recognised as an outstanding and very attractive individual.

Though presented in the first person, *Baba of Karo* differs from the more conventional autobiography in which the author deliberately presents, and creates, an image of the Self. In this study Baba is responding to questions raised by Mary Smith, questions directed at probing Baba's knowledge of the culture of her people as well as relating her personal story. In this interaction, Mary Smith is the initiator, the Self, and Baba, as informant, is the Other. Both have internalised their own cultural imprints. Baba's information covers a broad cultural spectrum—a virtual ethnographic index—with herself as the reference point, but the frame is designed by the anthropologist. Mary Smith records episodes and beliefs outside her own experience in the matter-of-fact way in which they were related. These are the vital and essential data of firsthand ethnography. Yet we are becoming increasingly aware that even in recording, and more so in the actual writing, the material itself is changed and reflects assumptions that are often implicit and unconscious.

Personal histories appear to have a universal appeal, but the modes in which they are expressed are culturally circumscribed. Autobiographies, biographies, case studies, and life histories are essentially constructs introduced from the outside. The complex interaction between an ethnographer and the central character of a study is of relevance to everyone interested in the methods of social research. In *Baba of Karo* we see the direct interaction between two remarkable women, compounded by the less direct participation of an alter ego, Michael Smith. The result is a book of high literary merit as well as a unique and stimulating contribution to social science.

March 1981   HILDA KUPER

INTRODUCTION

The following autobiography was recorded by my wife in Hausa, as far as possible *verbatim*, during a period of six weeks from November 1949 to January 1950, at Giwa and Zaria City in Zaria Province, Northern Nigeria, during the course of an eighteen-month field study provided by the Colonial Social Science Research Council, the assistance of which is gratefully acknowledged here.

How the Story was Written

Interviews with Baba occurred daily, for an average period of three hours, and questions were frequently asked to clarify various points. Prior to the start of the work on this autobiography, we had been living in Baba's community for four months, and my wife had collected more than a dozen case-histories from Hausa women in the village, some of whom were related to Baba. My wife undertook these case-studies to supplement my enquiries into Hausa life, since the practices of purdah marriage and the exclusion of men from compounds prohibited me from studying domestic units myself. In Hausa society, with its custom of secluding wives, it would have been extremely difficult, if not impossible, for a man anthropologist to have interviewed Baba daily and to have received such a complete and unreserved account. In the course of these studies, a friendship grew up between Baba and my wife, and when it appeared more valuable to obtain one detailed life-history from a woman of advanced years than to continue recording the shorter life-spans of younger wives, Baba was an obvious choice, for her intelligence, forthrightness, and faith in our good intentions. It may be worth pointing out that even where adults of opposite sex are not segregated as they are among the Moslem Hausa, a document of this character can only be obtained from a woman by a woman field worker. The following translation of an extract from my wife's notebook records the discussion which took place after Baba had been working with her on the autobiography for four weeks, and it became necessary to ask her to accompany us to

Zaria City and finish her story there; she willingly accepted, but made the following remarks.

Baba: 'I don't want the people of the town to know I am coming to Zaria because of our work. I have told them "I am going to Zaria to escort her", only. My kinswoman is there in her house at Tudun Wada, I will stay with her, and when I come back I will tell them I went to see her after we had parted. Don't let them say we have done anything. You know, the old women are afraid; they don't come here to see you. They say "Don't go to the Rest House, the Europeans will pick you up and take you home with them in an aeroplane. Don't go!" That was Azumi, Dantsoho's wife. Then there are *his* followers (*fadawa*—i.e. the District Head, Fagaci's, agents). They will trouble me, they will say I was always with the Europeans; I shall be annoyed.'

M.F.S.: 'Do you think they would do anything else to you?'

Baba: 'No. He wouldn't do anything—look at me, an old woman. But there will be words and gossip. When Fagaci (the District Head) came here yesterday, did you show him our book?

M.F.S.: 'No, I explained to him that we were working together and you were telling me your story from the time before the Europeans came, from when you lived in Zarewa, you were telling me all about your kinsfolk.'

Baba: 'That's good. He won't do anything.'

M.F.S.: 'We have asked Fagaci to look after our friends, and see that nothing whatever bothers them.'

Baba: 'That's excellent; my mind is at peace now. That is that. When they told me you would pick me up and take me away I said, "Come, come; my father isn't here, my mother isn't here, I have no master but Allah; what am I to be afraid of? Ai, I'm going to her —look at her, smiling and liking people, she is a slave of Allah, there is nothing wrong." Then I came.'

When the issue of the degree to which Baba is typical of Hausa women is raised, therefore, it may be said that she was bolder than many others of her generation at Giwa, but the younger wives, secluded in their husbands' compounds, also told their life-stories willingly, in private. The interviews with Baba were held in our quarters to ensure the necessary privacy, and also because it is a rule that people of higher rank should receive visits rather than make them. Baba might be regarded as a deviant in that she bore no children, but this is not uncommon among Hausa women.

INTRODUCTION

Baba's account of her life has been arranged as far as possible in chronological order, and where it was necessary for clarity, names have been substituted for pronouns where avoidance-relations are concerned, although Baba herself did not use the names of these relatives except in reply to a direct question; usually, of course, the context or an indirect allusion showed whom she meant. Approximate dates have been assigned to the major events of her life; the dating adopted is only one of two alternative schema worked out from various scattered references in the text; the alternative schema agrees with the estimated age for Baba given in the postscript by the schoolmaster at Giwa. On the evidence, the adopted dating seems preferable, but Baba's inaccuracy about the sequence of political events, which is characteristic of Hausa women, leaves room for error and doubt. However, it seems certain that she was married either shortly before or shortly after the British occupation of Northern Nigeria in 1900, and the record of her childhood has great value as a picture of Hausa life in the days of slavery, war, and rumours of war. The prosperity of her family was based on slave-ownership and was destroyed by slave-raiders. A vivid picture of the insecurity of small settlements is presented in the opening section. Pacification, to old people with such unforgettable memories, remains the greatest single blessing of British rule.

Apart from the diachronic perspective in which Hausa culture is placed here, Baba's story contains a number of significant themes, which are the themes of a Hausa woman's life: kinship, marriage, bond-friendship, spirit-worship, the rituals of childbirth and marriage, naming and widowhood, praise-songs and drumming, and the pleasure taken in traditional goods, in trade, farming, and craft production. Various incidents illustrate different aspects of these and many other important cultural attitudes and institutions. Time and again the instability of Hausa marriage and the high incidence of divorce is seen to be closely linked with the attachment of wives to their kin, an attachment which usually overrides any fondness they may feel for their husband when they conflict, which frequently happens at the instigation of kinswomen of a senior generation. Different contexts illustrate the prevailing bilaterality of Hausa kinship, while the strong patrilineal organization and solidarity at Anguwan Karo is evident. Cultural attitudes on farming, Koranic study, generosity, sexual deviance, spirit worship, and the proper fulfilment of the obligations of kinship, bond-friendship,

18

clientage and ritual behaviour, recur throughout the story. The influence of economic factors associated with the acquisition of new skills and crafts on the acculturation of children of pagan slaves to Hausa culture is indicated, and the symbolic character of the formal exchanges which are associated with different stages in the initiation of all institutionalized relations cannot be missed. The economic basis of wife-seclusion is illustrated, so is the method and sphere of ridicule and social ostracism and the basic element of reciprocity in informal relationships, particularly in relation to the adoption of children between kin. Where kinship norms are broken, the offended person suspends the relationship until the offender shows his penitence in some convincing way. The traditional dependence of markets on the spirits is illustrated in the tale from Old Giwa, and the role of *bori* in Hausa life as a principle of interpretation and of action on festive occasions, is referred to in several places. Proper behaviour is most strikingly illustrated by contrast in the tale of Hasana, who consistently broke all the rules and manipulated the obligations of kinship to her own advantage.

This autobiography is valuable from two different points of view: as a record of Hausa life it is unique in the detail, the time-span, the variety of aspects and events, and above all in its immediacy; but it is significant also to the social anthropologist with structural interests as a documentation of the extent to which, and the precise way in which, structure governs and shapes an individual life. A great deal has recently been written on a variety of postulated relationships between 'culture' and 'personality'; this record will have served a useful function if it suggests ways in which the individual's life-process and its relations to the social structure can be studied in greater detail, with a diachronic perspective.

Background to the Story: the Hausa of Northern Nigeria

When we talk to one another, usually we either make brief allusions to certain facts which are relevant to the subject, or completely omit any reference to them. We do this because a relation of such facts would be both tedious in view of their complexity, and unnecessary, since we can safely assume that they are known to our audience. The bulk of such omissions form the stable background of habits, relations and attitudes common to all parties in such a conversation. Such background information forms a large part of the 'culture' of a population, in the sense that the anthropologist uses that term, and must be given before the record of events characteristic of one cultural group may be fully appreciated by an audience composed principally of members of different cultural groups. This is particularly necessary with respect to autobiographies of individuals living in cultures widely different from ours. Facts which the narrator assumes that the anthropologist knows, are consequently omitted or briefly alluded to. It becomes the duty of the anthropologist to supplement the document with an outline of the background facts which receive such scanty reference, though they form the context of the tale. Similarly, it is necessary to give some account of the method by which the document was collected, and other relevant features of the field-work situation, and possibly to attempt an appraisal of its anthropological value.

The text records the life story of Baba, a Hausa woman who lived in the Nigerian states of Kano and Zaria, between approximately 1890 and 1951. As she tells us, her fathers and their fathers before them were Kanuri (also called Barebare) people from Kukawa, the nineteenth-century capital of Bornu, to the west of Lake Chad. But despite her Kanuri descent, Baba says time and again that she is a Hausa woman, describing herself as 'Habe' or 'Kado', which she distinguishes sharply from the Fulani, who, since their conquest of this area in 1804, have formed the ruling class in almost all the Hausa states. In fact 'Hausa' is a linguistic term referring to those people in Northern Nigeria and the neighbouring French territories who speak the Hausa language by birth; and besides Hausa proper, it includes people of such different origins as Kanuri, Arab and Tuareg where these have adopted the Hausa language and culture, as Baba's forefathers did. Adherence to the Mohammedan faith, membership of large centralized states, the practice of production for subsistence and exchange in local markets, and a high and varied level of technology are principal characteristics of the Hausa proper, differentiating them from pagan Hausa-speaking groups, who are known as Maguzawa and are scattered throughout the centre of Hausaland.

Environment and Economy

The Hausa live in open, rolling country with numerous rocky outcrops and thickly-wooded watercourses, a type of country usually described as 'orchard bush', or open parkland, merging into typical savannah country in the north, where it approache⌐ the southern fringes of the Sahara Desert. The area involved is vast, probably in excess of 100,000 square miles, and the population who speak Hausa as their native language in Northern Nigeria alone must number five million. The climate is hot but dry, except in the months of May to October, when the rains fall and there is intense activity on the farms. From December to February the harmattan wind blows from the desert, and the nights become colder as the days get hotter. In March and April the heat is intense at midday, and the scrub vegetation is parched and brown, while all but the principal watercourses are dry.

Although agriculture is the main economic activity of the Hausa, gathering is also important, and apart from wood and grass for thatch and mats, tree-crops such as those which locust-bean, baobab, tamarind, sheanut, horseradish-tree, deleb-palm, guttapercha and raffia provide are important as food, building materials, oils or commodities sold to European trading firms. Hunting is unimportant, though guineafowl and other birds are trapped, and fishing is an organized activity.

The staple food is grain, of which guineacorn (*Sorgum vulgare*) and bullrush-millet (*Pennisteum typhoideum*) are the principal Hausa crops, although varieties of late millets and maize have considerable regional importance. Other cereals include a type of upland rice (*iburu*) and marshland rice. Root crops, such as sweet potatoes, yam, coco-yam, cassava, *rizga* (Kaffir potatoes), bambarra nuts, *gurjiya* (*Voandzeia subterranea*) supplement and give variety to this diet of cereal. A variety of vegetables and spices are also farmed locally, and pulses such as cowpeas are a traditional crop. Farm products which are exported to Europe, such as cotton and groundnuts, are also used in large quantities locally, the cotton being made into thread by Hausa women, and woven on different types of looms by both sexes; while the groundnuts are processed locally to yield both oil and cake, which are put to a variety of uses. Hausa farmers also grow food crops, such as sugar-cane and onions for local markets, and other plants, such as indigo, henna, etc., which are used in craft processes.

Simultaneous cultivation of such a variety of crops requires a well-developed farming technique, in which intercropping and double-cropping are both practised. Cultivation is by hand, two different types and sizes of hoe being used. Manuring with green manure, house manure, and cattle manure purchased from the nomadic Fulani herdsmen, bush fallowing with the slash-and-burn technique, and irrigation along the banks of rivers and in marshes, are practised, as well as farming by means of cattle-drawn ploughs, which have been introduced by the Europeans. Soil-types vary, and planting is adjusted to this, but the principal distinction is between marshland, which permits of continuous cultivation throughout the year, and slope (*tudu*) farms, which can be cultivated only during the rainy season. The ratio of marsh to slope farms is generally low, so that for practical purposes Hausa farming can be regarded as limited to six or seven months of the year.

Mention has been made of the nomadic cattle-Fulani—the *Bororo*, or Bush Fulani, as they are known locally. Their movements follow the seasons in a broad way; during the rains they move north to the area of less rain, and during the dry season they move in a southerly direction in search of good grazing. Their dispersal and movements in smaller or larger groups brings supplies of meat, manure, sour milk and butter to the Hausa settlements, in return for which they purchase supplies of grain, salt, cloth and other goods and services. Wealthy Hausa merchants purchase cattle from these Fulani nomads for sale in southern Nigerian markets, such as Lagos or Enugu, but the Hausa themselves do not take to cattle-keeping. Their livestock is mainly sheep and goats and poultry, with donkeys as beasts of burden and the horse holding the place of honour.

Some idea of the complex and varied technological basis of Hausa economy may be gained from the following brief list of traditional occupational specialisms carried on for exchange in market conditions. Men are classified by Hausa as builders, thatchers, hunters, fishers, butchers, tanners, leatherworkers, saddlers, weavers, dyers, dye-beaters, native carpenters (i.e. those who use the adze as their main tool), blacksmiths, brass- and silver-smiths, calabash-decorators, drummers, praise-singers of various types, pot-makers, mat-weavers, *malams* (that is, Koranic scholars), officials and their agents, etc. Wage labour on farms, and transport by head-loading or by donkeys, are also recognized specialisms. It must be recognized that the preceding list refers only to crafts, and includes none of the trading specialisms, whether on commission or as independent retail or wholesale trade. Even the manufacture of chewing-tobacco or sweetmeats such as *allewa* are excluded, since these commodities are usually retailed by their manufacturers. Similarly, only traditional crafts are listed. The principal craft activities carried on by women are in the processing of a variety of foods for sale in the local market as snacks, and the manufacture of cotton thread and coarse-woven cotton blankets; but women also make pots, keep small stock, trade, are purveyors of medicines, devotees of the cult of spirit-possession (*bori*), praise-singers, and prostitutes (*karuwai*). Their role in the political system is limited to agency, as the messenger of a chief (the *jakadiya*) or as head (*magajiya*) of the prostitutes and *bori*-dancers of an administrative unit—village or district.

Trade is similarly complex and varied. Useful distinctions can be made between full-time specialists, trading with their own capital or for commission on behalf of others, and part-time specialists, some of whom also practise crafts. Generally, full-time specialist traders are found in greatest number at the principal commercial towns, that is, the capitals of the various states, or rural settlements which are very favourably sited in relation to a variety of factors, such as available markets and communications along which supplies are regularly moved. *Kasuwanci*, which means dealing in a particular market, must also be distinguished from *fatauci*, which is trade carried on by principals over long distances at a number of markets. *Fatauci* is generally two-way traffic, the merchant taking goods from his own country for sale at his terminus or in the markets *en route*, and returning with products from the places he has visited. In the nineteenth century *fatauci* linked Hausaland to Tripoli, Tunisia and the North African littoral, the Tuareg moving the goods across the Sahara by camel caravans. Within Hausaland, *fatauci* by caravan was also important, and took place along certain well-defined trade-routes, which were guarded and maintained by the heads of the various states through which they passed, in return for tolls levied by such rulers on the traders at established caravan-serai. Such long-distance trade enabled Hausa in the nineteenth century to obtain necessary commodities, such as salt and kolanuts, which were not produced in sufficient quantities in the area, and a variety of luxury goods besides. Within Hausaland, such traffic supplied regional deficiencies from the surpluses of nearby areas. The important point to grasp is that, in terms of the traditional scale of needs and market relations, nineteenth-century Hausaland was quite well able to meet all its requirements by its own production, by internal exchange, and by *fatauci* with neighbouring northern Sudanic communities. The presence of the Bush Fulani supplied the greatest single deficiency of Hausa food production, namely meat and dairy products.

Space does not permit detailed discussion of this complex and varied economy. All that can be done here is to draw attention to certain basic aspects. For instance, in the brief outline of *fatauci*, economic variations linked with regional differences are implied, with the corollary of the economic interdependence of such communities, and of producers within communities. This in turn implies some degree of participation in the exchange sector of the economy, whether by craft production, trading activity, or cultivation of crops for sale, by all Hausa men. The necessity for a combination of production for subsistence and for exchange is met by farming the bulk of household food requirements during the short farming season, and by plying non-agricultural occupations vigorously during the dry season; but craftsmen and traders whose exchange activity is sufficiently rewarding often engage in these occupations throughout the year. In the nineteenth century, when slave labour was available for farming, gathering, building and other heavy tasks, food production did not suffer from the preoccupation of slave-owners with non-agricultural activity. Generally, also, one finds a variety of such non-agricultural activities carried on to greater or less extent by the same person. Exceptions to this appear where continuous specialist activity is necessary, such as for instance among butchers at important markets, people on *fatauci*, or wealthy traders handling a variety of interests. Another important quality of this combination of production for subsistence and exchange is the high degree of freedom which it permits individuals, in adjusting their market requirements and degree of participation in the exchange sector to suit their circumstances.

Markets themselves are traditional Hausa institutions of great significance, socially as well as economically. It is possible to distinguish markets of greater or less importance, and the frequency with which they are held. The most important markets, and the largest, meet daily in the state capitals and certain very prosperous rural towns; less important markets usually meet twice weekly on set days, e.g. Sunday and Wednesday, in the walled towns which are the capitals and centres of local communities now given the administrative status of village-areas. The markets of neighbouring village-areas are held in rotation on different days, so as to enable specialist traders and craftsmen to attend each in turn. Markets are under the supervision of the appointed head of the local communities in which they are held, and are established under his leadership in a ritual context predominantly associated with the cult of spirit-possession (*bori*) which is a development from the pre-Islamic Hausa worship of spirits. Diffuse supervision was delegated to heads of craftsmen and commission-traders appointed by the chief for the local community, the head of each craft having limited influence only in relation to persons practising his craft; this is now much reduced since the abolition by the British of taxes on craft and trade. Craft products and services, such as barber-doctoring, form an important part of the turnover of market exchange.

Generally, persons selling the same goods or services sit together in their own part of the market; thus the sellers of pots share one section, the butchers another, the cloth-sellers another, and the measurers of grain and other foodstuffs, the leather-workers and so on are each grouped together in different market stalls. Markets are usually sited in the centre of the town, and are built, cleaned and kept in repair by communal labour under the chief's direction. On market-days, men from the town and the neighbouring communities assemble between ten and twelve o'clock not only to sell their wares and purchase household supplies (a man's job), but also to meet their friends and relatives and to discuss matters of interest. The Bush Fulani are there, their womenfolk selling sour milk and butter while the men, clad in their traditional knee-breeches and loose white shifts, remain a little apart from the crush of the market. There is a notable absence of Hausa women between the ages of about fifteen and forty-five, but apart from the various old women who are trading, the unmarried girls of the market town and of neighbouring settlements are present, usually trading on behalf of their mothers or aunts, but including many who visit the market in their best attire, waiting for the girls' dance which follows at night, where they will meet their suitors. At the market, Hausa find pleasure in the rich variety of manufactured and farm products, which have high value in their culture, in the constant hum of bargaining and gossip, the ethnic diversity of the teeming crowd, in the mobilization of individual contacts, the greeting of kinsfolk and friends, and in the handsome girls in their gay cotton prints with their powdered faces set off by necklaces and earrings and headkerchiefs, and in the sober elegance of prosperous men in their flowing robes and shining dark-blue turbans.

Kinship and Marriage

Hausa kinship is markedly bilateral—that is, traced through persons of either sex—both in terminology and behaviour. Marriage is virilocal, the woman coming to live with the man, usually in his father's compound if it is the man's first marriage. Cross-cousin marriages of both types are now made, though matrilateral cross-cousin marriage (i.e. that between a man and his mother's brother's daughter) was probably the traditional form. Parallel-cousin marriages of both types are also found, the marriages between children of brothers, which is preferred in Islam, being far more frequent than the marriages between children of sisters. Adoption is an important feature of Hausa kinship, and is most frequent for the first-born, being either maternal or paternal according to circumstances. Usually adoption takes place after weaning at two years. A rigid lifelong public avoidance is observed between parents and their first-born child of either sex, and use of their parents' names is forbidden to all children. The last-born child is the playmate of its parents, and has a special name—*auta*, the child of old age. Joking relationships, expressed by privileged behaviour such as teasing, and the right to appropriate certain possessions of the other party, obtain between children and their grandparents, and between children of a sister and a brother, in both cases the first-named parties being privileged to tease and take things from the last-named, who retaliate with good-natured abuse and more teasing. There are also certain other joking relations, such as a man and his elder brother's wife, who behave in a similar way.

As marriage is virilocal and usually patrilocal, the core of the co-residential unit is a group of males linked by ties of kinship traced through males. Where such a group exploits large resources together, or where important political office is vested in the patriline, groups emerge with greater or less degree of lineage structure, corporateness, and size. At the highest level, for instance in the case of the three principal Fulani dynasties of Zaria state, genealogies with a depth of seven generations are remembered, but generally the rule is that where trace of office is lacking, genealogical memory is shallow, and bilateral kinship connections with extensive lateral ramifications are emphasized, rather than unilineal descent beyond three generations.

Domestic groupings fall into two main types, extended and single families. Extended families may jointly hold and exploit economic resources, such as land, or they may not; when there is joint exploitation of such resources by two or more adult males on behalf of their wives and dependants, such a unit is described in modern Hausa as a *gandu*. In the nineteenth century, however, the *gandu*, which was the principal type of organization for farming, included slaves and their descendants. These were assimilated in some degree as kinsfolk of the *gandu*-head by employment of certain kinship terms between slaves and their owners. Sometimes the slaves' huts were situated within the same walled or fenced enclosure as those of the owners' family, though in a different section. Where holdings of slaves were large, the *gandu* ceased to be contained within a single compound, though it still functioned as a single unit for the production and consumption of food, the payment of tax, the provision of farm tools, and seed, the common exploitation of land, economic trees, and other resources, and the provision of brides for members of the group. When not working on the *gandu* farm, members were free to cultivate smaller plots allotted to them by the head of the *gandu*, or to practise craft or trade for their own individual profit, but the *gandu* head was traditionally responsible for meeting the group needs outlined above from the group resources over which he had control. An important aspect of the Hausa division of labour is the exclusion of Moslem Hausa women from active farming, in contrast to the pagan Hausa women, who participate in farming. Formerly when slavery obtained, free Hausa women and concubines neither farmed nor gathered firewood, though women of slave status were compelled to do both tasks. With the abolition of slavery under British rule, women formerly of slave status withdrew from the farms and as far as possible from wood-gathering, as an assertion of their new legal status as free persons, and in imitation of the traditional role of free Hausa women. Linked with this development is the spread of purdah-type marriage throughout the rural areas of Hausaland in recent years, for the seclusion of wives is closely connected with their refusal, wherever possible, either to farm or to gather sylvan produce, and their preference for the more rewarding craft and trade activities which they can carry out in their leisure time at home.

Despite the great variation between Hausa compounds, they follow a basic pattern, elaborations of which merely indicate differences of wealth and status of the household head, or structure of the domestic group. The compound (*gida*) is a rectangular enclosure; if the householder is wealthy or the compound is in the capital, it is surrounded by high mud walls; more common in rural areas are fences of guineacorn stalks. It is entered through a round mud hut with a conical thatched roof known as the *zaure* or *kofa* (see sketch plan, p. 36). Important men build elaborate two-storeyed entrances, with mud roofs and raised arabesques on the whitewashed walls, wooden windows and European-type doors. The *zaure* leads into a fenced or walled forecourt, wihch contains one or more round thatched huts as sleeping-quarters for the adolescent youths of the household, or male guests. Entrance to the interior of the compound (*cikin gida*), the women's quarters, may be through another hut, either circular or rectangular in shape, but with a partition preventing a direct view, or through a succession of such forecourts in the homes of wealthy or important men, or merely through a gap in the fence. The *cikin gida* itself may be partitioned by fence or wall, and the different sections, known as *sassa*, contain separate though closely-related families, sometimes forming a common unit of domestic economy, sometimes not. The partition itself may be taken into the forecourt, but if it is carried to the outer compound wall, there is a division into two compounds. The wives' huts are to be found in the *cikin gida*, and it is an important rule that each wife should have her own hut in which she keeps her possessions, and in which her young children sleep. The husband in a polygamous marriage may or may not have a separate sleeping-hut of his own, opposite those of his wives. Where he has such a hut, known as the *turaka*, his wives visit him in turn for two nights each, on the days when each is responsible for preparing the household food. When not occupied in preparing food for the common household, co-wives engage in craft activity, such as spinning, weaving, the making of processed foods for sale in the market by young girls, and so forth. Complete wife-seclusion (*auren kulle*) is only possible where the husband either fetches the water required by the household, or has it fetched, or has a well inside his compound; well-digging and repair is a traditional Hausa craft, with a wide market.

Hausa distinguish between marriages in two different ways: firstly, according to the degree or lack of wife-seclusion; secondly, according to the circumstances and relations of the spouses and their kin. It has been pointed out above that the reported increase in the practice of wife-seclusion is directly correlated with the abolition of slave-status, and the differentiation in the division of labour linked with different legal statuses; but this is not how the Hausa see the matter. To them, purdah marriage—complete seclusion of wives—is sanctioned by religious values and teaching, and the liberty of wives to go anywhere outside the compound is by implication an act of religious ignorance. But the necessity that wives should visit their kinsfolk and close friends, and receive visits from them, is incompatible with this rule ascribed to religion, and such visits, which usually take place with or without an escort, after dark, between compounds of the same village, or by day with an escort over long distances, are both frequent and obligatory on certain ceremonial occasions, such as marriages and naming ceremonies. It is significant that husbands permit their wives to go visiting after dark, despite the very great and well-founded suspicions that spouses entertain of each other's fidelity; night-time is the period when wives everywhere rest from their labours of grinding and cooking the household food, and are free to receive guests, while they spin or weave. That is to say, the general conditions of wife-seclusion among Hausa are more easily understood in terms of the economic interests and role of Hausa wives than the ascribed religious injunction, although prestige factors are of great importance, and the wives of chiefs and wealthy traders are permanently confined to their husband's compound.

The second classification of Hausa marriages distinguishes primarily between marriages of kinship or quasi-kinship and marriages between unrelated persons. The former type (*auren zumunci, auren dangintaka*) includes all forms of cousin-marriage, and holds between members of different occupational or even ethnic groups which are defined as joking relations, such as the Fulani and the Kanuri (Barebare). Apart from this, daughters are sometimes given by their parents in a marriage of alms to a selected man as a representative of the Prophet, no request being made for marriage-payments; this act of religious piety ensures local prestige. Infant-betrothal and marriage were sometimes practised, but the most singular of the remaining marriage types is that in which the wife lives in a separate compound and often in a separate village, and receives visits from her husband.

Unmarried girls are courted privately and at public ceremonial give-aways, over which certain praise-singers and drummers preside, both with a view to marriage and the institutionalized pre-marital love-making known as *tsarance*. Girls are married between the ages of thirteen and fourteen, and probably re-marry two or three times, on average, afterwards. The first marriage is always arranged by the bride's parents, her consent being purely formal, and later marriages may often be made at their behest also. Similarly divorce, which is frequent among Hausa, is often instigated by one or other of the wife's kinswomen, with a view to arranging a future marriage to somebody preferred by the instigator —often in discharge of some obligation. No linguistic distinction is made between divorcées and widows. The important social distinctions are between unmarried girls, married women, and women previously, but not at present, married.

Women of child-bearing age in this last group are known as *karuwai* if they remain unmarried after the termination of mourning or *Iddah*, the three months' period of celibacy enjoined on divorced Muslim women. The term *karuwa* is not adequately translated by its nearest English equivalent, prostitute, as it is also applied to adult males who are not married and are reputedly profligate. Female *karuwai*, besides practising prostitution, engage actively in craft and trade, and are the traditional supporters and exponents of the cult of spirit-possession (*bori*), for which their status suits them. As *karuwai* they are deviants from the Islamic norm of marriage for all adults, and as social deviants they are the traditional custodians of religious deviance in the spirit-possession cult.

A girl's first marriage is established by a *rite de passage*, and this is also carried out for a man's first marriage. By means of this rite, an individual exchanges the status of a youth or girl for that of an adult. To be an adult, it is therefore necessary to have been married. Consequently by definition, all Hausa prostitutes have been previously married, as the Hausa distinguish between *tsarance* (pre-marital love-making) and *karuwanci* (prostitution) according to the status of the female concerned, both relationships being identical in their economic and sexual aspects. Another *rite de passage* of critical importance takes place on the occasion of a woman's first childbirth. After the Muslim naming ceremony on the seventh day, the mother returns to her parents' home with her baby, and remains there for a period of six months or longer, during which she performs the prescribed post-natal ablutions daily for five months. This custom, known as *bangwalle*, has many different variations, but its performance for the first birth is normative. On completion of *bangwalle* the mother returns to her husband's compound loaded with gifts from her kin, and for the first time in her husband's home will suckle her infant without any pressure or compulsion being necessary. But throughout their lives, a parent of either sex and the first-born child observe a rigorous avoidance-relation, which is hardly relaxed even in private and when the child is fully grown. As the very full acount in the text illustrates (pp. 138 sqq.), social sanctions compel conformity to this behaviour, both during the period of ablutions and thereafter. The entire complex is best understood as a *rite de passage*, marking the transition in status to parenthood and full social maturity, and the lifelong avoidance-relation, which is extended by Fulani to the second and third child, and by Hausa-speaking Habe and Fulani to the next-born in greater or less degree, if the first child dies in infancy, gives a permanent expression to this new status. Similarly the post-natal ablutions, which are carried out for successive births, are probably best understood as extensions of ritual activity on the first childbirth rather than as measures of preventive hygiene (which the Hausa declare them to be), since such ablutions are not performed for stillbirths or miscarriages, and may be brought to an early conclusion if the mother is unable to bear the washing with nearly boiling water; if this happens, alternative 'medicines', herbal and Islamic, are employed.

The preoccupation of Hausa women with these two rituals is not to be ascribed merely to the facts of polygamy and motherhood, but to their importance in determining the status which women hold. One of the conditions of polygamous marriage is the ranking of co-wives within the household by seniority, in terms of their marriage order to the common husband. That is to say, ranking obtains between Hausa women in domestic polygamous units. As mentioned before, divorce occurs on average two to three times during a woman's life. Thus the domestic ranking of co-wives is impermanent, and provides no basis for the public ordering of their relative status; nor is it possible to extend such ranking to cover women of different households; nor, furthermore, does the rank of the husband apply to his wives, since divorce is so frequent. Consequently the statuses of marriage and parenthood define the adult Hausa women as a group within which further distinctions are made on grounds of age. In this context, parenthood includes adoptive as well as biological parenthood. The normal expectancy is, of course, that a married woman will have children of her own; but where, as in Baba's case, this does not occur, her kinsfolk or husband will provide her with children to foster and adopt, and she fulfils the role of their mother throughout her life. Thus one aspect of adoption is the provision of substitute offspring, which enables barren women to fulfil the normal expectations of parenthood, ritualized for those who bear children themselves in *bangwalle* and post-natal ablutions, and linked to the marriage ritual by annual gifts from the bride's parents to her until her first child is born.

The Political System

In Muslim law women are minors, but this is not a sufficient reason for their exclusion from the system of ranks which governs the political relations of men. Traditionally, before the Fulani conquest, women held titles and offices such as those of *Iya*, *Magajiya*, *Mardanni* in the various Habe states, and have continued to do so in the Habe state of Abuja. The husbands of such women acted on their behalf as agents in administrative affairs.

It is simplest to describe the political system from the territorial aspect, beginning with the smallest units. Local communities, as mentioned above, are territorial units centred on a walled town (*gari*) at which the chief resides, the market meets, the prayer-ground for the great annual Muslim festivals, Id-el-fitr and Id-el-kabir, is sited, and the community mosque and appointed Muslim priest are found. Bush hamlets, situated within the area under the administrative control of the town chief, are the parts of the community in which farming is most intensively practised; such bush hamlets are classed administratively as wards, though they may be of different status, some being settlements of free persons, and others having been privately owned slave villages, such as Anguwan

INTRODUCTION

Karo in this story. Within the town itself, further administrative sub-divisions exist, also known as wards. Ward-heads are appointed or confirmed by the town chief, and may be dismissed by him. Usually the heads of bush hamlets reside there, but in the towns the ward-head does not always live in his ward. Ward-heads are given titles on appointment, and can be classified as kinsmen of the chief, or as non-relatives, who are always his clients. Succession to chieftainship of local communities varied formerly; in some cases it was based on patrilineal descent, in others not, and in the same community different criteria of eligibility frequently obtained at different times. But the formal rule of patrilineal succession, where it obtained, only served to limit and define the field of effective competition since the chief was chosen from the patrilineage, with the result that patrilineal groups claiming rights of succession to hereditary chieftainship are split up by their rivalry into segments with great mutual independence as competitive units, and low corporate solidarity.

In the last century, as today, the main function of the chief was the collection and remission of the authorized tax to his superior, who in turn passed it on to the ruler of the state. Salaries were formerly unknown, but officials retained prescribed portions of the tax they had collected, as remuneration, and owing to lack of supervision, were free to over-collect and retain the surplus. The ward-heads were responsible for collecting the tax from their wards, and for the maintenance of good order and discipline in those units. The chiefs, traditionally, had limited judicial powers in civil cases such as marriage, divorce, debt, etc., which did not involve punishment by imprisonment, mutilation and so forth. They were also responsible for the repair of the town wall and defences, the mosque, and the markets and paths throughout their areas. In the nineteenth century the great majority of local communities had settled Fulani as their chiefs, consequent on the Fulani conquest of the Habe states in the *jihad* of 1804–10.

An interesting feature of Hausa community organization is the distribution of titles among the various occupational groups. These titles, like those of the ward-heads, repeat the principal ranks of the central political system, such as *Sarki* (chief), *Madaki, Galadima, Dangaladima, Ciroma*, etc. The particular titles and their order of precedence varied slightly from state to state, and over the years within the same state, but the principal distinction was that between royal ranks (i.e. titles held by kinsmen of the chief of the unit concerned, whether a state, local community, or occupational group at either level), and those held by non-relatives. In the nineteenth century an important duty of occupational title-holders was the collection of particular taxes from members of their occupational groups within the community, and remission of the prescribed portion to the heads of such groups throughout the state, at the capital.

The same principles and processes of political organization which have been described at the community level operate on a larger canvas for the state as a whole. From the perspective of the state, the local communities were administered in the last century as fiefs allotted to title-holders appointed by the king on bases of kinship or clientage. Certain trusted slaves were also given titles and fiefs as rewards for military and household services, and the territorial basis of rank held also for judicial and religious appointments in the central political system. Under British administration, fiefholders resident in the capital cities, administering their territories through agents known as *jakadu* (s. *jakada*), have been replaced by District Heads responsible to the Emir for compact areas, and resident in their districts; the traditional titles remain in use for these as for other officials of the state. Rulers of Hausa states are referred to in English as emirs; in the present text, however, the Hausa *Sarkin Zazzau*, *Sarkin Kano* etc., have been translated 'king of Zaria', 'king of Kano', as reproducing Baba's sense more clearly.

Variations in the pattern outlined above between different states are linked with the historical circumstances of their conquest by the Fulani during and after the *jihad* of 1804; thus, for instance, Kano emirate has one dynasty, the Suleibawa, from which all its kings are drawn; Zaria, on the other hand, has four dynasties, three of which had provided all the Fulani rulers except one. In a system of multiple dynasties such as that of Zaria, the different patrilines are permanently the effective units of political competition for the throne and the main subordinate offices of the central system. The situation is similar in a single-dynasty state, though not so permanently structured, and in 1893–4 a bitter war of succession was fought in Kano between the sons of two brothers. Katsina emirate provides another variation on the general structure, linked with historical factors; there, hereditary Fulani chiefs of large districts are recognized by the king, with a consequent reduction of his effective control.

In the nineteenth century the various Hausa states under Fulani rule themselves had the status of fiefs in relation to the empire administered by the sultan of Sokoto in north-western Nigeria, whose title was based on direct descent in the male line from the inspirer of the *jihad*, Shehu dan Fodio. The heads of these various states were appointed by the sultan from the principal candidates for office in the dynasties. In this way the sultan was able to control the chiefs under him, and frequently to order their deposition, with the certainty of support from their rivals. The efficacy of this administrative method is proven by the retention of effective overlordship by Sokoto from 1804 until the British occupation in 1900. In return for appointment, the chiefs of states paid tribute and gave allegiance to Sokoto, and provided military contingents when required. In their relations with their fiefholders or hereditary chiefs of vassal states, the kings of the principal Hausa-Fulani states acted in a similar manner and enjoyed similar rights. In the same way fiefholders, apart from collecting tax, stores, labour and military detachments from their fiefs, had the right to appoint or depose the community chiefs, as they in turn could do with their ward-heads. Thus there was a continuous chain of loyalty from Sokoto through the kings, their fiefholders or vassals, to the community chiefs and the ward-heads, and the principal relations of loyalty between subordinate and overlord were those of kinship or clientage. Before the British occupation an important distinction between vassal-chiefs and fiefholders, apart from the hereditary principle on which vassal-chieftainship was held, and the superior rights and status it involved, lay in the fact that fiefholders remained permanently in the capital, whereas vassal chiefs resided in their own country. Fiefholders administered distant territories by appointed and often titled intermediaries, known as *jakadu* (s. *jakada*) who carried their instructions to the community chiefs and supervised their execution.

Finally, the structural nature of the titles merits attention. Traditional titles are permanent corporations, to which territorial areas are attached for administration, as are permanent possessions such as farms, official residences, praise-songs and subordinate titles. Consequently it is common to find persons attached as clients to the title, as a permanent corporation, rather than to any particular holder of it; and the titles, as corporations, provide permanent principles of alignment and organization in all Hausa states. They provide the enduring structure of political relations, a framework of established offices and statuses which act as relatively fixed points about which political relations of authority and competition are articulated, at an individual level as well as between groups. As such, titles are extended to apply to all groups where traditional leadership is exercised through a hierarchy. Occupational titles, mentioned earlier, provide one illustration of this; another and clearer case is the play-associations of boys and girls, which are organized about ranked series of titles.

Clientage and Bond Friendship

The term 'clientage' has been used frequently above: it designates a variety of relationships, which all have inequality of status of the associated persons as a common characteristic. Only the main types of clientage will be distinguished here. In the political field, clientage as a permanent association between individuals and the titles as corporations has been instanced. Title-holders are themselves clients of their superior, and have subordinate community chiefs as their clients; thus chieftainship is itself a type of clientage, with limitation of the field of eligibility as a characteristic of hereditary chieftainship at any level. Similarly, a fiefholder's agents were bound by ties of clientage, kinship, slavery, or a combination of these to their lord and distinguished according to their specific function as *jakadu* (intermediaries to fiefs), *fadawa* (s. *bafada*, agents at the lord's court) and *barori* (s. *bara*, a term which describes all forms of clients, including menial attendants who farm and run errands at their lord's direction). A wider area of clientage is covered by the term *cafka* or traditional allegiance of territorial and kinship units to titles or dynasties.

Barantaka is the term used to denote any form of clientage, the domestic as well as the political. It will be seen that nowadays, with the prohibition of slavery, there is an overlap of domestic and political clientage in the associations centred on chiefs or holders of lesser offices. But domestic clientage can be distinguished as a separate type of relation when both parties are commoners, and may be of the same or different occupational class. Omitting for the moment ties of clientage involving wealthy merchants or

INTRODUCTION

women, domestic clientage can be summarily described as an association in which men not originally linked by ties of consanguinity of affinity adopt the relative statuses and roles of senior and junior kinsmen; that is, of father and son where the difference in age is pronounced, or of elder and younger brother where it is not. As such, domestic clientage is substitute kinship, and the junior or client (*bara*), in several cases which were studied, invariably lacked effective support from kinsfolk in the community, and was usually an immigrant. But whereas kinship is a permanent relation, clientage is an association terminable at the wish of either party. Enduring clientage, whether political or domestic is rewarded by the superior as best he can, with office and title if these are in his power, or with wives if he is a commoner. In both political and domestic clientage of proven value, the superior often gives his kinswoman, a daughter or a sister, in marriage to the client, thus changing the nature of their association and strengthening the bond. The same principle of marriage linkages is used between members of descent groups with hereditary claims to chieftainship.

Clientage with a specifically commercial function is a distinct class; two main types can be distinguished, that between a wealthy merchant (the *ubandaki* or *ubangida*) and his agent (*danarziki*), who trades independently at a distance with capital in cash or goods provided free of interest by the principal, which is paid off by deliveries of local products which the latter wants. Such an arrangement, if enduring, implies high standards of mutual loyalty and goodwill. Merchants are usually in subordinate relations of clientage to important officials charged with administration or supervision of their areas of interest. Such a superior is referred to by the merchant as his *ubandaki* or *ubangida*.

Clientage also obtains in a different form between women, whose diverse economic spheres and lack of political interests severely reduce the functional value of the association. In two forms described fully in the text, institutional relationships between women not linked by ties of kinship have aspects resembling certain features of male clientage, possibly in deliberate imitation. These relationships are firstly that in which the *yaya* (elder) occupies the senior status, and the *kanwar rana* (younger sister of the day) is the junior, and that in which the *uwar daki* (mother of the hut) or *uwar rana* (mother of the day) is senior to her '*yar arziki* (daughter of fortune). Three factors are present in these formalized asymmetrical relations between women, namely, degree of age-difference —if the parties are of fairly close age, and consequently status, the relation is that of elder to younger sister; if they are of different generations, of mother to daughter; secondly, use of kinship terms and exaggerated behavioural patterns associated with them; and, thirdly, the initiation of the relation by public action. In these two relationships, the element of clientage is prominent only on ceremonial occasions and during the stages of establishment of the bond, and the quasi-kinship behaviour is otherwise characteristic. In effect, as indicated above, domestic clientage among men is also patterned on kinship and provides substitutes for kinship relations. Hence the formation of such an association between adult males has a similar effect to adoption, and this act of adoption between two adult women is really the core of the two relationships discussed above.

Formal bond-friendship between persons of the same sex is a symmetrical relation of equals in status and age, with a variety of reciprocal obligations emphasizing the mutual identification of the partners. Between women, such bond-friends are known as *kawaye* (s. *kawa*), and they exchange gifts on ceremonial occasions, which progressively double their value at each exchange; other aspects of the *kawa* relation are fully documented in the text.

The rituals of kinship and bond-friendship which mark definite stages in the life-cycle, and create new roles and relationships, together form one field of ritual activity which is of great interest to all Hausa, but particularly to women. Apart from these rituals of kinship and association, there are three other systems of ritual and belief which together form a common system of cosmology and values for the Hausa. The principles contained in this total system compete with one another as bases of explanation and action in the magico-religious fields, and are actively championed by their exponents, who manipulate the statuses they enjoy to promote the beliefs traditionally attached to that status at the expense of competing principles. An example of this competition in the real world is given in the text (pp. 223 sqq.). These competing systems can be summarized briefly as 'medicines' (*boka*), which act by principles of sympathetic and contagious magic; animism, the worship of spirits (*iskoki*), particularly in the cult of spirit-possession (*bori*);*

* For *bori*, see Note (9) of Chapter III, and description on pp. 63–5.

and Islam, which incorporates animistic elements as *jinn* and magical elements in the charms and divinatory practices of learned scholars (the *malamai*), and subordinates both these to the will of Allah in terms of the concept of predestination and fate (H. *rabo*), in accordance with the teachings of the Kadiriya sect, which is the predominant Muslim teaching in Hausaland.

London, 1952   M. G. Smith

1981 Reprint Correction

For "dowry" read "wedding presents" throughout the book.

The Hausa word *gara*, which I mistakenly translated as "dowry" in 1950, refers to the traditional gifts of cooking utensils, household effects, and small sums of money which the bride's family and friends collect for her, especially on her first marriage, and which they carry in a procession to her new home as part of the wedding festivities.

M. F. S.
1981

PART ONE

HAUSA COMPOUND (GIDA)

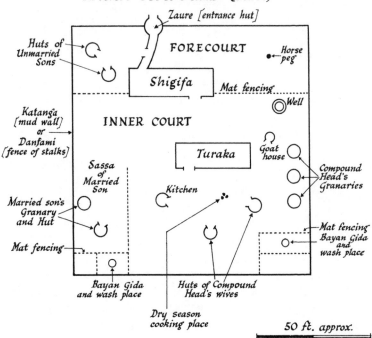

Zaure [entrance hut]

FORECOURT

Huts of Unmarried Sons

Horse peg

Shigifa

Mat fencing

Katanga [mud wall] or Danfami [fence of stalks]

INNER COURT

Well

Turaka

Goat house

Compound Head's Granaries

Sassa of Married Son

Kitchen

Married son's Granary and Hut

Mat fencing

Mat fencing Bayan Gida and wash place

Bayan Gida and wash place

Huts of Compound Head's wives

Dry season cooking place

50 ft. approx.

CHAPTER I

c. 1890–1904
CHILDHOOD

My Father's Family History

First I will tell you about my forefathers. The grandfather of our grandfather (1) was the Chief of Kukawa, a town away to the north in Bornu. When he died, his sons who were our great-grandfathers quarrelled, because all of them wanted to inherit his title and position. One of them, the Galadima of Kukawa, was made Chief of Kukawa (2) and two of the Galadima's half-brothers by a different mother, the Ciroma and the Turaki, left Kukawa in anger and came south to the kingdom of Kano, to Zarewa town, and it was they who built our hamlet of Karo. Turaki and Ciroma spoke no Hausa, but their children born in Hausa country understood the Hausa speech. They no longer marked their children's faces in the Bornu fashion, they adopted the lighter nose and eye marks like I have.

When our great-grandfathers Turaki and Ciroma came from Bornu they brought no slaves with them, and only the elder brother had a wife; their half-brother, the son of a different mother, had been awarded the title and they had failed, so they decided to leave the country, they sold their possessions and came south to the kingdom of Kano, and there they worked and worked and collected wealth. At Karo near Zarewa they cleared the bush, they cut down the trees and made farms; the younger brother got a wife, they worked and they begot children. The wife of the elder brother brought forth Dara, Ibrahim Dara my own grandfather, while the younger brother also had sons; Maidamishi, Mallam Husaini, Idirisu. Sadaka, I remember, was Idirisu's wife. There were daughters, too: Hajera, Rabo and Juma. I know the names of our grandparents, but I am not sure which of them were Ciroma's children and which were Turaki's. They all lived together, with their slaves, in their hamlet of Karo. We used to hear all about it from our parents, they would talk about the old days and we children would listen; it was good that we should know about our forefathers.

When Ciroma and Turaki had done, they died (3). Then their son Ibrahim Dara, my father's father, became the head of the house. The elder brother's compound was here, the younger brothers' compounds were there, all in the same hamlet. My grandfather Dara had four wives and twenty-three children, and he had as many as one hundred and thirty slaves; his younger brother Maidamishi had forty slaves. The slaves lived in their part of the hamlet (we call such a hamlet of slaves *rinji*), and the slaves worked on the farm while their wives made porridge for them to eat. They called their master 'Father'.

Grandfather Ibrahim Dara

Ibrahim Dara, my father's father, was killed by his own mare which he had bought himself. He always took her hay to her, and one evening while he was feeding her she kicked him; he fell on his back and lay still. Much later that evening his family started looking for him, but when they found him they saw that he was dead. Then there was crying and wailing, crying and wailing; that is what our parents told us.

After Ibrahim Dara died, everyone continued to farm; it's still the same, farming is the work at our hamlet of Karo. When we went out to the hamlet, we would see lots of granaries; the head of the house and his family would go out from Zarewa to Karo to farm in the wet season, and at harvest time when the farm was fruitful the harvest was divided in two, the slaves were left in the hamlet with one part and the master and his family returned with the other to Zarewa, the walled town. Ibrahim Dara had three houses, one at Karo, one at Zarewa, and one in Zaria City. If they had to flee from Zarewa in time of war, they went to Zaria and took refuge inside the walls of the city. The master and all his family would flee, taking all their slaves with them so that the raiders could not seize them. They would leave behind a few strong, reliable slaves, who would run away into the bush if they saw raiders coming and hide in the trees. The invaders would go into the compounds and when they found no one, burn them. The corn

would all burn, and that household would go hungry. When they
went away the slaves would come back to the compound at night,
and find no one; the raiders had gone—till next year. They never
returned the same year. Most of the raiders who came to Zarewa
were Maradawa or 'Mbutawa. When the slaves returned they would
look around the house—it wasn't all burnt—and they would clean
it up and settle down. The master stayed in Zaria City with all his
valuable possessions, and after three or four months, when that war
was over, he returned to his hamlet.

When Ibrahim Dara died his sons abandoned the house in Zaria
City and only used their compounds in Zarewa and Karo. Zarewa
is a big town now with a great many people—a great many Kano
people. At Karo our kinsfolk are still there, lots of them, elder
brother's son and younger brother's son all living near to one
another. When I was young at Karo the *rinji* was to the west of us
and our compounds were to the east, the slaves lived in one place
and we in another; they used to come and greet us and bring
bundles of guineacorn, groundnuts and yams, cotton and sweet
potatoes. There were more than 250 of them, and there were crowds
of us. Everyone in our family had his part of the *rinji*. Even now
we are still there—last year I went and visited them all.

Ibrahim Dara collected money and went to Zaria market and
bought some of his slaves, then they had children. When he died
some of them fled, and the remainder were divided up and given to
his children. He had one big *rinji*, the only *rinji* in our family,
Anguwan Karo. He freed Sarkin Gandu; Sharo, Kado's father
(raiders caught Kado's wife much later) he freed. He freed Hajera
and gave her a dowry and arranged a marriage for her because of
her goodness; whatever you said to her, she said 'Yes, very well'.
Her father and mother were Dangwari and Mada, but they were
not freed. When Dara died at Karo he left 130 slaves. Eighty fled,
in the morning we saw they had gone—they did not want to stay
with his children. The family was wailing because he was dead and
the slaves saw their chance and ran away. About fifty were divided
up among Ibrahim Dara's heirs; everyone took his share to his
house, and they did his farm work for him. Men inherited two parts,
women one part. While Dara was alive all his sons were in one
place, working in his *gandu* (4) at Karo; all the slaves were in their
father's hand. When he died each son took his own slaves, and they
built their separate compounds in Karo and the nearby hamlets.

Their father's farmland was divided among them and each son worked his own land. Those hamlets were not *rinjoji*. After Dara's death there were a great many sons but there was no quarrelling; since their father had been wealthy they divided up his wealth, but if a man leaves nothing his children stay together in one *gandu* and keep on working, they are seeking food. But since when Dara died there was plenty, each son took his own share of the inheritance.

Malam Buhari, the eldest son of Ibrahim Dara, remained at Karo with about twenty slaves. His younger brother Audu and his family and Tsoho, our father, were with him at Karo, but each had his own house and farm separately. Sa'idu and Ubangida were at Wawaye, Alfa was at Ruwanbago, Balarabe was at Dankusuba, Audu dan Kunza was at Guga, Audu dan Ayashe was at Maicibi, Audu dan Ayashe (another of the same name) was at Kuriareji. They all lived in the hamlets and if war came they went into Zarewa town.

Slave Estates

When the children of slaves grew up, they were married, they were joined in a marriage of kinship. (5) When anyone in the *rinji* had a child, there was a naming ceremony (6) and a ram was killed and porridge made. (7) The child was freed (8) and it came into our family. We took part in one another's ceremonies, there was 'kinship'. When the *malams* (9) had come in the morning and given the infant its name, the grown-ups collected us children together and the head of the family got up and told us: 'You see your brother so-and-so; he is your younger brother.' They became kinsfolk, they were not called *dimajai*, sons of slaves, they were called brothers. In the evening of the naming-day, porridge would be made, and the rams cooked and everyone feasted. When they grew up some of these children of our slaves married us and some of them married outside the family.

That is, the slaves in our *rinji* were the ones who had been bought in the market; all their children were freed. Sarkin Gandu (whom Ibrahim Dara freed) had four wives; his children were married in the town, one married a blacksmith and one married a praise-singer. The reason why Dara freed his slaves was because he wanted to be rewarded when he died—because of religion. It is like giving alms. But if masters of slaves did not attend to religion, they did not do it at all.

CHILDHOOD

This is what we heard, about the inheritance of a slave's posses-sions, but we never saw it happen. If a slave died, his master took his possessions, they were his property. When the slave's children grew up the master arranged marriages for them and gave them houses and farmland. If a slave married a free woman, she remained free and her children would be free—'they have sucked milk from a free woman'. She would not work in the house of her husband's master, she would work in her own house and on her own farmland. If a slave asks a woman to marry him, and she sees a compound and money and good farming and ornaments, will she refuse? No. If a man-slave married a woman-slave who belonged to another family, she continued to work in her master's house in the day, and she came home to her husband at night. Her children belonged to her master, they followed the milk side; even if she had ten or more children they wouldn't belong to her husband's master. My family did not mind their men-slaves marrying women who belonged to another family; when the children grew up their mother's master would take them. If a free man bought a slave woman he would give two male slaves in exchange for her and she would be his concubine, but never his wife. When she had children by him she became free, and she could leave his house and marry someone else. We called the man who bought her and made her his concubine her 'father'—she was his property. If she ran away and married another man, he was her real husband. But if a concubine had children she would hardly ever leave. If she had no children she might run away into the world.

This is how the slaves worked: each slave had his own farming land, if he had a wife she helped him, if he had none he worked alone, and if he had children they helped him too. In the early morning the slaves and their sons would go to their own farms. At this time of day (9.30 a.m.) they came back and went to the master's farm, the *gandu* fields, until Azahar (2.30) when they returned. At noon food was taken out to them at the *gandu* farm. At Azahar they came in and rested, then in the afternoon the men slaves went to their own farm-plots, and their wives and children went to their little plots too. Everyone grew guineacorn, cotton, millet, cowpeas, sweet potatoes, pumpkins, groundnuts, peppers, bitter tomatoes, sugar-cane, rice, *iburu*, (10) okras, tomatoes and green peppers.

In the morning the slaves ate in their own compounds. At mid-day porridge made from the *gandu* grain was taken out to the slaves on the farm, while their wives ate grain from their own store at home. In the evening they all came to the front of our house and ate the *gandu* food of the master's house, each one took his own and they ate it there in front of our compound. The grain was divided out amongst the slaves' wives and they would grind it and bring back the flour to our compound and make the porridge. Everyone ate it, men and women and children—they did no cooking in their own homes except in the early morning. At midday and in the evening they all ate the *gandu* porridge. (11) In the morning the master's head wife distributed grain to them and the slaves' wives ground the flour for the midday meal; then after that was eaten she gave them more grain and they ground the flour for the evening meal. It was cooked in a giant pot in our compound.

Whatever the slaves grew on their own farm-plots was their own, they took it to market to sell and bought gowns; their wives bought cloth and made ceremonial exchange-gifts. (12) The slaves did not give their master any of their own farm produce, they did his work for him and that was that. If we had a ceremony, they all brought things to give us; if they had one we all took things to them, we took part in each other's ceremonies. When I was married they collected a bag of rice and a bag of grain, they packed the bags tight and gave them to the master as reinforcements. (13) If the master's wife had a child, the slaves ground flour and made porridge and millet-balls, (14) they killed a chicken and brought gifts on the naming-day. They would all come to our entrance-hut on the naming-day and eat.

In the afternoons after work on the *gandu* farm was finished, some of the slaves worked at crafts. Some wove on the men's narrow loom, some were brokers in the market, some were salt-sellers, some sold kolanuts or sugar-cane or sweet potatoes or cotton, or other things. Some were dyers, some grew onions or sugar-cane in marsh-plots. Some just farmed their own plots. Those who did crafts had been born in the *rinji*; slaves who were bought in the market could not do anything except farming. If a slave had a son he would see a craftsman working, he would go and watch him and he would learn. The bought slaves spoke 'Gwari', but their children spoke Hausa.

I remember when a slave known as the Chief of Adamawa came touring the country, he came to our market-place, riding his horse; he filled his hand with tobacco-flour and put it all into his mouth.

He came with his praise-singers, he dismounted and danced. We were all laughing. The king of Kano had bought him and appointed him 'Chief of Adamawa'; he went about the country and every slave who had been caught in Adamawa country came running to him and crouched down and greeted him with gifts of money. He couldn't talk (Hausa) properly and his praise-singers couldn't talk properly. He sang a song saying he only wanted groundnuts. The Chief of Adamawa, the groundnut-eater! The king of Kano sent him on this ridiculous tour—the king didn't get a tenth of a penny out of it, but it amused him. If you bought an Adamawa man, and he heard their drumming you would see his head going like this, like this until he went to them and danced.

Our slaves were from many tribes, there was no sort of slave that we hadn't got in our *rinji*. When they had children, the children were given our inherited facial marks, the Barebare mark down their nose. Not all masters gave their slaves' children their own marks. When the boys were seven years old they were taught to say their prayers and they went to the Koran school and learnt to recite passages from the Koran; some of the girls went, too. There were several teachers, Malam Yusufu and Malam Tanko and Malam Audu Bawan Allah. There was no *bori* (15) dancing in our hamlet except for one of our slaves, Mada, a Gwari, who was sometimes possessed. We used to go to the compounds of the prostitutes in Zarewa town and watch them *bori*-dancing.

Slaves sometimes escaped, our Tagwayi escaped and so did Hasada. Hasada ran away one night. You would hunt and hunt for them, and then one day you would hear that someone had seen them in a far-away town. If anyone questioned him the slave would say he had been sent to do an errand for his master. You never caught them again.

The Family after Grandfather Ibrahim's Death

When Ibrahim Dara died, our own father, Tsoho, went to live with his maternal grandfather, Mai Anguwa, (16) at Gwibi. Mai Anguwa was the father of Anja, our father's mother. He was wealthy, but he had only one son, Danyaya, and one daughter, Anja, so he had great possessions but no children—only a lot of slaves. My father's sister Alahamdi also went with him to live with Mai Anguwa, and he arranged marriages for both of them; he gave

Tsoho two wives and he arranged Alahamdi's marriage; she had nine children, four of them are still alive. Mai Anguwa's craft was dyeing, and after that farming, he would go round his farm encouraging his slaves while they were working. He died before I can remember, I didn't know him, I only heard about him; he was rich, and he arranged our father's marriage. Our father's father was wealthy, and then his maternal grandfather also was wealthy. Mai Anguwa arranged a marriage for Tsoho with a daughter of the Gwibi blacksmiths, the makers of farm tools.

When our father Tsoho had lived in Gwibi for three years with his two wives and they were both pregnant, he said he would return to his family at Karo. His grandfather wept bitterly because he wanted Tsoho to become his son, but he had not begotten him and he wished to return to his father's house. Father's family back in Zarewa were delighted, they put on their finest clothes and rejoiced because their kinsman had come home with his two wives —our parents. They were glad and they gave him the land that he had inherited, and he farmed. He had inherited slaves, every son of Dara had ten or fifteen men and women who farmed for him. They grew cotton, they grew tobacco and groundnuts, pumpkins and rice, sugar-cane in the stream bed, and guineacorn. Tsoho worked too. Some owners of slaves worked together, the master and his sons and his slaves; some of them put on their best clothes and sat in the shade and watched. Our father worked.

When father returned home from Gwibi it was the brothers' custom every market-day to go and trade; they would put on their best robes and mount their horses, the horses went *kan-kan kankan*. They went to Makarfi market on their horses, they sat down in the market—about twenty of them—with their slaves who had carried the loads and their children, all in their fine clothes. They bought and sold, they sold cotton and sugar-cane and they bought food and kolanuts and tobacco-flowers to take home to the women. They sold their farm produce and bought food and luxuries. When it was market-day in Kudan, they went there to trade; at Dan Sambo market too they would trade and wear their fine clothes and ride their horses.

They all farmed, our family have no other craft to this day except farming; one or two weave, but most of them dislike weaving, they prefer farming. After their father Dara died, each son farmed on his own instead of in one *gandu*, but on market-day all the brothers

went to market together to trade. When they came home we
children were happy—'Father has come home! Father has come
home! Welcome home, Father!' He brought bean-cakes and sugar-
cane and yams and pumpkins and all sorts of food, it would be put
down in the baskets and the children carried it to the door of the
compound. Our father gave us fine things, he bought us rings and
bangles and cloth. His younger sister made stew for us, Father said
'All of you come and eat'. His elder brother was Malam Buhari,
and Malam Buhari's horse was called Bikili, Tsoho's was Danda,
Sa'i's horse was Tantabara, Audi's horse was Sari—they all had
horses and we knew all their names; there was Fari Biyar too, with
five white marks. The five horses of Dara's sons. Their compounds
were close, close together. Malam Bawa was there with his wives
Maria and Iya—he was a younger brother of our grandfather Dara.
There were about thirty compounds belonging to our family.
'Tantabara's father has come home, Fari Biyar's father has come
home, Danda's father has come home'—that was our own father—
and Fari Biyar's father was Audu. That is what we called our
fathers. We grew up with all their children.

If we saw our grandfathers, (17) when they had come back from
the farm and put on their gowns. then we seized them and hung
onto them until they put their hands in their pockets and threw us
some cowries (18)—our own money, in the old days. There were
twenty of us children, we used to plan to catch our grandfathers.
We knew Malam Bawa and Mai Yana, the others had died. If their
wives had mixed them some millet-balls then we came along to
grandfather's entrance-hut, and peeped, we peeped in, then when
we saw that it was ready, we came in and they gave us some to
eat. Malam Bawa was tall and dark, Mai Yana was light-skinned.
Malam Bawa was fiercer, if he saw us afar off he would pick up his
stick and say 'Come on, I'll beat you!' We would come, and he
would throw us some cowries and we would run away. We called
him Father of the Gwari, his slaves, and we called his sons 'Father'.
Mai Yana was the laughing one. He had one wife, Hajera, and one,
Taku. We grew up with them, we saw them all die. If our grandfathers went to market, we would meet them on the road and try
to take away the things they had bought—bean-cakes and root-
vegetables and all sorts of food. Our grandfathers only gave us
food and money, they didn't give us cloth.

CHAPTER II

FIRST MEMORIES

When I was two years old and it was time to wean me from my mother, Zetanku my father's old slave took me to live with her until I forgot about the breast. She said I cried a lot, I was with her for three months. She liked her master's baby and when it was time to wean me she came and said she wanted to take me. Father said 'Yes, you may take her'. Then she took me to her compound in the *rinji* where she lived with her husband Danku-rama. She vaccinated (1) me for smallpox; they used to scratch your arm until the blood came, then they got the fluid from some-one who had smallpox and rubbed it in. It all swelled up and you covered it until it healed. Some children used to die; your way of doing it is better. After three months Zetanku took me back to my mother.

About that time Dan Barahiya came with war:

> Dan Barahiya the oppressor,
> He seized the women of Giwa,
> He seized the children of Giwa,
> He seized the men of Giwa,
> Dan Barahiya the oppressor.

There had been a birth in our compound at Karo, and we were about to have the naming ceremony. We all fled to Zarewa from Karo, we went inside the town and held the naming ceremony there. Our mother put me on her back and covered up her head and face and went out. The men of the family told the slaves to gather up all our possessions and take them inside the town. When the rainy season came the war stopped and they took us back to our hamlet; that war didn't reach Zarewa, Giwa was its limit. When the raiders came in the dry season we used to take up the corn and hide it inside the town so that they should not come and burn it. The granaries were inside the town, then when the rains came the corn was taken out to the hamlet and everyone went out there to work and eat. It was taken out on donkeys. When war came they closed the town gates, they beat the big drum (like yours on the wall there), the men of the town hurried to man the walls and shoot at the enemy. When the Maradawa, Dan Barahiya's men, came one year they went all round the town walls but they could see no way in. Then they called out 'Peace! Peace! We have come so that you may sell us tobacco. Greet the young children for us! Peace!' The women were in the compounds, the men mounted the walls. One woman picked up her cotton-carder and said she would shoot them with it! The men had hunting bows and quivers of arrows. The raiders had come from Fatika, they were looking around and they saw our town. When they saw they were stopped, they went away. You know Gwamma, my brother Kadiri's wife? Well, the Maradawa seized her grandmother, her father's mother, out in the hamlet and her kinsfolk ransomed her from away beyond Sokoto. The Maradawa didn't kill their slaves, they took them home, and if you brought money they gave them up. The 'Mbatawa, the Ningi, always killed people. In those days there was always fear; war, war, war—they caught a man and they made him a slave, or else they killed him. Now the world is repaired, we are thankful.

About the time that they weaned me all the cattle were dying, one year they all died: (2) it was about four years after Dan Barahiya's war that the cattle all died and the Fulani went mad looking for them, so that we had to tell them to look somewhere else so that they should go away.

I lived happily in my mother's hut for two years, then my grandmother A'i came and begged my parents to let her adopt me. She was the sister of my mother's mother Cibi, who had already adopted my elder sister Dije. Mother knew that A'i was ill-natured, but when she came to ask if she could adopt me, Mother was afraid of my father's kinsmen who wanted to give me to A'i, so she said nothing; they did not know her disposition, she was not of their kin. Much later, when my fathers brought me home again, Mother said, 'Mm. I knew she wouldn't be able to keep the child.'

A'i took me to live with her, she beat me, she made me miserable with her scolding. She took me when I was four years old and I was with her for two years. She had a sister Cibi, my mother's own mother, and another sister Mairo. A'i took me first to Kaura. After about two months at Kaura she divorced her husband and went to Mahuta and married someone else. After five months there she left and broke up the marriage—her husband didn't know what she was like, if he had known he would never have married her, he would have said he did not want her. She returned to Kaura. When she came back to Kaura her son came to visit her from his father's house in Katsina, but he ran away after ten days, she scolded him so much. When she had finished her *Idda* (3) she married the chief of Gwibi, near Kaura, Sarkin Gwibi. (4) When Sarki saw her beating me, I was crying, he said 'Leave her alone, don't beat their daughter like that'. She abused him and said 'Is she your daughter then?' He was afraid of her, her co-wife Tagudu was afraid of her; if I went to her co-wife's hut she would give me food, if A'i had gone out. 'Quick, eat quickly!' Tagudu would say. When A'i came back she would start nagging—'Get up and do your spinning, get up and fetch some water'. Then she caught me and took me to her hut. Her co-wife was afraid of her, she did not want her to quarrel with her. If A'i was scolding me or Sarki, her co-wife Tagudu would go into her hut and stay there, quite quiet. 'Tagudu, stop running, your head will break!' we used to sing to her. In that compound there was me and there was Lantana and Juma, the children of Sarki's younger brother, their part of the compound was next to ours. We would be playing together, then A'i would come: 'Come on, come on and do your work!' I was only a little girl, I wasn't very strong. The boys too used to sing about her in secret, they were frightened of her.

> *A'i who scolds, A'i who scolds,*
> *A'i who beats, A'i who curses!*

They wouldn't even go near her hut.

One day my mother came to her mother Cibi's house, she sent for me and I went and she gave me porridge to eat. I was crying. She came once to Mahuta and three times to Kaura. She saw that I wasn't happy, she said 'You must be patient and bear it'. When she went home she didn't tell my father, she was afraid to. It was my grandmother Cibi who told them, she went to our home and appealed to my father, she said 'Take away your daughter, she is very unhappy'. Then the four fathers came on their horses; they went to grandmother Cibi's house, they did not go to the house of

A'i who ill-treated me. They sent for me, my sister Dije came and called me—'Come, we have visitors'. I went, and then I saw the horses, I said 'Ap! There's Bikili, there's Tantabara, there's Akawal, there's Dandana—exactly like our fathers' horses!' Then Dije said 'Yes, it's they'. Then I peeped into the entrance-hut, and I saw a lot of people and a great many of my father's kinsmen, then I ran away. Then they said 'Come in'. While Dije was explaining it to me I was saying 'Hallo Bikili, hallo Akawal, hallo Tantabara, hallo Dandana', I was singing to the horses and dancing about. Dije laughed and said 'They have come and you're happy'. Then I was singing 'Welcome, father, welcome, welcome!' They were sitting with grandmother Cibi's husband. They called me and I went in, they said 'You've come? We're going.' I had no proper cloth, only a ragged one. Dije gave me a cloth to put on. My father Ubangida took me and said 'Ah, our little Baba, trouble's finished and we're going home—are we?' I said 'M-hm'. Then Father of Danda, that was Ubangida, (5) set me on his horse, I looked around from side to side; Father of Gwibi and Father of Madunguri and Father of Tantabara took me away.

About this time of day (5 p.m.) we arrived home, we went into the compound and Mother drew water and washed me and tidied me up and put my antimony on my eyes; in our own hut they gave me food and I ate a little, but I had got used to trouble, grandmother A'i did not give me enough to eat. Then my brothers and sisters came and played with me, they took me to this house and they took me to that house. My mother was rejoicing and her co-wife was rejoicing, my father was rejoicing—'Today they have brought Baba home, Allah be praised! Today her troubles are over!' Grandmother A'i cried, she broke up her marriage and came to Karo, saying she wanted me back, but my kinsmen refused. Everywhere there was food. 'Look at that child, she is thin, they have been ill-treating her!' There were my younger brothers, all fat, and I was small and thin. But after seven days I began to eat properly. A'i used to give me yesterday's food and say 'Eat it!' I said 'I cannot eat it', then she would beat me. She would give me spinning to do, I couldn't do it. I was there in her compound for two years, just me in her hut. Later on she adopted another child in Zarewa, but after two years they took her away; it was her nature, you see. When my brothers and sisters came and said 'Come and play', I would take out my spinning, then Mother would say 'Go and play'. Then I would get a little water-pot to go to the river, and she would say 'Put that down and go and play'. I had got used to working, but now my troubles were over.

We used to sing this song about our villages:

> *Ya-re, a-ye, ya-re, a-ye,*
> *Let's go to Ruwanbago and see the chief's son like the white men,*
> *Where shall I return? I always return to Karo.*
> *Habibu's town, Habibu Mama's grandson,*
> *I'll go back to Ruwanbago.*
> *When you see Bagudu, look behind him, Hari will be there.*
> *I'll return to Zarewa, at Zarewa I will stay.*

Then we sang this song:

> *May Allah give me a true friend, whether he's small or big,*
> *Even an infant sucking at the breast, or one lying in the womb,*
> *When he comes forth we'll be friends.*
> *Allah give me a true friend, whether he is small or big.*

When I came home I found my little brother Tanko in our hut. Then Tanko died and later on my mother's other children, A'i, Mairo, Balarabe and Shetu also died. My elder sister Dije was eight years old then and I was six, but Dije was living in grandmother Cibi's house, Cibi had adopted her. Dije was happy because that grandmother was very kind, she didn't scold. Dije stayed with her until Cibi died, and the year Cibi died Dije was married. In our own compound there was no disagreement, nothing of that kind. My father's wives joked and laughed together, they had nothing to do with quarrelling. They made food, they used to give me nice things, they would say 'Let's do this', or 'Let's do that', and they did not bicker. My father farmed and he was a Koranic student, a *malam*, he taught the boys to recite from the Book. When we went to Karo, the slaves would sweep the compound and the grain would be distributed, they would come and say 'Greetings, blessings on you! The people from the town have come back.' Then there would be games and rejoicing and we would play together. They used to have double names, if you called the first part of the name they answered and completed it, like this: there was 'Gift of Allah', you would call 'Gift!' and she would answer 'of Allah!' There was 'Wealth belongs to'—'Allah', 'Life in this world'—'patience', 'The Lord of all slaves'—'Allah', those were all women slaves. The men were called 'May Allah prolong'—'our father's life', 'Gift of Allah', and many others. The slaves called us daughters of the house 'Yaya', as we call our elder brothers and sisters; they called my brothers 'Yaya' too, or 'Kawu' as we call our mother's brothers. We didn't play with them much, if they did something wrong we hit them. I played with my ten 'sisters', and when the dry season came round we went to live inside the town and left the slaves there in the hamlet. Sarkin Gandu was in charge of them, he and his wives and children always lived at Karo. When he went to the farm he gathered them all together to work, when they had finished they went to their homes and did their own work, each one had his own farmland. When we went in to Zarewa in the dry season, the season of marriage feasts, we found everyone making marriage porridge, killing chickens and goats, and taking food to the men to eat, taking food to the girls to eat, taking food to the parents and elders to eat, and taking food to the drummers so that they should eat and we should enjoy their drumming.

A Day in my Childhood

In the morning when the sun got up our mothers would rise and start making bean-cakes; we would get up and wash our faces and put on our cloths and they would give us the bean-cakes and we would go round the village selling them. When we had sold them we came back and Mother gave us some grain to grind. She did a lot and we did a little. We sang our songs at the door of her hut, we were grinding away, one of us would start the song and the others would answer.

When I returned from grandmother A'i's house I found many people in our compound; Tsoho our father, our own mother Fatsuma (her elder daughter Dije my sister, was at grandmother Cibi's house until Cibi died and Dije came home for two years until she was married). There was me. There was my younger brother Tanko, Mother was carrying him about on her back when I came home from Gwibi, he was less than two years old. Mother's co-wife Rabi had Tanimu, she was carrying him on her back, while her other sons, Mika'ilu and Kadiri, could walk. The other compounds in Karo were the homes of our parents, there was Bare's house, there was Audu's house, Sa'i's house and Ubangida's house (he was very fond of me, my father's brother), Malam Idi's house,

Malam Bawa's house and seven more. We had kinsfolk living in
Dutsenkura, in Kaura, in Zarewa, in Makarfi—in all the towns and
villages round there were members of our family. One would marry
a kinswoman and she would have children, another would marry a
kinswoman and she would have children. They liked to arrange
family marriages.

So when we came back from selling our bean-cakes we would
eat millet-balls with sour milk, then when the afternoon brought a
shadow across the compound we would settle down to grind the
corn—'I'm going to take that stone!', 'I'm going to have that one!'
Then we would sing as we worked. We sang the song of the Madaki,
a son of the king of Zaria who ruled Giwa; we heard his praise-song
from the Giwa people who came to our town. He was wandering
about somewhere in the west when his father won the throne. His
father called him back and gave him Giwa district and made him
Madaki. (6)

> *Lord of the broad world,*
> *Son of Ali with the* dodo.
> *We will go to Giwa,*
>   *They're the goats of your house;*
> *We will go to Makarfi,*
>   *They're the goats of your father;*
> *We'll come back to Likoro country,*
>   *They're the chickens of your house;*
> *We will go to Gimi,*
>   *They're the ducks of your father;*
> *We will go to Makarfi,*
>   *She's your father's pigeon.*
> *Lord of the broad world,*
> *Son of Ali with the* dodo.

Isn't a great chief a *dodo*? All the towns of Zaria were just like his
household goats and chickens, you see—so his praise-singers told
him. You know Dangaladiman Busa who plays the pipe (7) here
now—well, his father played for this Madaki, he was very generous
to his musicians, he gave them money and gowns and turbans.
That is why they liked him. He was a good-humoured man. The
European we called 'Kwatamassa' came when he was ruling Giwa.

When we had finished grinding we gave our mothers the flour.
They cooked a big pot of porridge and a pot of stew; then they

would put out the porridge and pour the stew over it, 'Take this to so-and-so', 'Take this to so-and-so'. We picked it up and took it to the men, and then we came back and ate ours with the other children; if we weren't full we got some more. When we were satisfied we put down our wooden bowls and calabashes (there were no enamel bowls then), then we ran off and played. At nightfall we came back and spread our mats in Mother's hut; the wife who was cooking that day went to the husband's hut, the maker of porridge took fire to the husband's hut, she drew water and she lit the lamp and took it. He would be at the house-door talking to his friends, when he came in he shut the door and went to his hut. The children filled up their mother's hut. In the morning she would wake us up and we all washed our faces.

We didn't play or joke with our 'fathers', only with our grand-fathers. We went to grandfather Malam Bawa's house, if we saw they were cooking porridge we peeped in; if Grandfather saw us he would say 'Come in and eat millet-balls'. When we had eaten he would give us some money and send us away. Then to grandfather Mai Yana's house, we would say 'We've been to grandfather Malam Bawa's house and he's given us millet-balls; now we've come here to get some food'. He would say 'There's none'. Then we would say 'Give us some money and we will buy bean-cakes'. Then he gave us some and we went inside his compound, they made bean-cakes in his house. We bought some. We did not play with our fathers, we just bowed down and greeted them politely. But grandfathers— we were always giving them trouble, we ate up their money and we ate up their food, then we would say 'Come on, we'll leave him!' Next day we would come back, he would pick up his stick and say 'Run away and leave me alone'. We made faces at him then, 'Rowo rowo rowo rowo!' We knew three of our grandfathers, the others had died. If he didn't give us any money we would sing

> *Malam Bawa of Karo,*
> *He always comes laughing,*
> *Hurrying along, round-shouldered,*
> *He always comes scolding,*
> *Malam Bawa of Karo!*

'Go away, go away!' Then he would take out some money and throw it to us. Then off we went to the sellers of groundnuts and bean-cakes.

We brothers and sisters all lived in our mother's hut and at night we would tell stories and talk, then we would go to sleep. When day came we got up and washed our faces, we made porridge and we made millet-balls. When we were able to make porridge and pound grain in the mortar and grind it on the stone, we used to tell Mother to sit down and we would do it for her. When we had slaves they did the house-work, ours was only play. My mother and her co-wife spun thread for sale, they made millet-balls for sale, they made bean-cakes, groundnut cakes, roasted salted groundnuts, fried groundnuts and groundnut oil—they sold them all. At that time our mothers did not know how to weave as we do now, on broad looms. The wives used to make porridge and stew for their husband, they made it very tasty, with meat. The slaves made their own food separately, and we made a little bit of porridge and a little bit of stew in a very small pot. Boys follow their fathers, they learn to farm and recite the Koran; girls follow their mothers, they spin and cook. Father was dark, short like his father Dara, with long thin hands and feet. When we got up in the morning we used to go to his hut and greet him. 'How did you sleep? Have you rested?' 'I am quite well, I am quite rested.' When he had dressed he went out to the entrance-hut and ate his food with his brothers, they would all come, one would spread his mat here, one would spread his there, and his son would bring him food, millet-balls or porridge. Malam Buhari would come, Audu would come, they would sit down and eat. When they had finished we brought them water to wash their hands, and picked up the things and ate up the remains until we were quite full. We had already had our food inside the compound, then we came and ate what they had left, we picked it all up and took it away. If they were going out to the farm and it was the work season, then they would get up and go; if it was not the farming season they would go to the market, until the afternoon when everyone went home.

After the morning meal we went into the compound and if Mother had things to sell we went to market and sold them for her. If she made you beanflour cakes you took them, if she made bean-cakes wrapped in leaves you took them, if she made cornflour cakes you took them, or little bean-cakes. We went to market and walked about selling our wares, and brought home the money. Our sisters and cousins would say 'Put your basket on your head and come with me, pick it up quickly and let's go along together!' Then off we went, when we got to the market-place we settled down to sell: 'Look at my cakes—give me your money!' When we sold some we were happy, we put away the money and covered it up. A little later someone else would come along to buy. It was in the time of our cowrie-money, three hundred shells were a penny-halfpenny, two hundred were a penny; four hundred cowries was twopence and fourpence-halfpenny was nine hundred cowries. A buyer would come with his cowries, and you counted them and counted them, then he took away what he had bought. You know how we put things to sell, such as cakes, in a calabash, then we keep the money in a different part of the calabash. When you had sold everything you went back home with your cowries and your mother counted them—that's all till tomorrow! She hid them in a cooking-pot, and if you saw something you wanted she would buy it and give it to you. My mother was a secluded wife, (8) she didn't leave the compound. If we sold our wares quickly we came back home at once, if they didn't sell we brought it home at night and gave them to the children to eat. When we came home they would be making millet-balls or porridge or bean-cakes steamed in leaves or whatever was wanted for the evening meal. We were given a little grinding to do, we were learning. Then at night we would play and dance and sing our songs—the old-fashioned songs, not the ones they sing now.

Sometimes Mother went to visit her kinsfolk in Katsina at Kahuta, then she would take us with her to see her own grandmother, an old woman whom we called Iya. (9) Iya's husband was a barber-doctor, they called him Wanemutum. If we left home about now in the early morning, at the afternoon prayer we would reach their village. We used to take flour and cakes and salt and all kinds of food to divide among the people of the household. It wasn't far away. When we arrived at their house we rested, and they were very pleased that visitors had come. Iya used to make locust-bean cakes and her husband shaved men's heads. We would find her making her locust-bean cakes and we would chat to her, then when she got up to take them to market to sell we would go too. She sold them, then we bought food and ate it. She would sit and talk to Mother—'You run away and play!' Then we would come back and peep in—'You run off and do your own things!'

CHAPTER III

A GIRL'S FRIENDS

I had four *kawaye* at Zarewa; a *kawa* (1) is your special girl-friend. There was Kande, a Maguzawa girl, Zaila a daughter of butchers, Matan Sarki who was my 'sister'; Matan Sarki's mother was married and Matan Sarki was born in that house, then her mother broke up that marriage and came to our ward and married one of our 'fathers'; she brought Matan Sarki with her. She was nine years old and I was nine at the time, too. When we put on our best clothes and went to market, our mothers looked at us and saw that we were both handsome, so they said it would be nice to make us *kawaye*. Since I was already living here in the town, I bought ten kolanuts and some perfume and henna and I called my younger sister and gave them to her to take to Matan Sarki's mother who had married our 'father'. They gave her the gift-bearer's dues, a small share of the gift she had brought them. The following Friday Matan Sarki sent her younger sister to bring gifts to me. There we were, then when the Great Festival came round one friend would get out her money and buy oil and perfume and henna and kolanuts and take them to the other, so that she could dress her hair for the Feast. Matan Sarki would send her younger sister, who would come to our mother's hut. Mother would give her threepence or sixpence, her dues, and say to me 'Here are your things'. She was pleased.

This sort of friendship between women who are *kawaye* has nothing to do with men—men have their own sorts of friends. (2) In the morning we would go off to market together, the five of us, and when we came back we would take each other home and all eat food together. At night we used to go dancing. When one *kawa* got married, the others escorted her to her husband's home.

There was Zaila—they used to drum to her a lot, I remember her song: (3)

A GIRL'S FRIENDS

Zaila from a distant town,
Zaila from a distant town,
Whoever sees Zaila gives a thousand (cowries),
Even if it breaks a poor man,
Or he gives her five hundred.

This was my drum-rhythm:

Baba with many Gwari, (4)
Baba with many Gwari,
Everyone sees Baba with many Gwari.
In your house they don't say 'yar kwaliya
                    They say dan kwaliya,
In your house they don't say dan koko,
                    They say dan koko.
Baba with many Gwari.

Zaila was a daughter of the Zarewa butchers, she lived in their ward. We met in the market and we exchanged gifts. She died four years ago over at Jos. I liked Zaila, she was handsome. Matan Sarki, in our own kin, was dark like me but she had a longer nose. Among us all there wasn't one ugly one. Kande lived near the market, when we went to market we used to see her, the daughter of the sellers of salt. One day she said 'Do you like me?' I said 'Yes I like you'. I said '*Kawa*?' she said '*Kawa*'. There was no more discussion, we liked one another. It had nothing to do with our parents, Kande and I became *kawaye* on our own. I had been seeing her for a long time, then the day that desire came we became *kawaye*.

The girls of our family did not go to a Koran school, we were a farmer's family. At that time our male relatives did not farm, the slaves did that. The boys of the family went to Koran school.

In the evenings we used to play and dance and sing songs; there was one I remember about Maikano the *jakada's* (5) grandson, he was a young man who used to steal and give the stolen goods to the drummers and singers; when he gave them things they made songs about him.

There was a splendid drummer, and there was a song about him:

The drum drums health,
The drum drums wealth,
He takes his wife six hundred thousand cowries.
The drum drums health,

> *The drum drums wealth,*
> *He takes his son six hundred thousand cowries,*
> *The drum drums health,*
> *The drum drums wealth . . .*

Then we danced. Another of Mai Zaria the drummer's songs went like this:

> *If I were like Mai Zaria*
> *I would not farm, I would not hoe,*
> *I would not even go to market,*
> *If I were like Mai Zaria!*

His drumming was so good that everyone gave him money, they gave him gowns, and he felt good. Then the praise-singers would sing:

> *Son of the house, take out your money,*
> *Take it out and give me some,*
> *Take out your money and give it to me,*
> *Indeed friends are made with laughter,*
> *Cheeriness is what takes a man.*
> *You aren't like the orphan*
> *On whom Allah turned his back,*
> *Because you have your parents*
> *You have gifts in your house,*
> *You have inherited happiness.*
> *For your mother looks at her son,*
> *Your father looks at his son,*
> *Indeed you've inherited gifts in your house.*
> *Because your mother sees her son—*
> *Because your father sees his son—*
> *Take out your money and give it to the singers,*
> *Because you inherited such gifts in your house.*

The praise-singers are cunning—they undoubtedly are. I don't remember all the words of their songs, those are what I remember.

The Children's Play-associations at Zarewa (6)

At Zarewa we had titles among ourselves when we were young, the youths and the girls appointed their officials. The chief of the boys, *Sarkin Samari*, was given a turban by the Chief of Zarewa, and there were the chief's officials, Galadima, Ciroma, Madaki, Ma'aji, Magatakarda and Danmori. In my time there was Sarkin Samari Tanko and Sarkin Samari Bawa. The girls' chief was called Mama or chief of the girls, and the girls had other titled officials like those of the boys. One Friday in the dry season all the youths and girls would gather together in front of the Chief of Zarewa's palace, the boys in one place and the girls in another. The elders who appointed the Sarkin Samari sat with the Chief of Zarewa. Sarki would instal the Sarkin Samari and give him a turban to wear. The young men selected their leader because he was popular and good-tempered, not because he was wealthy; when they had chosen him they would go to Sarkin Zarewa and say 'We want so-and-so to be Sarkin Samari'. He would say 'Very well, we will instal him next Friday'. That boy would remain chief of the young men for about four years, then when he started to shave they would choose another one. We girls used to go out and sing to the boys as they worked in the fields, 'Work is new, Work is hard, We greet you at your work . . .' The young men put on their ornaments, they slung their hoes over their shoulders and we went with them in our best clothes, then we would take food out to the farms and give it to them.

When the boys' chief had been appointed, the boys and girls went and toured the country round, singing songs, so that everyone should see Sarkin Samari and Mama. Those with titles mounted horses, as they do for a bridegroom, and the rest went on foot round the wards of the town and out to the hamlets. When they arrived in a place everyone dismounted, stools were brought and millet-balls and sour milk, everyone ate. That is, the hamlet recognized his rank. Sarkin Samari and his titled officials sat on stools, and Mama sat on a stool opposite to him; those who had no titles, the commoners, sat on the ground. Mama would send a girl over to Sarki, she knelt down before him and said 'May Allah prolong Sarki's life, I want to leave this place and go home'. He would answer, 'No, we are going to stay here until tomorrow'. They did what Sarki said. When the people of the ward brought porridge and kolanuts to Sarki and Mama he would distribute them among his followers and she would distribute them among hers. Our Sarkin Samari was a son of the onion-farmers and Mama was a daughter of the butchers; they were both tall and very good-looking. At night the young men would be shown a resting place in the forecourts of the houses of the hamlet, and the girls would be shown a resting place. Everyone chose the girl he liked best for *tsarance*. They stroked one another and talked and told stories, then they went to sleep. They don't do anything more until they get married.

In the morning the girls washed and put on their fine clothes, they all got up and the boys escorted their chief while the girls escorted Mama, (7) and with the drummers and praise-singers they returned to the town. Sarki had a bodyguard and attendants who walked in front of his horse, everyone greeted him like a chief, 'May your life be long, Sarkin Samari!' Mama had an attendant in front and one behind, one on her left hand and one on her right, they walked slowly while the drummers drummed:

> *See Mama, the chief's mother,*
> *See Mama, the chief's mother,*
> *See the chief, see the chief,*
> *See the chief, see the chief,*
> *See the chief, see Mama,*
> *See Mama, the chief's mother.*

For seven days after he was installed there would be dancing and drumming, and after that Sarkin Samari's ceremony was over. Every market-day there would be dancing to the large deep drum; Sarki would come and take his place, Mama would take hers, then the drummers drummed to them and they got up and danced. We would all dance until dawn.

If someone called a farming bee he would tell the boys' chief to bring his young men; the girls did not work, they just put on their best clothes and followed the young men to the farms, the young men went with their hoes and the girls went too, singing farming songs and encouraging them at their work.

Our parents forbade us to go to these girls' games, but we went secretly and watched, we went secretly and danced. They did not approve, they said we were to play our own games at home, Zarewa was too far away. But when we lived in Zarewa, in the dry season, our parents allowed us to go to the dancing but they did not let us sleep with the boys. Girls would be in the group from the time they were nine or ten years old until they got married, at thirteen or fourteen. They could have titles at any time. Each ward of the town had its little group, the Ward of the Fulani had theirs, our Ward of the Farmers had theirs, each part of the town had its own groups of girls and boys, they danced and their drum was played for them. Asama'a was Mama from the time she was ten years old until she was married; then they appointed her younger sister Asabe, she was nine, and after she was married there was Ladi. When Ladi got married there was Gwamma. They were all girls from the Chief Butcher's compound in the Butchers' Ward. In our ward we had no Mama, we just watched when one was appointed. There was only one Mama in the town, and one Sarkin Samari, and no Mama was appointed except from the Ward of the Butchers, it was their inheritance. Sarkin Samari was always from the Onion-farmers' Ward where they all farmed in the marsh by the river. Ciroma, Galadima, Turaki, Madaki, Ma'aji, Shentali and Majidadi —all the boys' titles were held by boys from the Onion-growers' Ward. The other young men of the town followed them, they didn't object. If one Sarki grew too old they would appoint his younger brother or his kinsman, they wouldn't lack a suitable boy in the family; the boys and youths of the town would follow him.

They used to drum to Mama—I remember one Mama who even took her father's gown and gave it to the drummer! When she came to take her place for the evening's dancing the girls would all greet her, 'Greetings at your coming!' If the boys or girls quarrelled in the town they would be taken before Sarki or Mama and fined, the chief's money would be exacted. Sarki dealt with the boys, Mama with the girls, that was the limit of their authority; they did not help one another. If the boys annoyed people in the market with their quarrelling and fighting the elders would take them to the chief of the boys. The boys did not consult the girls about appointing Sarkin Samari, and the girls didn't ask the boys about Mama.

At the New Year festival, the Feast of the Full Stomach, we eat chickens and meat until we are quite full. When we were young, the boys would go out that night and draw water from twelve wells, then we took the water home and drank it and washed in it. Then we would put on our best clothes and lie down in them and go to sleep. You feel how good the world is.

Girls' Trading Expeditions (8)

The thing I remember best before I was married was our girls' trading expeditions. We took our money and our big calabashes, we went to Doka and bought yams, we went to Fillata and got groundnuts, we went and bought sweet potatoes from our hamlet, Karo, and from Dankusuba, Sundu, Wawaye, Guga. . . . When we had been to a lot of different villages and bought things, we came home and cooked them. When they were ready we took them to market. This had nothing to do with our parents, we went and sold our goods and put by our money. In the dry season we traded like this. When we had been to market in the morning with our mothers' cakes, eight or ten of us, we would meet our friends and come back, twenty of us, all singing, crowds of girls. Then we would put our heads together, we would go on an expedition. 'Are you coming?' 'Yes, I'm coming.' In the morning we got up early and we went along singing, twenty of us, thirty of us. When we arrived at a village we would go to the market and see things for sale. 'Oh, look at that! It's cheap, we'll go and make a profit.' And we bought it. One girl would buy groundnuts, one would buy yams, one sweet potatoes—each one bought her own produce. The little girls came along too with little loads, about three-pennyworth. We older ones took about a shillingsworth. The country people said 'Welcome, daughters of the village, welcome!' We answered 'M-hm'. 'Daughters of the town, welcome!' We said 'M-hm'. Then the country people would laugh, 'Ha! ha! ha!', they never laugh softly. We weren't exactly village children, we used to live in the town. They were country bumpkins, they hadn't got much sense, they weren't used to seeing a lot of people.

When we got back home we would cook the food we had bought, and next day we sold it in the market. The third day we returned to the hamlets. We were traders all right! For instance, if you got something for sixpence you would sell it for a shilling—but it was in our old kind of money, cowries. Then at night you danced and gave the praise-singers money, you danced and gave the drummers cloths. Next day you would go to your mother and say 'I haven't any money, I spent it all on the praise-singers!' If she is annoyed she says 'I haven't got any money'. Then you say 'Give me some, I'll return it to you'. Then she gives it to you and you go to market, you make a profit and come home and give her money back to her. When you hear drumming, you hear the deep drum and you hear the praise-singers—you'll give them money! One girl would give them a cloth, then they would go on singing about her until she gave them another, and she has to go seeking for one to wear. But they don't do that nowadays. . . .

A GIRL'S FRIENDS

Bori

In Zarewa we used to watch the *bori* dancers. (9) One day I was watching and one of the dancers became possessed by Dandambe, the Boxer. She bound up her hand in a cloth as boxers do, and she came over to me, singing. She liked me. She was handsome in her fine clothes. The Boxer's song is:

> *Whoever succeeds takes something to his* sarki,
> *Also if he wins he takes something to Baba.*
> *I am Madambaci, son of the Boxer,*
> *I am Madambaci the Boxer's son.*

The onlookers gave him money and he gave it to me, then when the spirit had left the dancer I gave the money to the praise-singers. Then I went home.

I often saw *bori* dancing at the compound of Magajiya, (10) the head of the prostitutes, (11) they were the *bori*-dancers. Among married women you would find one here and there, but most dancers were prostitutes. At Zarewa when we were young there were many prostitutes, they had their large huts in Magajiya's house. A man who went to their compound would take one of them home with him, and in the morning he would give her a little money and she would return to Magajiya's compound. There was Lemo's compound, Magajiya's and Auta's in the Butchers' Ward, they were all houses of prostitutes. The prostitutes came to the town and stayed two or three nights, then they went and some others came. We used to see their huts full of men and women. At night if a thief had stolen something he would sleep with a prostitute and give her money, then he would flee so as not to be caught; but the prostitutes didn't steal.

Some prostitutes were the daughters of *malams*, some were the daughters of noblemen, some were the daughters of commoners; if their parents had arranged marriages for them against their will they ran away and became prostitutes. Then and now, it's all the same; there have always been prostitutes. Magajiya is their mother, when any of them get money they take her a little. A man will come to Magajiya and say 'I desire your daughter'. She says 'Bring your money'. If he hasn't any money, she says 'She does not desire you'. If he has enough money she will desire him. If a prostitute comes to her house without anything, Magajiya will help her.

Lemo and Auta had prostitutes in their compounds, too. The men were always coming, they had their wives, they had their concubines, then they went out and had prostitutes too.

Sometimes a wife, if her husband is away, will steal her own body (12) and go off to other men; whoever sees her going along the road desires her, he sends a message by an old woman: 'I have come to greet you. How is the master of the house?' 'He is very well thank you, he has gone away to work.' 'When will he return?' 'Tomorrow.' 'Ap. See, here are some kolanuts, here is some money; so-and-so sent them to you.' 'I'll come tonight.' Then quickly, quickly the wife pays her visit and returns. In the compound of his bond-friend the man will borrow a hut and take her in; his own wives would beat the woman if they saw her in his compound! If the faithless wife has a co-wife she will say to her 'I am going to visit my family'. The co-wife will keep her secret. A married woman may have ten lovers, or even twenty—then or nowadays. She will go and tell her *kawa* about it. They desire men and they desire money. I never behaved like that.

In the old days *bori*-dancing was prostitutes' work, but there were some men dancers, too; there were two in my family, Dogo and Dan Auta, my father's 'younger brother', a son of Malam Bawa. Their *bori* was good, but there are more women than men.

I remember when I was about ten years old, after my mother had died, a prostitute was chosen to be Magajiya and she was installed in front of the Chief of Zarewa's palace; we went and watched. The prostitutes all danced in the morning, then they went to the house of Sarkin Zarewa, where he gave her a turban and appointed her Magajiya. He said that if any man took a prostitute to his house and did not give her any money, she was to take a complaint to Magajiya, who would make the man pay the woman her money and also fine him. That is, he gave her authority to do this.

We used to go to their compound and watch the dancing, their ward of the town was near to ours. When they were dancing at night their drumming prevented us from sleeping. In Zarewa, when I was eight or nine years old, there was Dandaudu's compound in Illalawa Ward, there was Auta's house at the North Gate, Lemo's at the South Gate and Magajiya's near the Butchers' Ward. '*Yandauda* (13) aren't healthy, they are men but they become like women, some of them even put on women's clothes.

A GIRL'S FRIENDS

They build women's huts for rent in a compound of prostitutes. The prostitutes give them a little money. I remember Danjuma, Citama, a son of the blacksmiths, Balarabe and Dandaudu; there they were, very beautiful to look at, like women. But they had no health, they could not go to women or to men. They put on fine clothes and ate nice food, that's all. The prostitutes would hire huts from them and pay them money, and in the day they would go to market and sell farm produce on commission, as the Chief Food-broker does here—but he's healthy all right, there's nothing wrong with him, he's always out hunting women!

CHAPTER IV

WARS, RAIDS, AND THE COMING
OF THE BRITISH (1)

When I was a maiden the Europeans first arrived. Ever since we were quite small the *malams* had been saying that the Europeans would come with a thing called a train, they would come with a thing called a motor-car, in them you would go and come back in a trice. They would stop wars, they would repair the world, they would stop oppression and lawlessness, we should live at peace with them. We used to go and sit quietly and listen to the prophecies. They would come, fine handsome people, they would not kill anyone, they would not oppress anyone, they would bring all their strange things. We were young girls when a European came with his attendants—'See, there's a white man, what has brought him?' He was asking the way to some town, we ran away and shut the door and he passed by and went on his way. Then the Tejani came, (2) they came from the edge of the river far away, the Christians had driven them out so that they came to our town, to Zarewa. They were fleeing, they came and said 'Peace, peace, we do not come with war, we are Tejani, the Christians (3) have driven us here'. They came into the town and rested. Some had lost their legs, some had no arms, some were ill; some rode horses, some came on foot. They had left Zaria the day before and slept at Kudan, then they came and stayed two nights at Zarewa with their horses and camels and goats and guns; from there they went to Makarfi, they said they were going south. They were light people with reddish skins, all ruling Fulani; their wives had fine clothes. They weren't like Mai Sudan's people—those were Gwari, very black— these were beautiful people.

Before the Tejani came there had been civil war in Kano, sons and brothers fought, ward fought against ward in the same town. (4)

WARS, RAIDS, AND THE COMING OF THE BRITISH

We were taken inside Zarewa town for fear of the war. Yusufu was the king of Kano, Tukur was his younger brother, the two of them made war in the one city, elder brother and younger brother fought one another. The Sultan of Sokoto settled the quarrel, then after that was over Mai Sudan's raids started up. (5)

I remember when a European came to Karo on a horse, and some of his foot soldiers went into the town. Everyone came out to look at them, but in Zarewa they didn't see the European. Everyone at Karo ran away—'There's a European, there's a European!' He came from Zaria with a few black men, two on horses and four on foot. We were inside the town. Later on we heard that they were there in Zaria in crowds, clearing spaces and building houses. One of my younger 'sisters' was at Karo, she was pregnant, and when she saw the European she ran away and shut the door.

At that time Yusufu was the king of Kano. (6) He did not like the Europeans, he did not wish them, he would not sign their treaty. Then he saw that perforce he would have to agree, so he did. We Habe wanted them to come, it was the Fulani who did not like it. When the Europeans came the Habe saw that if you worked for them they paid you for it, they didn't say, like the Fulani, 'Commoner, give me this! Commoner, bring me that!' Yes, the Habe wanted them; they saw no harm in them. From Zaria they came to Rogo, they were building their big road to Kano City. They called out the people and said they were to come and make the road, if there were trees in the way they cut them down. The Europeans paid them with goods, they collected the villagers together and each man brought his large hoe. Money was not much use to them, so the Europeans paid them with food and other things.

The Europeans said that there were to be no more slaves; (7) if someone said 'Slave!' you could complain to the *alkali* who would punish the master who said it, the judge said 'That is what the Europeans have decreed'. The first order said that any slave, if he was younger than you, was your younger brother, if he was older than you he was your elder brother—they were all brothers of their master's family. No one used the word 'slave' any more. When slavery was stopped, nothing much happened at our *rinji* except that some slaves whom we had bought in the market ran away. Our own father went to his farm and worked, he and his son took up their large hoes; they loaned out their spare farms. Tsoho our father and Kadiri my brother with whom I live now and

Babambo worked, they farmed guineacorn and millet and ground-nuts and everything; before this they had supervised the slaves' work—now they did their own. When the midday food was ready, the women of the compound would give us children the food, one of us drew water, and off we went to the farm to take the men their food at the foot of a tree; I was about eight or nine at that time, I think. (8)

About a year later Mai Sudan's men kidnapped Kadiri's mother, our father's wife Rabi, and later our father's sister who was also called Rabi was caught and sold into slavery at Abuja. (9) In Kano they had stopped slavery then, and in Zaria they had stopped it, but in Katsina it still continued; later the Europeans conquered Katsina and stopped it. (10) When they opened the big road all was quiet.

In the old days if the chief liked the look of your daughter he would take her and put her in his house; you could do nothing about it. Now they don't do that.

Two years after the people inside the town had begun to go out to the bush and farm, my mother died, she was killed in a fire; she died three or four years before I was married. (11)

Slave-raiders at Karo

At the time of Mai Sudan's raids I and my *kawaye* were young girls, our breasts had not begun to grow big. Mai Sudan came to Kaya and Fatika and Danmahawaye, he laid them all in ruins, he carried off the people and sold them. I remember how when the world was made peaceful he went off somewhere and his followers came to Zarewa, *tim-tim tim-tim*—crowds of horses—they stayed for seven nights, then they rose up and fled from the Europeans; they went southwards, or was it towards Ikara? The Europeans don't like oppression but they found a lot of tyranny and oppression here, people being beaten and killed and sold into slavery. Mai Sudan had a ram with four horns, and his horse was fat—*kong-ko-kong, kong-ko-kong* it went along.

One day Mai Sudan's men kidnapped Kado's wife and the bride and a little girl called Laraba and Rabi our father's wife, Kadiri's mother—they caught them all as they were working in the rice-field. The raiders were scouting around looking for people to kidnap, they seized women and children and men too if they were unarmed.

WARS, RAIDS, AND THE COMING OF THE BRITISH

On that raid they went first to Wawaye, the hamlet of my father's brother Ubangida. The raiders came at night, Mai Sudan's men, they broke into the compound and took away three of his children and Gambo his wife, who was long pregnant, and about ten of his slaves; Ubangida and two of his wives hid in the fireplaces under the beds. (12) There were about twenty horsemen and ten men on foot. They banged on the entrance-door, everyone rushed out terrified and they caught them. When Ubangida came out he shouted and shouted, they hit him with a stick and he fell down and he could hardly drag himself into the hut near the house-door, he hid and they didn't see him. No one nearby heard anything, they were all asleep and they didn't hear the men come. The wicked men, the kidnappers came at night and seized the house—Mai Sudan's men.

In time of war the men of one town would send a sensible boy to take a message to the chief of the next town, he would say 'There is fighting away over there at so-and-so', then the chief would order the drummer to climb up on a high place and beat the deep drum (nowadays we only use it for farming and dancing) so that the villagers and people in the surrounding hamlets should come inside the town walls. The drum-rhythm said 'Come in, come in, come in. . . .'

Ubangida got back his wife and children, he paid ransom, 400,000 cowries for his wife, (13) 400,000 for his three children, 400,000 for her unborn child. The man who had bought her when the kidnappers sold her into slavery said he would not give her up until he saw what she brought forth, so Ubangida said he would pay for her child within her. For three months after the raid everyone was miserable, they wailed and cried and could do nothing. Then they met and discussed the matter at the compound of Malam Buhari, the eldest brother. They heard that Gambo and the children had been sold in Bakori in Katsina, to the chief of Bakori's house. Mai Sudan's men never kept their captives, they sold them and took the money. Then Malam Buhari went to the chief of Zarewa, who gave him a letter to take to the chief of Bakori; but Sarkin Bakori refused to return them, they were fine children and their mother was lovely. Malam Buhari came back to Sarkin Zarewa, and they appealed to the king of Katsina; he was great and he felt compassion—doesn't one carry complaints to the lord of the land? The king wrote an order, he said Malam Buhari should pay the ransom money and get his family back. Malam Buhari returned home once more and called the kinsmen together, they consulted together and discussed the matter, then for three months they were collecting money. All our parents gathered at Maidamishi's compound inside the town, one brought chickens, one brought ten shillings, one twenty shillings, one forty shillings, one fifty shillings, one eighty shillings, one a hundred shillings. Some brought seven or eight pounds. (14) Some fell into debt. They counted it all and calculated that they had collected two thousand thousand cowries—forty-four pounds. The kinsmen and kinswomen had all brought what they could. At the end of three months when it was gathered together, all the cowries were sewn up in mats, the Chief of Zarewa was told that it was ready and he summoned young men to carry the loads. Sarkin Zarewa and Malam Buhari went with them. Three times they went and on the third journey they completed the ransom and Malam Buhari and Ubangida and Sarkin Zarewa went to Bakori to fetch Gambo; they brought her and the children home. When she had been fourteen nights at home she brought forth her child, a boy. She came home on foot, she was too far pregnant to mount a horse; the others came on horseback.

We heard that some of the slaves in Ubangida's house had been sold by Mai Sudan's men, but we did not hear where they were. Aljimma and Zaman Duniya and Ku-bar-wahala and Asada, Dangwari and Baregi were all killed, and the others were sold; we used to play with them all, then in one night they were seized and taken far away. . . .

I was about ten years old when all this happened. (15) Not long after the raid on Ubangida's house, about thirty days later, we heard that the raiders had gone away, and Father said they could go out of the town to look at his rice-field near the river—there were father's wife Rabi, Kado's bride and ten men who were working amongst the high rice. Silence, they were all working, then suddenly *gom-gom-gom*—there were horsemen and men on foot surrounding them. (16) The farm slaves ran away but the raiders caught Rabi and Kado's bride, they tied their hands across their breasts, each hand on the opposite shoulder, with rope, and they carried them off to Katsina. The slaves were afraid and fled into the bush. We were in our compound inside the town, when the slaves came back and said Rabi and the others had been seized. We cried and wailed. 'There's war near Karo hamlet!' Then the

drumming started—'Come in, come in, come in, come in!' Father
took up his bow and arrows and went out, he alone, to search on the
farm. When he saw the rice all trampled down he began to weep and
wail, they had taken away his family. Our own mother, Fatsuma,
who had been with them, was hiding in the water amongst the rice,
then she crept out and hid among the grass. She saw someone come
and thought it was another raider, but she was shaking with cold
and she couldn't keep still. Then she heard him wailing and she
knew raiders don't wail, so she peeped out. When Father saw her
amongst the rice he said 'Is it indeed you? Haven't they taken
you then?' Then he looked round and said 'In the name of Allah,
where is Rabi?' She said 'They seized her, she cried, she cried
bitterly, they caught her and carried her off'. Tsoho said 'And that
daughter?' Then Dije heard his voice, she was hiding too, near our
mother, she came out and he said 'Ah, this daughter, didn't Allah
count you all?' Dije was going to be married that year, she was a
young girl and her breasts were rounded. Then Father went searching all around but he only found four people and his boy Tagwai
and two girls who had been farming too, Dantine and Laraba.
All the other slaves had been captured, or they had run away. Back
at home we were crying, we had heard that everyone had been
carried off.

Our father took them back home, as they went they heard the
drums beating, they were drumming the war alarm at Zarewa and
everyone was hurrying inside the town walls. It was towards evening that he came back with them, when he brought the news that
Rabi had been captured, her children cried and wailed, they threw
themselves on the ground again and again; the mother of our hut,
who had been spared, was wailing for her sister Rabi who had
been taken away. People came to greet our mother who had come
back safely—'Blessings on your coming, blessings!'—and then they
were wailing and crying for our lost Rabi. After that Rabi's children went on living in her hut, but our mother gave all of us food.
Those two co-wives had liked one another.

After about seven days the rice was harvested and put in baskets
—at that time there were no sacks. Those men were Mai Sudan's
followers, they weren't ordinary kidnappers.

We waited for news, we didn't know what had happened to
Rabi and the others who had been captured; only a few weeks
earlier Ubangida's family had been captured in the night. We

heard our parents saying 'Where will we find them? They must have gone to Katsina with them.' Everyone was wary of Katsina —a Kano man didn't go to Katsina openly. (17) But Katsina people would not seize a Zaria man—Dan Barahiya was not a Katsina man. We were there thus for one or two months before we heard that Ubangida's wife Gambo was a slave in Bakori; about a month after that we heard news of Rabi, a traveller came to our house and said 'Someone has seen Malam Tsoho's wife in Maicibi's house in Maska, (18) but the women are not allowed to come out'. He had gone secretly to visit his kinsmen in Katsina, and he had heard of our mother in the town, so he came back and gave us the news. People used to talk, 'So-and-so, the wife of so-and-so, is in that compound'. Then if someone from the captive's own town heard, he would say 'I greet them, tell them certainly I will take back the news'. The women would not be allowed to leave the compound, but a woman of the ward would go in and greet them, (19) she would say 'May Allah assist you!', the captive would say 'Amen!' Then her visitor would say 'I'll give the news'. She would answer 'Thank you'.

Rabi was in the house of Malam Maicibi, a wealthy man in Maska. Wives of commoners went in, and when they returned home they said to their menfolk 'Malam Tsoho's wife from Zarewa is in Maicibi's house'. When the traveller came and told Father he rejoiced, he brought kolanuts and gave them to him, he gave him money so that he could buy more kolanuts. Father and his kinsmen went to the *malams* and took them money, so that they should work for them and make them charms and writing. Then they started to collect money for the ransom, they were collecting money in our house and in Ubangida's at the same time. They took the matter to the Chief of Zarewa, they told him they wished to ransom Rabi and get her home. Sarkin Zarewa sent his retainers to escort our father to Maska. They said to the Chief of Maska, 'Malam Tsoho's wife is here in Malam Maicibi's house'. Sarkin Maska sent for Malam Maicibi and told him that Rabi's family wished to ransom her. Maicibi said he would not give her up to them. He had put her to grinding corn, she refused to do it; he wanted her as his wife, but she refused. She was two months pregnant with child, so he left her alone. He said he required 400,000 cowries; father said he could not pay so much, and he returned home with Sarkin Zarewa's retainer and told our fathers. When Father saw her she was very happy that he had come; after Sarkin Maska had coaxed him, Malam Maicibi agreed to let her go; when Tsoho came home he told the kinsmen and they decided to try and collect the money. Our father and his kin and her kin sought for the 400,000 cowries, and when they had collected it they went to Maska and took it. Only the *karemari* of 40,000 cowries (20) remained to be paid before they could bring Rabi home. At the time Father took the ransom, Malam Maicibi and his boy escorted Rabi and Tsoho and his brother Audi and Rabi's elder brother Danbaki to the gate of Maska; when they had collected the *karemari* they could come and take her home. But Rabi kept feeling a pain in her head, and when she got back to her master's house she lay down as if she was going to rest; in the morning she died. From Maska they sent a message to Sarkin Zarewa to say she was dead. Sarki sent for our fathers, when they came and did obeisance he said: 'There is news from Maska. We have paid the ransom, 400,000 cowries; only the *karemari* of 40,000 remains. Today they have sent to say Malam Tsoho's wife has died.' Malam Maicibi kept the money, the 400,000 cowries were his. We were full of grief; Rabi had been ransomed but she died before she could be brought home. 'No money, no man.' Her master had nothing to worry about, he bought her for 100,000 and he got a ransom of 400,000 for her—he made a profit. (21) A year later her son died in our own mother's hut in the fire. Only one of her sons died, the other is still here, my younger brother Kadiri.

After six months of bringing money and still more money we ransomed the four of them from Ubangida's house. That day they came on their horses, and there was nothing but joy. Some of the horses had been sold to get the money—Bikili and Dandana had been sold—everyone brought money to our fathers and it was tied up in mats. We went to the gate of the town to meet them, there they were, our fathers and Ubangida's children on horses, we all rejoiced. Laraba, who was born on my naming-day, (22) came back and she and I played and were happy together. Soon afterwards their mother had her child.

After this our father didn't go back to the hamlet, he lived inside the town walls; at that time our slaves ran away, and in the morning he went to Karo to farm, and at night he came back to our compound inside Zarewa town. (23)

My Mother Dies; Aunt Rabi is Enslaved

Not long after all this my own mother was killed by lightning; there was a storm on the fourteenth day of the month of the Great Feast, (24) she came hurrying back from the river with water and went into her hut with her two younger children. Then lightning struck the hut and it blazed up *pa-a-a-a-a*. The people of the house came rushing in from the entrance-hut, but they found them dead. I was playing with the other children when the storm came; the rain poured down and we went into the house of Makadi the drummer. The market was empty, everyone was sheltering and watching the storm. While I was in the drummer's house they brought the bodies out and took them behind the hut. At that time if someone died they were buried behind their hut. (25) The *malams* were called, we children hid; the wife of our 'father' Sa'i came and took us to her hut in her compound nearby, she stayed with us. When they brought us some food I said 'I can't eat'. After my mother had done my hair and washed me and looked after me, after she had done all that for me, she died in the fire. When they brought her out, quite still, I fell down and cried, when I rose up I threw myself on the ground again, I cried and cried. . . . (26) My younger brother Tanko died with her. She was a beautiful woman with lovely hair and light skin; one day at Azahar she went to the well to draw water, then the storm came and her hut caught fire and she could not get out, she died. I was about ten years old and my brother Kadiri was about seven. (27)

The next day we washed our faces and they took us home; we found all the parents and kinsfolk sitting round, they had all assembled, the men in the entrance-hut and the women inside the compound. Our father was sitting in the entrance-hut, they had come to greet him. When we came we went straight into the compound and they called him to come in. When he saw us he began to weep, he felt sorry for us, we were so small. At first he had thought we were all dead, but when they saw we weren't in the hut they told him we weren't dead, but he didn't grasp it. Then when he saw us he knew we were alive, he said 'Allah has raised them up?' Then he wept. Our 'mothers' were all there. Our father's sister Rabi brought her slave Ajuji, a beautiful daughter of the Buzaye, she gave her to our father so that he should not live like a bachelor with no one to grind his corn. (28) Father gave Aunt Rabi his own man-slave in exchange, he went to work in the *gandu* of Rabi's husband. Ajuji was married, (29) it was a slave marriage because there was no order in force at that time, so she took up her belongings and left her husband's compound and came to live with us. Her mother was called Aso, she had facial marks like this, and her father was Dandare. Ajuji was nice. The day the funeral was over they said she was to come and sweep out our hut and make food and live with us. She was light-skinned, (30) like my mother; my mother was very beautiful and light-skinned. Look at me—black, like my father! Ajuji came and lived in the hut that had belonged to Rabi, who died at Maska. It was a little hut, and besides that one there was another in the compound belonging to an old lady, a sister of our father's mother Anja—she and Anja were brothers' children; she was our 'grandmother', and we played in her hut and ate our food in Ajuji's.

We lived thus with Ajuji, then after a little she became pregnant. When the nine months were up she bore a son. She was carrying him around on her back, then she said she wanted to go to Farakasa, over near Zaria City, to visit her mother's kin. (31) Her father and her mother were slaves of our grandparents. Father said 'Yes, you may go'. Then we collected gifts for her, sweetmeats, salt and potash and locust-bean cakes. She said she would soon be back. But she died there; they sent a messenger to say she had died, then they sent home her son, she had died in their house. When we heard she was dead we cried till we were weary, we loved her very much and our father loved her; she was a pretty light-skinned girl with a straight nose. She and our father's sister Rabi started out together and parted at Zaria City; Ajuji went to Farakasa, while Aunt Rabi and her husband went on a trading expedition to the south. Away near Abuja the kidnappers caught Aunt Rabi, we heard the news of her capture at the same time as we heard of Ajuji's death. Rabi, our father's sister who had given him her slave Ajuji. Rabi inherited about six slaves when her father Ibrahim Dara died, and her brothers inherited twelve each; they had children and increased. Men inherit two parts and women one part; if a woman's father dies she inherits; if her husband dies, she inherits; if her mother dies, she inherits. (32)

After Ajuji died Anja our father's mother came to live in our compound, she made food for us and we lived in her hut. When our father had been alone for three months, he married Tumbadi, he

lived with her for two years in Zarewa before he arose and came
here with her to Giwa. When our father married Tumbadi his
mother Anja moved to Giwa to live with her youngest son. (33)
But before Tumbadi became my father's wife I was married to
Duma, I was married four years after my mother died.

My Maternal Kinsfolk

My mother's family were drummers and blacksmiths. There was
Gambo's house at Sunjir near Gwibi, he had ten children himself
and in his compound there were more than fifty children; in every
hut they could drum. (34) They were our cross-cousins, our joking
relations. (35) I went to their home very often, I learnt all their
songs. I was the sister's child, they were the children of the brothers,
kinsfolk on the milk side. There was Sarkin Makada, the chief
drummer, (36) my cross-cousin; even now if I go to his home I
snatch off his turban and he calls me 'Slave!', I answer 'Yes?'
They all have drumming titles, like Galadiman Makada and
Ciroman Makada. They drum and they farm. I didn't know my
mother's father Sarkin Makera, chief of the Gwibi blacksmiths,
but I knew his brothers Magawata and Mijinhaji, they were our
grandfathers. Those two were the fathers of a great many children,
but Sarkin Makera hadn't very many. Our grandfathers we called
Kaka, their children we called *Yani* and the women *Babanni*, this
is Barebare speech. (37) On the father's side we called our fathers
and their brothers *Abba* and our father's sisters *Goggo*. Then we
would call our 'fathers' each by the name of his horse, we said
'Abba baban Bikili', or 'Abba baban Tantabara'.

More about my Mother's Kinsfolk

I will tell you a story about a girl who wanted to marry my kinsman on my mother's side in the home of Gambo, the drummers'
compound. She was a young girl who had never been married, her
name was Anci, her mother Gaje and her father Danladi. She came
and hid in the compound of the drummers' children. For about ten
days her parents were searching for her, then it was said that she
had hidden in the drummers' house. They said the drummers were
to bring out their daughter and give her back to them. My mother's
brother said she must come out, Gambo said 'Here is your daugh-

ter, but you can't take her away, my children like her'. Her mother said 'Come along, let us go'. She said 'I'm not coming'. Her father said 'Come along, we are going home'. She said 'I'm not coming'. Then she ran away and hid in a hut. Her parents returned after seven days and Gambo said 'Give us your daughter so that she may marry Ahmadu, whom she desires'. Ahmadu with the farming drum. . . . They said his family were to give 200,000 cowries to her family. Her father said she was to come out of hiding, and they would set the day. Then she went to her parents' home, she agreed to go with them.

> She went to the house of the drummers, there she would sleep,
> She was ready for marriage, she said to the house of the drummers she would go
> Her mother said 'O dear, come home to Gaje's house!'
> Her father said 'O dear, come home to Gaje's house!'
> She said she would sleep in the house of the drummers,
> She had come to be married in the drummers' house.

Then they made another song about Ahmadu, who married her:

> Ahmadu with the farming drum,
> For the sake of Allah take out your drum,
> We will go to Saurawa
> So that we may go and see wealthy people,
> At your house there is farming,
> At your house there's no useless wood
> Ahmadu with the farming drum.

Anci is still living with Ahmadu, she has three children.

When I was a girl Sarkin Makada, the chief of those drummers, my mother's kinsmen, wanted to arrange a marriage of kinship for me, but the people at Karo refused; he had wanted my elder sister Dije, but they refused, then he wanted me, but my father's people would not agree. My mother's people were drummers of the farming drum, they were not praise-singers, but my father's family said I was not to go wandering around with them and singing. I liked them and their songs. But later I got Malam Maigari and he loved me.

I often went with my mother to visit her kinsfolk, I used to play with them all. When my elder sister Dije was going to be married, we went to see them so that she could greet them before she went to her new home. Dije was married earlier in the year that Mother died. (38) I took part in the marriage ceremonies as Dije's younger sister, I went to *Mawankiya's* house with her; (39) her *Mawankiya* was Karimatu, our mother's younger sister, a daughter of grandfather Magawata. The grandmother who put henna on her was Abinda her maternal grandmother, a younger sister of our mother's father, Sarkin Makera. Her paternal grandmother was Aso, the mother of Ajuji, our slave, father's concubine; some slaves have been with your family so long that they become like your grandmothers.

The day of the wedding-feast, Dije and I were quarrelling. I was rejoicing because she was going to go away and leave us our hut. We were wrestling, she kept beating me with a stick until our mother drove us out into the compound. Then we went on fighting outside, she slapped me then I caught her and wrestled with her, then I bit her. But if we were anywhere together and someone else quarrelled with me and was going to hit me, Dije would drive her off and say 'Come on, we are going home'. She didn't like anyone to beat me but herself! When we were at it, Mother would say 'Go outside!' and Dije would pull me out—I didn't want to go— then *kichi-kichi* we would fight. I would go into our mother's hut, crying, then Mother would send Dije away and give me a sugar-cane and tell me to wait. I went to the door of the hut and spied Dije outside in the compound. Then when she heard her coming Mother would say 'Give me the cane and I'll keep it'. Then when Dije came in I would say 'There she is, beat her!' Then Mother would burst out laughing and pick up the cane, Dije would rush out, and I would start singing 'She's running away from a beating! She's running away from a beating!'

After Dije was married I returned to our hut rejoicing because she had gone away and left us our own hut. I was very pleased about it. Mother said 'Are you pleased? Oh, she'll certainly be coming back'. I said 'Oh no she won't come back, see they've taken her away to her husband's house'. She was married to one of our kinsmen, he was a young man and she a young girl, she desired him. He was the younger paternal half-brother of Duma, whom I married later. Before I married his elder brother I joked with him because he was my elder sister's husband; (40) when I married Duma, his elder brother, I still joked with him because he was my husband's younger brother. But supposing I had married his younger brother, I should have had to stop joking with him, because he would be my husband's elder brother, with whom one does not joke. When Dije was being married, I saw them taking all the things from our hut to give her. They bought her cooking-pots, water-pots, spindles, cloth, calabashes—a great many things. I said 'Ap. Are they going to take her all these things? I'm going to hide mine!' Then I went off and hid my possessions.

Dije and I had disagreed ever since she came back from Grandmother Cibi's house when Cibi died; (41) Dije came home a short time before she was married. When she returned, Father said she was to keep slapping me so that I shouldn't despise her, since she was the elder sister. For two days we were delighted that she had come home, after that we fought. Mother didn't like it either. That hut had become ours, Mother's and mine, then she came. Dije was hitting me and I was crying, Mother said 'Go away and do your work!'—she was their eldest child. If Father sent us to carry a message for him, we would run, and he would greet the one who got back first with 'Well done, Chief of Speed!' Dije was annoyed and went along slowly, slowly, and I raced her. Father said to me 'Well done!' Dije was very cross. I didn't quarrel with Kadiri. (42) If someone slapped him I retaliated and took him home. There were just the three of us, the rest died when they were small.

If there was a lot of crying inside the compound, Father would hear and come in, when I saw him I cried hard, I said 'She's beating me, she's hit me in the eye', and Dije said 'It's she who's hit me!' then Father would say 'Hit her again!' and he would look at us both like this. Then I would jump up and run into Mother's hut. He liked me and Kadiri best. He had seventeen children. He said to Malam Buhari, their eldest brother, 'We are always having children, but they keep dying'. Malam Buhari said 'Allah grant they may live'. Father said 'Perhaps the youngest will remain to us'. Then we were there, the three of us, and we didn't die. But fourteen children died. (43) Some were a year old, some had already been weaned. They used to make a bitter medicine in which they washed them, and they gave it to them to drink. Now we know what causes them to die, but in the past we didn't. The children just died. When Mother died she left Dije five months pregnant, and when she had her child, Danlami, he died. After Dije was married, if I went to her compound and she sent me to buy her something in the market, I wouldn't go!

My Aunt Rabi

Our Aunt Rabi was our father's elder sister. She was adopted by her father Dara's younger sister, Rakia. When Rabi reached marriageable age (she was married six times in all), Rakia married her to her co-wife's son Rabi'u, because Rakia had no children herself, and if her adopted daughter Rabi married her co-wife's son in the same compound, she hoped to acquire grandchildren. (44) Rakia and her co-wife liked one another. When Rabi and Rabi'u had had seven children, she left him and married Malam Barau, a man from Doka, a hamlet like Karo. She had more children by him, Mijiniya and Nasammai and the others. Then Rabi left Barau and married Mai Koko, the *jakada* of the king of Kano. He used to come to fetch the tax of the country, he was the retainer of the king's *jakada*. One day he saw Aunt Rabi carrying her baby on her back, looking very handsome. He desired her. She also liked him, so she broke up her marriage with Malam Barau and when Mai Koko returned he married her and took her away to Kano City, where he shut her up. All the men of Kano City lock up their wives completely, so that no one shall see them. He brought her nice food to eat, he brought her lovely clothes to wear, but she could not visit her kinsfolk, she could not see her children. When he came to Zarewa to collect the tax we used to make him porridge and cook chickens for him, we would ask him 'How is Rabi?' and he answered 'Very well', but he would not bring her to see us. After four years in Kano she slipped out one night and ran away to a village; in the morning she asked the way home. She walked and walked, there were no lorries then as there are now; she passed about fifteen walled towns before she came to Zarewa. At that time her mother Anja was still alive, she had re-married after Ibrahim Dara's death and was carrying her youngest son, Haleru, on her back. (45) Aunt Rabi went to Anja's hut in the compound of Haleru's father, she had returned to her kinsfolk and her children, she couldn't bear to stay away there and not see them. I was quite small when Aunt Rabi came home from Kano.

When Mai Koko came to collect it, the tax was paid in cowries. They counted them in 'mats'—*keso daya*, one mat, was one large Bornu mat, sewn up, containing 20,000 cowries. Ten 'mats' was 200,000 cowries. When they were turned into your money there were 100 cowries for a halfpenny, one thousand cowries was five-pence, so 20,000 cowries was one hundred pennies, that's eight-and-fourpence. The Chief of Zarewa would send his men to collect the money. His courtiers went to each house and collected the money for tax. In those days there was not only the household tax, *gandu* tax, there were also taxes on all sorts of different farming—groundnut tax, sweet potato tax, sugar-cane tax, and others; we called them *kudin noma-nomi*, the farming taxes; there were craft taxes, too, for instance, a dyer paid 2,000 cowries for every dyepit he had. Only the household tax went to the king of Kano, the other taxes were kept by the town chiefs. If they used up all the money themselves, the common people had to pay. Sarkin Zarewa would sometimes spend all the tax, then when he was tired of spending money he would take a gift of greeting to the king of Kano. After you came all those taxes were stopped, now there is only the household tax to pay; that is to say, we can rest. You don't like that sort of thing. The fiefholder had a share of the tax too, but I don't know how it was arranged. (46) When Mai Koko had collected the household taxes, about thirty or forty *keso*—'mats'—he took the money to the Chief of Karaye; when Sarkin Karaye had collected the tax from all his towns he took it to Sarkin Kano, the king. They couldn't touch one shell, the king kept an eye on them! Then they took his share to the Sultan of Sokoto, and the balance belonged to the king of Kano. (47)

To count cowrie-shells they spread them out on the floor. They counted in groups of five; ten groups of five were fifty. Then they collected the groups of fifty into groups of two hundred. Ten 'compounds' of two hundred were two thousand. When they were arranged in 'compounds' you started to sew up mats and pour in the cowries. One mat, twenty thousand cowries; that was a man's load, and a strong man would soon get tired of carrying it. Now you see eight shillings like this in your hand! Counting money was the work of a chief's retainers—you can imagine that there were a lot of them!

After our father's sister Rabi came back from Mai Koko's house at Kano, she married a man called Madu from Bornu and they set out for the south on a trading expedition, at the same time as Father's concubine Ajuji went to see her parents at Farakasa. Then at the same time as we heard about Ajuji's death, we heard that Aunt Rabi and her husband had been surprised by kidnappers on the road, they knocked Madu senseless and left him for dead,

Aunt Rabi they carried off to Abuja where they sold her to the king's wife as a slave. But we did not hear this until three years later, when a traveller brought the news; the kidnappers had beaten up Madu, but he recovered and late at night he got up and went on his way, he had no idea where his wife was. The trader who had heard the story secretly in Abuja came to our house and told us that the Chief of Abuja's wife had bought Rabi and she was there in his palace. She was captured in the year I was married.

PART TWO

CHAPTER V

c. 1904–1907
A GIRL'S FIRST MARRIAGE (1)

When a young girl was going to be married for the first time, this is what happened. If both the man and the girl were free people, he gave her these presents while he was courting her: at each of the two *Salla* festivals he gave her 20,000 cowries, a short petticoat, a blouse and a head-scarf. Then on market-days he gave her her market-gift, he gave this to her once weekly, although markets were held more often. When he saw her in the market-place he called her *kawa* and gave her a thousand or two thousand or even three thousand cowries. At Zarewa the market was held every other day, and at Karo there was a little market under the tree every day. The following week the young man would give his girl two thousand cowries, after another week three thousand, after another week four thousand, after another week five thousand. Then he would give her no more, he would leave them alone. Then they would go to his compound, the *kawa* would catch hold of him and say 'Give me the market-gift!' After about two months he collected six thousand or eight thousand cowries and gave them to her. He continued to give them gifts every week for a time. Then when the wedding was near he stopped again.

When slaves married they did not pay as much money to the bride's family as we did, but otherwise the marriage customs for slaves were the same as ours. The slave would come and kneel down before his master and say 'There is a woman in so-and-so's compound, I desire her'. Then the master would say 'Go and talk to her'. When the slave had been, he would come to his master and say 'Indeed, she desires me'. If the slave was a young man he would be too shy to tell his master himself, but if he had talked to the girl and knew she desired him, he would get a little old lady who would go and tell his master. When she told him, the master would say

'Very well'. Then the old lady would tell the slave and he would start giving the girl presents. On market-days he would give her her market-gift, first two hundred or three hundred cowries, then four hundred then five hundred then six hundred, perhaps up to one thousand; he would give her a gift every week for some time. At the two festivals he would give her two thousand cowries and some henna, some oil and some blue cloth. The old lady would take the gift to the master so that he should see, and he would say 'Splendid!' His wives would be shown the gift, and then he would say 'Right, take it', and his wife would give it all to the girl. At the Greater feast (2) the slave gave the girl more than at the Lesser feast, he gave her henna, blue cloth, oil, three thousand cowries, a blouse, a head-kerchief and a little petticoat.

When her breasts had grown and she had reached the age of marriage, the master would say to the families concerned, 'Come and we will set the day'. If she were not old enough he would say 'Wait until next year'. But the girl must receive her gifts at two feasts, and if the marriage was postponed till the next year she would have gifts at four feasts.

First the betrothal ceremony would take place at the master's compound; the payments were all half those for free men. The man's family would bring a calabash of kolanuts, a little salt, locust-bean cakes, and millet; fifty of the sweetmeats called *nakia*, and a little meat. The girl's grandparents would receive four thousand cowries, and the girl's 'parents' on her mother's side two thousand cowries, and on her father's side two thousand cowries. The bridegroom's family would also bring a little gift to their master, 20 kolanuts, one thousand cowries, ten *nakia* sweets, and handfuls of salt, millet and guineacorn. The master would say 'I give this girl to you. Come next Friday and we will set the day for the marriage ceremony'. At this betrothal the 'parents' and 'grandparents', both men and women, of the bride and bridegroom came to the master's compound, but the bride and bridegroom hid, and their own fathers and mothers who begot them did not come. The praise-singers and drummers (3) came and played.

The following week, when they came to set the day for the wedding, the master's entrance-hut was swept out and mats were laid down on the floor. When the kinsmen of the bride and the bridegroom arrived at Azahar, the afternoon prayer time, they entered the master's entrance-hut and knelt down to greet him.

A GIRL'S FIRST MARRIAGE

He named a day in the following month for the wedding. (For our marriages, that is if the man and woman were free, it would be in the month after next.) When the day had been set, the younger sister of the man's father and the younger sister of his mother (4) came into the entrance-hut from where they had been waiting with the women inside the compound, they bowed down and said 'Which day have you arranged? We will go and tell the women.' Then they would be told 'Such-and-such a day in next month'. Then the man's family brought their gifts and set them down and the sisters of the girl's father and mother came and took them up and carried them into the compound to be divided up. For 'setting the day' the bridegroom's family brought gifts for the bride's father's kin, fifty *nakia* sweets, half a basket each of salt, millet and guineacorn; some locust-bean cakes and rice; four white Kano mats, and three thousand cowries. They would bring the same for the bride's mother's kin. Then they brought gifts for her grandparents, big handfuls of peppers, bitter tomatoes, flour, salt, locust-bean cakes; and five hundred cowries for her maternal and five hundred for her paternal grandparents. They brought the master a gift too —two thousand cowries, twenty kolanuts, ten *nakia* sweets; with handfuls of rice, salt, millet, guineacorn, and locust-bean cakes.

The same people would come to this ceremony as attended the betrothal; the man and woman concerned, with their own parents who begot them, would not come. At all these ceremonies, then and now, the women always go inside the compound and the men remain in the entrance-hut, they are never together. The women-folk used to bring the gifts and take them into the compound to the hut of the master's head wife, then the master was called in to look at them and he would say 'Excellent, that is very nice'. When such ceremonies were for slaves, they would all sit outside the master's entrance-hut, they would not sit inside; the master and his own relatives sat inside.

The gifts set aside for the girl's mother's family are divided like this: her own mother gets a large portion; her mother's younger sister also gets a large portion; the rest is divided among her mother's 'brothers' and 'sisters'. The bride's maternal cross-cousins come and seize their share while the dividing-up is going on, and they run away and get chased and beaten with sugar-canes— everyone laughs. In the same way the gifts to the father's side are divided up among his kin. When the ceremony is over they all get up and go outside, and there is drumming and dancing until dusk, when everyone goes home.

Seven days before the marriage-day, the bride's kinswomen catch her and rub her skin with henna; (5) when they come to do this she runs away, and when they get her she cries and wails, she throws herself to the ground again and again crying because the time for marriage has come. (6) When she is exhausted with weeping, her kinswomen call her chief *kawa* to come and comfort her. The *kawa* calls ten other friends, the bridegroom's relations bring millet, guineacorn, cotton and money, which are given to the chief *kawa*, with a chicken to eat and money for sour milk. Then the *kawa* and the ten friends come to the bride's father's compound, the *kawa* distributes the grain among the other girls, and they all grind it up. During all this the bride hides her face in her cloth and sits down, the bride feels shy; she will laugh and play with her friends and the other children, but with older people she feels shy and covers up her face. The ten girls are given a hut to themselves in the bride's father's compound and they spend the time preparing their food and playing and dancing; they call the drummer with his deep drum to the compound-entrance, and there is drumming and dancing, both in the day and at night. They make millet-balls and porridge and eat until they are full.

If the marriage was between slaves, the same things would happen, but first, when the month came round, the bride's grandmother would go to the master and say 'When shall we stain the bride with henna?' and he would reply 'Tomorrow night'. Then the bride's friends find out and tell her, 'They're going to put on your henna today'. Then she runs away and hide in the house of a *kawa*, and the old lady follows her and catches her; the girls hit her grandmother and run away. All day they are hiding from the bride's grandmother, but at night the old lady gets her in somebody's compound, and rubs a little henna on her skin before her friends can hide her; then the grandmother runs away. (7) This is the same for slaves or free people; Zetanku my father's old slave was my grandmother when I was married—it doesn't have to be your father's own mother or your mother's own mother, it can be any of your 'grandmothers'. When the little bit of henna has been rubbed on the bride, all her friends fall on top of her, crying, they cover her up. Then the grown-ups, the bride's 'mothers' come along and tell them to be calm—'Be quiet, be quiet; run and call a drummer'. He comes to the door of the compound (the master's compound if it is a marriage of slaves), the *kawa* brings a cloth like a turban and ties it round the bride's head, (8) then out they come for the playing and drumming. At night the slaves would go back to the *rinji*, to sleep at their own compound. Food is brought from the bridegroom's house for the bride and her friends to eat. Between that day of first putting on henna and the day of the marriage feast, it was four days for us—free people— and two days for them, the slaves.

The *kawaye* stay for a night at the bride's house; they make porridge and eat till they are full. At night henna is put on her arms and legs for the second time. In the morning the bride's grandmother, her mother's mother, washes her all over with warm water. When she brings the bride round from behind her hut (she doesn't hit the old lady this time, she merely cries), her *kawa* comes and puts a cloth over the bride's head, she takes her hand and leads her along. (9) They all go to the compound of the 'mother' who has been chosen to wash her—one of her mother's younger sisters. The praise-singers and drummers lead the procession, then follow the bride and her chief *kawa*, then the girls, round them and behind them. The bride is crying and all her friends sing this song:

The *kawa* begins:

> *From this year you won't go dancing,*
> *From this year you won't go to the dance,*
> *From this year you won't go dancing,*
> *You'll only dance on the path to the river.*

The other girls reply:

> *From where you're tossing cowrie-shells* (10)
> *From where you're tossing cowrie-shells,*
> *From your compound you'll hear our drumming under the*
> *   silk-cotton tree,*
> *From your compound you'll hear our drumming,*
> *But you won't be able to come.*

The songs make the bride angry and she starts crying again. When they arrive at the compound of her mother's younger sister, her friends lead the bride to her mother's sister's hut, she is her *Mawankiya*, the 'mother' who will wash her for marriage. She talks to the bride and lectures her about behaving properly, while all her friends sit round and stop singing and are quiet. Then *Mawankiya* hands the girls the grain that has been sent from the bridegroom's house, and they set to work to grind it, they cook it and everyone eats the evening meal. Then henna is brought from the compound of the bride's father and the grandmother comes again to put it on. Outside *Mawankiya's* hut the girls are preparing the henna-leaves, and the drummers and singers are busy at the front of the compound. When *Mawankiya* leads the bride out from her hut, her friends seize her arms and legs and hold her while she struggles. The girls begin to sing again, while the grandmother is putting on the bride's henna they sing this song:

> *Save my life*, hankaka, *save my life*,
> *Save my life*, hankaka, *save my life*
> *On the day of marriage;*
> *Save my life*, hankaka, *save my life*,
> Bazara *has come*,
> Hankaka *with the white breast*,
> *White-breasted one, marriage has come.*

The bride wants hankaka, the pied crow, to rescue her, so that they shall not give her in marriage. There are a lot of people in the compound, the younger sister of the bride's mother, her mother's mother, all her friends and the drummers and praise-singers and onlookers; they are all inside the compound, unless it is a house where the women are secluded, in which case they would only come as far as the forecourt. The young men, the bridegroom's friends, come, and his younger brother (the bride's joking relation) they come and help to hold her. Some of the girls, and the bride's younger sister, go over to the bridegroom's compound, if it is his first marriage too they will be putting henna on him; (11) he has a *mawankiya*, his mother's younger sister. When the henna has been put on, the drummers drum and the girls play, there is dancing—even the bride joins in. The young men from the bridegroom's compound and the village come and watch. When it is time to eat their food, the girls go into a hut and close the door, so that the young men can't come and take away their food.

The bride stays in her *mawankiya's* compound for four nights; *mawankiya* puts henna on the bride's arms and legs every day, and ties them up in leaves, but she doesn't put the long henna-gourd on her hand and arm, so the girl just unties the leaves and pulls them off and runs off to play. When the girls cook food in *mawankiya's* compound they give some to the drummers and singers.

I remember my first marriage—Zetanku, our old slave who had weaned me, was my 'grandmother' who washed me, while Muna-yebo, another slave, poured out the water. My mother's elder sister Dije was my *mawankiya*. (12) They took me into Dije's hut, just the three of them and me, and they talked to me and gave me good advice, they said 'You must do this, you mustn't do that; he desires you and you desire him, you must settle down happily and be content'. They sent away the little girls. Then I went off to dance. If the bridegroom has been married before they don't put henna on him, it is like a previously-married woman.

All this was the same for slaves, except that their *Mawankiya's* compound would be in the *rinji*, and they would not take so long over the ceremonies as we did.

The seventh day is the marriage day; the bride's maternal grandmother washes her at her *mawankiya's* house, then her mother's younger sister, her *mawankiya*, takes her to her father's compound. (If they are slaves, the bride would be taken to the master's compound, he is like her father.) (13) The bride covers her head with a cloth, her *kawa* takes her hand, and off they go, kinswomen and girls, with the drummers and singers leading, and the girls singing this song:

> *The lucky one, the favourite,*
> *The lucky one of the kin,*
> *The lucky one was betrothed,*
> *The lucky one got her!*
> *Resign yourself, patient girl,*
> *Marriage is an ill you can't revenge,*
> *Only death will bring relief.* (14)

When they arrive at her father's home (15) they find her kinsmen, both her father's kinsmen and her mother's, in the entrance-hut, with the bridegroom's kinsmen. The women of her father's and her mother's kin, and the kinswomen of the bridegroom, are inside the compound in the women's quarters. The *mawankiya* presents the bride to her own father, who says 'Wash the bride and give her to the bridegroom's kin'. Then *mawankiya* leads her into her father's compound, if they were slaves she would lead the bride to the hut of the master's head wife. Then the gifts from the bridegroom's home are brought—a calabash of grain with a chicken on top of it, and a calabash of porridge with stew, some millet-balls and sour milk. The bride's mother's younger sister eats some of the food and then gives it to the bride. The bride's father sends the same food, and the *mawankiya* eats some of that also, and then feeds the bride. When they have eaten they give the remainder to the bride's friends and they eat it up. The bridegroom's kinswomen have brought the food, they are there—his mother and her co-wife and another woman of his kin. 'Come,' they say, 'let's go to the bride's home', and they take up the gifts and go. Besides the food, they bring the bride four cloths, a pair of slippers, some soap, a washing-calabash, another little calabash, a blouse, a petticoat and a spindle. If slaves were being married, all these things would be shown to the master before they were taken into the women's quarters of his compound.

Then it is time to wash the bride; they seat her on an upturned mortar that is used for pounding corn, they cover her head with a cloak, her mother's mother washes her while her father's mother pours out the water. They wash her all over thoroughly with soap, while her friends sing 'Save my life, *hankaka*, save my life!' They try to get in the way of the grandmothers, they sing:

> *Old one with the little calabash,*
> *May Allah put a stop to your work!*

and the chief *kawa* seizes the washing-bowl before the grandmothers have finished, they throw it away, they smash the calabash, they don't like the old lady who put henna on the bride and is now trying to wash her. Then *Mawankiya* brings the clothes which the bridegroom sent, she dresses the bride in her new clothes, she puts on her head-kerchief and her slippers. When she is dressed her *mawankiya* leads her out to the entrance-hut, where her father speaks to her. She kneels down before him and covers up her head. He says 'May Allah grant you His blessing; be patient, don't be mean, do not be disrespectful, do not abuse anyone, do not go wandering about, but settle down to married life, make good porridge and divide it properly among the household, be content and live in peace'. He talks to her like that. Then he turns to the younger brother of the bridegroom's father and the younger sister of his mother, who are there, and says 'I give her to you, I entrust her to you, take good care of her'. If slaves were being married, the master would take the place of the bride's father, her kinsmen and kinswomen would come to his compound, but her own father and mother would remain at home.

Then the bridegroom's special friend comes forward with a horse, all the bridegroom's friends have come to fetch the bride. Slaves used to carry the bride themselves, they didn't have horses —the groom's chief friend would carry the bride home on his back. *Mawankiya* dresses the bride in a man's trousers and a short petticoat, she wraps her cloth round her on top and puts her kerchief on her head, then she is set on the horse with her younger sister behind her; the groom's friend holds the reins, the girls and young men surround them, and off they go. The girls hold up the bridegroom's friend, they won't let him start off until he has given them some money—three times he has to give them money before they will let him go, with the bride on her horse. Then on the way to the bridegroom's home the girls try to stop his friends from taking away the bride. The drummers and singers lead the procession, the drum-rhythm says:

> *You have had your gifts,*
> *Get to your house,*
> *Go and taste the chickens of your husband's house!*

All the girls sing:

> *The great hunt was a good hunt,*
> *The great hunt brought meat,*
> *In the great hunt we caught—*
> *(The great hunt was a good hunt)—*
> *We caught, we caught*
> *Ten hares, ten ground-squirrels,*
> *Ten buffaloes, ten gazelles,*
> *Ten elephants, ten antelopes,*
> *And ten hyenas—we caught them.*
> *The great hunt was good.*

They are singing this when the procession arrives at the bridegroom's compound, then the girls block up the entrance and say they won't let the bridegroom's friends bring the bride in. Then the bridegroom's kinsfolk bring some corn and salt for the horse to eat (if his friend has brought the bride on his back, he pretends to eat the corn and spits it out), when he has eaten the horse enters the compound with the bride on his back. The friends and kinsfolk who have brought her all follow her in. The bride is helped to dismount, and taken into her new hut; her kinswomen fill her hut, the bridegroom's kinswomen are inside the compound too, all the men remain without at the front of the house. But when they arrive at her hut door they find her new joking relations, the bridegroom's grandmothers, sitting there and saying that they can't come in with the bride! When they are given a little money they get up and let her in. Then it is the turn of the bride's girl-friends to prevent her from entering her hut, they sing and the chief *kawa* hangs onto the bride.

> *Bring the bridegroom's water,*
> *Bring water with a threepence,*
> *Bring the younger sister's water,*
> *Bring water with a threepence.*
> *One always gives water.*
> > *We'll drink from the stream,*
> > *We'll drink from the river—*
> *Bring the bridegroom's water,*
> *Bring water with a threepence!*

Then the groom's younger sister, the bride's new joking relation, comes quickly with a vessel of water with a threepenny piece in it, she puts it down at the door of the hut and runs away. They try to catch her and pour the water over her. If she is slow and doesn't come at once, then the bride and her friends rush off and run away towards the river, while the older people chase them to get her back. Some brides run right away and go home, then the bridegroom's chief friend has to go after her—he always brings her back, because he is stronger than she is. The bride's friends and the groom's younger sisters are playing and teasing, the friends won't let the bridegroom's younger sisters enter the bride's hut, and when food is being eaten, if the younger sisters come near, the bride's friends will smear them with porridge and stew and oil and they will have to run away and wash. If the bridegroom's younger brothers come in, they get into trouble too. Meanwhile the bride's grandmothers are busy washing her again behind her hut—quietly this time, with no drumming—and then they clothe her in her best things and put on her ornaments, and take her back into her hut. The chief *kawa* steals the bride's slippers and hides them, and her *mawankiya* has to pay her to bring them back. Then the *kawa* sweeps out the bride's hut, she puts the sweepings into a beautiful bowl and takes it, covered up, to the bridegroom; she says he is to buy the bowl. If he refuses she pours the sweepings all over him; if he pays then she takes the money and leaves him. They all run away—the bride's *kawa* and her younger sisters and all the girls. Meanwhile the older women are preparing the food and getting the bride's hut ready.

Then the bride's dowry is brought, her kinswomen on both her father's and her mother's side bring it all to the bridegroom's compound. The bride's family will try to bring a sack of guineacorn, a sack of millet, and one of rice, and the bridegroom's family will give the couple the same, and they will give the bridegroom a new gown to put on. The bride's family will also bring salt and tins of oil. The chief *kawa* brings her gifts, the bride's younger and her elder sisters bring theirs, they all come about the time of La'asar (5.30 p.m.). They arrange all her things in her hut. A *kawa* brings one large pot for cooling water, one plate with a cover, one big ladle, and later when there were metal coins she would bring a shillingsworth of *aninai* (tenths of a penny) to be used as ornaments. (16) The bride's younger sister brings a small mat, a white mat and a mat to hang before the door of the hut. She puts these things into a woven cloth and takes them to her elder sister. Then the bride's elder sister brings hers, a huge basin of very white rice, ten thousand cowries and one cloth. After a year the bride will buy two or three chickens and a small goat and send them to her elder sister, to thank her for the hard work she did. The bride shows her gratitude to her younger sister and her *kawa* on their wedding-days when they come, but she cannot do that to her elder sister, as she is already married; so she waits a year and then takes her a present. In addition to the sacks of grain and rice and the oil and salt, the bride's parents will also collect bowls and plates for her and earthenware pots for water and for cooking, and baskets of different kinds of food—locust-bean cakes, peppers, okras, onions, the ingredients of stew, and a basket of *wasa-wasa*. (17)

After a year she does not take the same gift to her parents as she does to her elder sister, but after she has been married for a year or two she buys a gown and a ram to give to her father; he gives alms with the ram, and he wears his gown. She buys a cloth and a ram to give to her mother. This is called the 'payment for bearing her', and they say 'May Allah bless you!' This is done because they brought her forth and reared her, even until she reached marriage. Whether she has a child or not, she will give these gifts to her parents. If her grandmother is alive, her father's or her mother's mother, the bride will give her a cloth; if her grandfathers are alive she gives them millet-balls or perfume. For good-natured grandparents whom she likes, she will prepare millet-balls to take to their house, she will put on her best clothes and take it along and spend the day with them—if it is a long way away she will stay for a night too. When she is returning home, the grandparents fill up a calabash with locust-bean cakes, and another with salt and one with cotton, one with corn, and one with okras; they give it all to her as a present to take home. When she arrives at her husband's compound she distributes the gifts to the people of the house.

After a bride has been married a year or two, the bridegroom's father or mother say 'This daughter must go home to see her parents'. They give her grain, she makes millet-balls, her husband's mother escorts her and they travel together. She goes from one house to another to visit her kinsfolk, and they all rejoice, 'So-and-so has come, so-and-so has come . . .' She stays with them for two or three nights, or seven nights if it is far away. She has been spinning and weaving and saving up money to buy them their gifts; now she greets her mother and father with the cloths and goats, she greets her grandparents with gifts and millet-balls, she greets the kinsfolk, father's and mother's sisters, with millet-balls. As for her brothers and sisters and cross-cousins, she waits until the day they have children. The reason for all this is that her parents brought her forth and cared for her, and her kinsfolk gave her many things, they filled up her hut with their gifts.

When the dowry and gifts have been brought to the bride's new hut, her kinswomen arrange them for her and make her hut look nice. Only her kinswomen are doing it—the bridegroom's kin are busy with him. They decorate the bride's hut and they adorn her with cloths and bracelets and ornaments. While they are arranging her dowry, the bride sits on the bed and watches. She has cried until she is weary, now she is pleased—she looks at the lovely clothes, and her hut full of good things. While they are arranging her possessions, there is drumming and feasting outside. Then your mother's younger sister comes and seizes you and ties

you on her back like a child, she covers your head with a big cloth
and dances with you where they are drumming. Ten of my 'mothers'
danced with me like that, they felt joyful and they danced in the
courtyard of the compound. Then they gave me a stick and a bowl
and told me to go begging, while they drummed the song of the
malams—my father was a *malam*.

> *House of blessings, house of the Book,*
> *House that is filled with ablution-jars,*
> *House of blessings, house of the Book.*

Then my 'parents' on my mother's side pretended they were angry,
and said I must do the dance of the blacksmiths—they put a
tomato in my mouth for the red-hot iron.

> *You eat fire* bel-bel, *the blacksmiths' game,*
> *You eat fire* bel-bel-bel, *the blacksmiths' game,*
> *Sons of the blacksmiths, you eat medicine,*
> *Playing with fire, only the blacksmiths,*
> *You sons of the blacksmiths, you eat medicine,*
> *Only the blacksmiths can play with fire!*

Then my father's kin said 'Drum the Barebare song to the bride!'
I filled my mouth with *damus*, the Barebare food, and they
drummed the song of the Bornu people.

Everyone has his special dance for feasts like this; the blacksmiths heat iron until it is red, red, then they play with it in their
hands and against their bodies and heads until there is lots of smoke.
They have magic, it doesn't burn them. The onlookers give them
money. Buzaye, the people from the north, put a wooden mortar
on their stomachs, the man will lie down and put it on his stomach
then they pound the corn in it! If it is a wedding-feast they give the
grain when it is ground to the bride's father's younger brother, or
to the bride's cross-cousin, and they give it to the bride to eat.
Katukawa (18) from the south eat sun-baked bricks. For us, the
Barebare from Bornu, they set a cooking-pot in the middle of the
compound, and fill it with millet and porridge and red sorrel, then
we have our feast. We fill our mouths with the sorrel-juice, it is
very bitter, we fill our mouth then we drink water, and we dance
with our mouths full of our food. At a butchers' feast they fill
their mouths with porridge and dance; they sit down and pretend

that they are selling their meat in the market. Cattle Fulani just collect milk and butter and drink it.

When the bridegroom's friends came in, they gave me money, they filled up my bowl with money and they gave money to the drummers and singers. The bridegroom stays outside at the entrance-hut of the compound, he doesn't come in. Weeping was over, I was happy—here were gifts and money and my parents and kinsfolk. My husband's senior wife presided over the feast, she collected the money. In the afternoon everyone went home to rest, the feast was over. My *kawaye* and I sat down in my hut, and we did our spinning. That night we all slept in my hut. In the morning the bridegroom and his friends mounted horses, those who had none borrowed them, and they went off 'mounting the bridegroom' in their best clothes, through all the nearby villages.

If the bride is her mother's first child, her mother will come at night to visit her, but if she is a later child her mother will come in the daytime to see her daughter's gifts. Her father comes to see the bridegroom's father, and says 'We thank you, we thank you'. They converse together in the entrance-hut, the bride's father says 'If she does anything wrong, come and tell us, she is your daughter'. At night when her mother sits there and sees the decorated hut she rejoices over her daughter, she is happy. Then she gets up and greets the people of the compound and she says 'Now I am going home', then she goes back to her own home, till tomorrow. The bridegroom's father gives the bride ten thousand white cowries in a calabash—she dips in and gives her mother her share. The bridegroom's mother cooks porridge for her for three months, until she is accustomed to the house. The first night in her new hut, the bride doesn't go to sleep, she sits and spins with her *kawaye*, they gossip and tell stories. If you have come as a stranger, will you go to sleep? No, quietly, quietly until you grow used to it.

When they have finished 'mounting the bridegroom', the bridegroom sleeps in the compound of his best friend. Next night, his friends bring him to the bride's hut and try to push him in, but he resists and runs away. For about seven nights they bring him like that, struggling, and he always resists and runs away. After seven nights three of his friends bring him, they fight and struggle and they push him into the hut; when the bride sees him she opens the door and rushes out and hides elsewhere in the compound. He lies down in her hut and goes to sleep, then when dawn is close she goes in, and he runs away to the compound of a kinsman. For seven nights when it is dark he comes, and she runs away. After two weeks he comes one night and brings her money, he buys kola-nuts, sugar-cane, dumplings, cassava, and sweetmeats; he gives them to her younger sister to take to her. They eat and eat, then at night the women send the younger sister away to the husband's mother's hut or some other hut—the elders of the compound drive her out of the bride's hut. He is wooing her with food and money. When the elders of the compound are asleep, and the girls have all gone home, it is all quiet; then he goes into her hut. That means that the marriage has 'taken'; they live together. On that night he brings the 'money to open her mouth', and then she can speak to him. That is how it was when I was a girl; nowadays the young people are not so shy, some of the bridegrooms will sleep with their brides almost as soon as they are married.

Before the marriage had 'taken' the bridegroom's younger brother would come and tease the bride, he would look at her spinning and say 'It's no good!' he would break the thread and she would get up and hit him and chase him away. He is her joking relation. For three months the bride does no housework, except that she will help a little in grinding the grain. This allows her to become accustomed to her new home.

When women-slaves got married, their master was their *wali*. (19) If he freed one of his woman-slaves, her own parents could act as her *wali*, otherwise it was her master.

Marriage of Almsgiving (20)

There is another kind of marriage where the bridegroom's kin pay nothing for the bride; this is called a marriage of alms. If a man wishes to give another a gift, whether it is a *malam* or just someone he likes, then he will collect cloth, guineacorn, millet, rice, and the other marriage gifts, and put them together. He says nothing to the man who is to be bridegroom. He tells his daughter what he wants to do; if she refuses to be married to the man her father has chosen, they try to persuade her, but if she keeps on refusing, they drop the matter—she would not settle down. If she agrees, then one morning the marriage ceremony is held, and she is married to a representative of the Prophet. Late that night her mother's younger brother and her father's or her mother's mother take her to the compound of the *malam* who is to receive her. They call out 'Peace be upon you!' The door is opened, 'Upon you be peace!' 'Here is alms, we have brought alms to so-and-so'. They take the bride into the compound. Next morning the *malam* who has received this gift collects twenty thousand cowries—nowadays he would take about £1—he assembles about ten *malams* and they take the money and some cloth and go to the entrance-hut of the bride's father. They give him the money as the gift we always give to one who brings presents, and the cloth is for the bride. My younger 'sister' Barmo was married like that, and my elder 'sister' Bagura, they were married in Zarewa. Barmo was given to Yusufu, Bagura was given to Balarabe. There was Kande, she was given to Dalhatu. Some of the girls refuse to be given as alms, then they will be married to the man they prefer.

Bond-friends and Marriage

My four *kawaye* got married at about the same time as I did; first Zaila, then Tagadago, then me, then Matansarki then Kande. Zaila was married first, in the Butchers' Ward. She died at Jos recently, she was light-skinned and lovely. We all took her to her *mawankiya's* house and then to her new hut. We were crying, we didn't want to part with her. When we went to *mawankiya's* compound we ate food, then her grandmother came with the henna and the drummers came and drummed. We sang that we would kill the old lady, and we hit her and tried to stop her putting the marriage henna on Zaila.

We Bare-bare women have a special custom: if your husband gives you kola-nuts and tobacco-flowers, you know that he desires you. You sit in your hut in the evening, eating kolanuts and rubbing the tobacco-flowers on your teeth, and you feel good. As you finish with the tobacco-flowers you put them in a flat basket and hang it up on your wall. You do this for seven days, you collect them. On the following Friday you send a young girl to your *kawa* with the used tobacco-flowers. If your *kawa's* husband has also been giving her tobacco-flowers and kolanuts, she hangs your little basket on the wall, and for seven days she collects her used flowers. Then when the Friday comes she puts them all together, yours and hers, and sends them back to you. Then you both know that your marriages are going well. After dark the *kawaye* will go to visit each other, they laugh and are glad because each one knows her husband desires her. But if the husband of one of them does not give her kolanuts and tobacco-flowers, and the other one sends her a little basket full of used flowers, then the neglected one will break up her marriage—that is, it is her *kawa* who has caused the marriage to break up. One wants to be treated as well as one's friend. That is a custom of Bornu women.

If a husband is not wealthy and cannot give her presents, then the wife's family will say 'Leave him, leave him! It isn't a marriage. No gifts, no marriage.' The things which make a good marriage are these: a man desires you, you desire him, he marries you. He keeps giving you gifts, he buys you cloth and kolanuts. If he is earning money, he takes out a little of it at the festival and buys you a cloth. A townswoman prefers money, a countrywoman prefers grain—give a countrywoman a hoe and she will do her own farming and eat her corn. But with a wealthy man who is quarrelsome, no woman will settle—what is the use of quarrelling? A good-tempered man is better. Yet one desires money. . . . You see?

CHAPTER VI

I MARRY MY COUSIN DUMA

When I was about fourteen years old it was time for me to be married; (1) I had grown up with our six 'fathers', the sons of Ibrahim Dara and his younger brother Maidamishi, and when the time came they arranged my marriage within the family, a marriage of kinsfolk. I was married to Duma the son of Sidi; Sidi was the son of my grandfather Mai Yana, Mai Yana and Ibrahim Dara being the sons of two brothers. I called Sidi 'father' and his son Duma was my elder brother; I called him 'Yaya'. Duma's father Sidi and my father put their heads together, the elder brother said to my father, 'We will marry them to one another', and his younger brother replied 'Very well'. They were always arranging marriages between kinsfolk in our family, everyone married his kinswoman and took her to his compound. My mother was dead at that time, and my father's sister Rabi was like my mother, (2) but she had been kidnapped. My father sent for me and I went to him and curtsied. 'Your kinsman desires you,' he said; 'I also desire him,' I replied.

Dabo, the son of Sarkin Zarewa our town chief, loved me and I wanted him, but my family would not agree to our marrying, they did not like titles and title-holders; they were farmers, they liked their daughters to marry farmers. (3) We often married into the families of blacksmiths, too; blacksmiths are the farmers' friends, they make our tools. Blacksmiths and farmers like to join their children in marriage. (4) But the chief of the town was a Fulani, and we are Kado—Habe, the people who have been here since long before the Fulani came; Habe are free, not like a *dimajo* or a *bacucane*, they are two names for the same thing—the son of a slave, a man born in captivity. We came from Bornu but we were like Habe, and my family did not like to marry into families who

102

held ruling titles, in spite of the fact that Bornu people and Fulani are joking relations—Barebare and Fulani. (5) That was why I could not marry Sarkin Zarewa's son. There was also Malam Maigari who wished to marry me, I promised him I would come to him later.

The chiefs of Zarewa were Habu, who died; then Usuman, who went mad; then Danfangi Aliyu, (6) then Abubakar, then Danfangi Ibrahim, then Hanciji, then Garba, then Danfangi Yerbi—he is there now. Danfangi Ibrahim was born in Giwa, but he became Chief of Zarewa; the Giwa and Zarewa Fulani are related to one another. When Ibrahim left Zarewa he came back here to Giwa and they made him Danfangi Giwa—he was the father of the present village Chief of Giwa, he was Chief of Zarewa before he came back and got appointed here. This Danfangi who is the village Chief of Giwa now was a young man living in Zarewa when we were young.

When my kinsman Duma came to visit me, (7) I sent for my *kawa* 'Yariya, her home wasn't far away, and she came to our entrance-hut. I took out two mats and we gave them one and sat on one ourselves. Duma came with his special friend, another man, and I talked to his friend while 'Yariya talked to Duma, we were all laughing and joking. Then his friend took out some money and placed it on our mat. Then we arose and escorted them on their way home, and when we returned home we rolled up the mats and went into the compound. 'Yariya picked up the money and put it into a flat basket, and I took my share, which was bigger than hers. When her cross-cousin was courting her (she was daughter of the sister, he was son of the brother), she used to call me to go to her compound in the same way, and I used to go. His name was Inusa. We all talked together, then Inusa's friend Yero came and put down the money in front of me. When we had escorted them homewards, we came back to 'Yariya's compound and I took up the money while she rolled up the mats, then we went into her mother's hut and laid out the money. 'Yariya gave me my share, a little, and kept her share, which was the greater part. Then she escorted me home. We always showed our mothers the gift, but the money was ours. If you like the man, you say to his friend 'Yes, I like him'. Then they put down the money and your *kawa* takes it. If you don't like him, you say 'Get on with your work. You are too strong for us'. They put down their money, and your *kawa* says 'Take away your things, she does not desire you'. Then you leave the money alone, you don't accept it. If they come back the next day you run away. But if you agree, they come every week to visit you and bring money, they keep on coming for a whole year.

When they were arranging my first marriage, my father talked to me and persuaded me to accept Duma, he wanted his kinsman to marry me. Since he wished it, I said 'Yes, very well'. When Duma came to visit me we chatted and laughed a lot—we knew each other well; then I accepted his money because Father wanted me to do so. But because I didn't really love him I left him after a few years. Parents always hope their daughter will have children and settle down; if she doesn't have children she does not settle down—and some, even if they do have children, leave them and break up the marriage. (8)

When it was time for me to be married the elders of our family met for the betrothal ceremony; a month later they 'set the day'; and two months after that was the wedding feast. That is three months altogether. At the *Salla* feast before our marriage Duma came to visit me, he could come inside our compound—wasn't it also his father's house? (9)—and he brought me money and kola-nuts and perfume, and told me to go and buy cloth. I went to market and bought cloth. He came and we conversed together. I bought bowls and some flat baskets and a few plates. Then on the marriage day my father's family and my mother's family all came. They brought sacks of guineacorn, sacks of rice, baskets of salt, of onions and of locust-bean cakes, and oil. They decorated my new hut with all my things, they set out my plates and bowls and spread mats on the bed and the floor—both the mats the pagan tribes make, and the ones from Bornu. Then they spread my blanket on the bed and set down the pillow. If you are going to be taken to your hut today, there is drumming and drumming, and tomorrow your kinsfolk will bring you all sorts of lovely things. The men load their donkeys with sacks of corn and rice, and the women put on their best cloths and carry the plates and bowls, they bring it all to you and put your dowry in your hut. (10) Yesterday evening you were in your hut, you covered your head and wept—no more going to play with the young girls, you would hear their drumming, you would hear it but you wouldn't be able to go out and dance. You feel very angry. Then your mother comes and talks to you, 'Be quiet, be calm, stop crying!' One of my aunts came (my mother was dead and Aunt Rabi was lost), she sent away

the children, 'Run away!' Then she talked to me and I was quiet.
Then my husband's wife, my co-wife (11) came and took me to my
new hut, she gave me some food and said to me 'Take out your
spinning'. We sat there spinning, and she coaxed me, and I felt
better. Her name was Ture and when I married Duma she had a
daughter Marka—that means steady rain, she was born in the
rainy season—and a son called Ciwake, which means 'Eat-beans';
they were eating beans when he was born. (12) She was a very good-
tempered woman. Duma was tall and handsome and sensible, we
lived together in peace with no quarrelling or anything of that
kind.

The Rescue of Aunt Rabi

When I had been married for some time to my kinsman Duma,
we heard news of my father's sister Rabi, who had been kidnapped.
When her children and relatives heard the news, they heard from
a traveller that she had been sold in Abuja, they pledged one of
her twin slaves, they collected money, and they gave it to her eldest
son to give to the *malams* so that they should make charms for
him. He went to Abuja to fetch her, but on the way he wasted the
money on women, and came home to say that he had not found
her. Then again they collected money, and they gave it to Nasamai,
her second son. He sold a female slave to some rich people—the
rich man made her a concubine in his house, he had had no children
until she came, then she bore him eight. Nasamai took money to
the *malams*, who did their work and said 'She is in the palace of
the king of Abuja'. Nasamai made ready and set out, the *malams*
gave him charms to take both in his hand and in his mouth; (13)
baduhu for washing his eyes, *layan zana* so that he shouldn't be seen,
charms to put in his mouth and charms to hold in his hand. He got
them both for himself and his mother. When he got to Abuja—the
malams had looked and said 'Go to the king's palace'—he went to
the king's palace, he passed through the first entrance-hut, there
were many courtyards and many entrance-huts, each with a lamp
burning in it, the courtyards that kings' houses have. When he got
inside he heard the king's chief wife calling 'Woman of the Hausa,
bring me fire, bring me water, come and light the lamp'. The slave
answered 'Very well'. When he heard her voice (he knew where to
look for her because of his charms), he went and touched her, she

said 'What brings you here?' Then he put a charm in her mouth. The king's wife called 'Bring the lamp!' She picked up only one cloth, Nasamai said 'Be silent!' He tied her on his back with a blanket, like a child—he was tall, she was very small. Swiftly he slipped out and carried her away. Only one man saw them; he went 'a-hem!' and he said nothing; late that night he told the king, 'I saw a man leave the palace today carrying a woman on his back'. When the king's chief wife called and there was no answer, then she began to look for her slave; she didn't see her. She went to the king and she said 'The Hausa woman is not here'. Then the king called out his men and told them to search for her; there was a storm with pouring rain, at daybreak the men hunted for them on the road, but they could not find them. Nasamai took her to Gobirawa and there they ate; after three days they reached Zaria, and they sent a message to Zarewa to say Nasamai had found his mother.

We were at Karo, our hamlet, then we heard that there was war; we all went in to Zarewa town, and it was then that she returned. We were delighted, we all gave her cloths, we gave her head-scarves. As for Nasamai, everyone praised and blessed him, he was a determined man and everyone in the town rejoiced at him. Rabi had no husband, because he had escaped from the kidnappers and gone off somewhere and there was no news of him; so when she came home she married her kinsman Mamman—he and she were the children of two brothers. She had been exactly three years at Abuja; she did their grinding and spinning, they gave her food, she ate and was satisfied.

At that time I had been married for three years to my kinsman. His chief wife had two children when I married him, she was carrying one on her back and the other could walk. When father's sister Rabi (we called her 'Baba's mother') (14) was brought home from Abuja I was very happy. Everyone came to say 'Blessings on your fortune, Baba's mother!' Everyone praised her resourceful son. Then the war-alarm came and Duma sent us into Zarewa while he stayed out at Karo. All the village was fleeing from the war. (15) When we got into Zarewa we heard that the mother of Baba had come home, so we went to her compound, we were all over her— you couldn't see her! She was staying in her son's compound, he had two wives; there were kinsfolk and friends and *kawaye*, like a whole town.

I MARRY MY COUSIN DUMA

When she came home I no longer wanted to live in the hamlet, I preferred the town; (16) it is nicer in a town, there are more people—Karo was four miles from Zarewa. My 'parents' told me to go back to him, but I refused. Then my husband's 'parents' came and said I must go back. When I still said I would not go, then all the elders, men and women, came to Aunt Rabi's (17) compound and assembled in the entrance-hut. The old women sat with the men in the entrance-hut. Some of them said 'She must have patience and return', others said 'Since she dislikes the marriage it is better that they part'. Then they sent for me, I came in and they said 'You must put up with it, you must have patience; your husband is your kinsman, you must go on with your marriage'. I said 'No'. Anja, Ayashe, Kunza—they were my grandmothers, wives of Ibrahim Dara, who liked me. Duma was there, it was he who had said 'I want her to calm down and come home; send for her'. I came and knelt down, and he asked me 'What have I done to you? Be sensible and come back. You know I want you, stop being angry and come home.' I said 'No'. He wanted me very much, but I didn't want him, I desired a son of the blacksmiths, Maigari of the South Gate. When I was a girl he used to give me money on market-days; he wanted to marry me, but I refused so that my parents should not be angry with me and beat me. I had promised him I would come, I said 'Be patient, I will not remain there'. When Aunt Rabi came home I knew she would help me; (18) before she was taken to Abuja Maigari had begun to court me, then when she was not there they had married me to someone else. When she came back I felt good, I told her that I didn't like the marriage and she said 'Very well, go and break it up'. 'You didn't want him,' she said, 'and they did that to you. Very well, go and get divorced, I am back.' Aunt Rabi's daughter and I were born on the same day.

Aunt Rabi was there in the entrance-hut where they were discussing my marriage; she said to them, 'She said she did not wish to marry Duma. Very well, you forced her. Now I have come back and she is not going to stay married to him.' Then my father said 'What business is it of mine? It has nothing to do with me.' That was that. Then to the Chief's compound. (19) All the fathers had come to Aunt Rabi's compound and she had told them off soundly. There were ten of them on Duma's side, we all went to Sarkin Zarewa's compound. But before that I had paid a visit to the chief's house, I went to see his head wife, I knew his wives. She said 'What brings you?' I said 'I have come to break off my marriage'. She explained the matter to Sarki. When I went to his house officially, to start the divorce proceedings, I went inside the compound to his own hut, I knelt down and greeted him.

'Allah preserve your life.'

'Good. Woman of Karo, what brings you here?'

'I want to break off my marriage.'

He said 'Indeed! Be patient and go back. What is his fault?' I said 'He hasn't done anything, but I don't like the hamlet, I prefer the town'. Then he looked at me, then he said 'Very well'. We had known him ever since his father held the chieftainship, they were the Fulani of our town. (20) When he returned to the entrance of the compound he sent his courtiers to Karo to call Duma's people. When they came, Duma said I was angry and he did not know the reason. Sarki questioned me, I said it was nobody's fault, I was just tired of village life. I did not mention the matter of Maigari. Sarki gave me a document (21) and my marriage with Duma was over. Duma and I remained friends, our kinship did not die. When I had been married to Maigari for two years Duma's daughter, his head wife's child, came and spent twenty days with me, I gave her a small cloth and head-kerchief when she returned home. When she was married I went and stayed for two nights in Duma's compound, Maigari did not prevent it, because of the kinship between us.

When I had ended the marriage I went to Aunt Rabi's compound. (22) We were delighted, we had triumphed. I helped to grind the corn, the wives of my 'brother' made porridge, we used to eat ours together, and we gave Rabi hers separately. (23) After she had lived in her son's house for a year, her kinsman Mamman came from Karo, they were the children of two brothers, he was Maidamishi's son and she Ibrahim Dara's daughter; he desired her, and she married him.

PART THREE

CHAPTER VII

c. 1907–1922
SECOND MARRIAGE

Arrangements for my Second Marriage (1)

I stayed for three months, ninety days, during my *Iddah*, in Aunt Rabi's home, then the one who desired me came forward, a son of the blacksmiths, whom I also desired. A son of the Zarewa blacksmiths, he had known me when I was a maiden and he was a young man. Aunt Rabi didn't like him, she preferred Musa, but I did not like Musa. Then the day I had finished *Iddah* she said Musa was to be my husband. I said 'No'. Then she was angry so I left her compound and went to Haleru's, to his wife's hut. Haleru was my grandmother Anja's youngest son, she had married again after grandfather Ibrahim Dara's death. Malam Maigari sought me there, he came with his friend Mentari. I received them alone, I bowed down and welcomed them. He said 'We desire you, but your mother Rabi does not want us. We have come to hear from your own mouth what you wish.' I said 'Yes, I wish it'. They returned in the evening and greeted Haleru. Haleru told them to go to Karo in the morning and take their money and greet my father. My five 'fathers' were there, Tsoho my own father, Sa'i, Ubangida, Audu and Malam Buhari, the eldest. On the day of asking for me, they went to Ubangida's compound with the gifts of seeking a bride, they found him there and he took them to Malam Buhari's compound. When they arrived they greeted the 'fathers', then Malam Maigari's friend said 'We desire Baba'. Father said 'Ap!' Then Mentari, Maigari's friend, said 'She has left Rabi's hut, Rabi does not like us, she is staying in Haleru's house and she says she desires us'.

My father's elder brother Ubangida used to arrange our marriages, our father arranged Ubangida's children's marriages. That

111

is why Malam Maigari and his friend went with their gifts to Ubangida. Then I was sent for to Karo and my father Ubangida questioned me; I told him I wanted Maigari. After that my fathers discussed the matter, they said 'She sent them and Haleru sent them; he is the man she wants. Then shouldn't we give her to them?' Then they brought millet-balls and milk and gave it to Malam Maigari and his friend and told them to return on Monday, the marriage would be performed. You don't 'set the day' for the marriage of a woman who has already been married, (2) you just say 'The marriage will be on such-and-such a day'. The gifts and the marriage payments are just the same as for a maiden. On the day of the marriage I was taken to my new hut. After seven days the dowry was brought. Seven days after Malam Maigari had asked my family for my hand, we were married; and after seven more days they brought my dowry.

I didn't cry because I liked him. I did not love Duma, but my fathers said they would beat me, they would tie my legs and beat me again and again, so I said nothing more, I agreed. Your mothers never beat you, but fathers do. Your own father wouldn't do it, he would call his younger brother and say 'Beat her', his younger brother ties you up tightly like a thief; your father calls him, so that no one shall say that he who begot you did it. But he is there, looking on. If a man is very angry with his son, he will beat him himself, but if he is not as angry as all that he will send for his younger brother and tell him to beat the son, and then the son runs away. But if the boy is sensible he will kneel down and keep on saying to his father 'Allah make you forbearing, may Allah give you patience!' and then his father calms down. Formerly boys used to be beaten a good deal, but now they don't do it much—in the past a boy couldn't run away from home for fear of wars and slave-raiders. Duma never beat me at all, husbands aren't supposed to do it, only fathers. But some husbands do, if you do something wrong.

The Wedding

For seven days the bridegroom's kin collected the gifts, then the old women and children of Malam Maigari's compound carried them to Ubangida. On the marriage day they brought a calabash of salt, the 'salt of seeking', a calabash of kolanuts, the 'meat of seeking' and three cloths. These were divided between my father's and my mother's kin. Then they brought ten thousand cowries *sadaki*, this was mine. There was money for greeting the kin, eighty thousand cowries, half for my father's and half for my mother's kin. When my representatives and Malam Maigari's had solemnized the marriage they came back from Karo. All these things are divided up amongst the kinsfolk and friends, they all have a very little so that they may 'feel the marriage'. I was not present at the marriage ceremony, neither was Maigari, our parents went to Malam Buhari's house at Karo, and when they returned they said 'We have performed the ceremony'. For this ceremony at Malam Buhari's compound there were the five fathers and my father's and my mother's kinsmen, and about thirty of Malam Maigari's. Malam Buhari said 'I give her to you; when Monday comes round she will join him'. That was that, until the day of the feast came. Everyone took up a full calabash, and plates, some with rice, some with guineacorn. The bridegroom also sent food for the bride. I remained in Haleru's compound for seven nights.

The morning after the marriage had been performed an old woman brought me the *aunaka* (3) grain from the bridegroom's house; we ground it and made flour and a woman of our compound made porridge and stew. Malam Maigari sent a big basket of guineacorn from his own granary—if he had been a youth it would have been from his father's granary—two chickens, some salt, locust-bean cakes, baobab leaves, okras and a bottle of oil—the ingredients of stew. In the morning the bride cooks porridge and stew, and two old women go and take the *tuwon aunaka* to the husband, he tastes the bride's porridge and he sees that she knows how to make it. When he gets it he distributes it amongst his family and friends, they all taste the bride's porridge before she comes to join him. When they have tasted this porridge two of the bridegroom's 'parents' come to ask when she will come to his compound. They went to Ubangida, he took them to his eldest brother Malam Buhari, they considered it and they said 'When Monday comes round again'. When they returned home the bridegroom bought a calabash of kolanuts, and sent it to the bride to give to her friends, he bought another one to distribute among his friends to announce the day when the bride would enter his household.

On the day that she will go to him, the 'day of coming together', the bride heats water in the morning and washes all her clothes, except for her new marriage ones, which she puts aside. You wash all your ordinary ones. You make some millet-paste and hide it, that millet-paste is called 'the love of the two'. When noon has passed, the afternoon comes, your *kawaye* bring their gifts. Your parents collect for you two sacks of rice, one from your mother's and one from your father's kin; two sacks of guineacorn, one from each side; all the ingredients for stew, ten bottles of palm oil and ten of groundnut oil. It was all collected at Ubangida's compound over at Karo; then they took it to Buhari's house, he saw it and said 'Allah be praised!', then they brought all the gifts to Zarewa, to Haleru's house. When my kinswomen and friends arrived with my dowry, the drummers came. In the evening the old women and children from the bridegroom's house brought *tuwon jere* (4)— the food that is set out in a row, the food for a bride who has been married before. They brought five huge millet-balls, a goat, ten chickens, a big calabash of milk and ten bowls of porridge. I was in my hut with my *kawa* Kande, my parents divided the *tuwon jere* and everyone ate it, saying 'May Allah grant she conceives! May Allah give her children!' Then they took it and divided it up, they gave the women and children who had brought it a little porridge and a little meat for their trouble, the gift-bringer's dues. All my mothers and sisters came over from Karo, the *tuwon jere* was shared out in Haleru's house, while I hid in my hut with Kande. We sent food to Malam Buhari's house at Karo, and there they settled down to apportion it out. Their wives came from Karo, but the menfolk didn't come, men don't come to a woman's marriage—she is going to be taken to someone else's house. For a girl's first marriage, both men and women come, but for an adult woman, women only. The bridegroom's menfolk were there in his house. Haleru was in our compound with his friends, in the entrance-hut. The bride—there was I with my chief *kawa* Kande. Haleru made food-gifts of rice, his wives cooked it. My Aunt Rabi, 'mother of Baba', (5) did not come, she was cross, but my fathers were not angry. Haleru was one of my fathers, he was about twenty-five years old, he was the youngest child of my father's mother Anja, the son of Malam Barau whom she married after Ibrahim Dara's death.

When they had eaten and were satisfied, the women picked up the dowry and took it all to Malam Maigari's compound. There were ten full calabashes of corn, five bowls of millet-balls, ten chickens. The kinsfolk had collected it, *chip*. The women took the grinding-stones, the cooking-pots, all the dowry—everything was new. Everyone who came brought something, men and women; one brought money, one brought oil, one brought guineacorn, everyone brought something. Then the food was distributed among them. It isn't like a girl's first marriage, you bring what you can to a woman's marriage. As they carried it along the kinswomen and friends were singing:

> *See your dowry that we've brought,*
> *See your daughter whom we've brought.*

As they went along they sang the song about the hunt, then at the door of the bridegroom's compound they sang 'See your daughter whom we've brought!' I and my *kawa* Kande and my younger sister Lami covered up our heads, and when they had gone with the dowry we started out for his house. The entrance-hut was full, there were crowds of men, we covered our faces and went in quietly; they said 'Here is the bride'. We entered the compound and I went and hid in my hut while Kande seized the beams of the hut and threatened to pull it all down if they didn't bring the water with money in it—she wouldn't let any of the older women in. When they had brought the water, everyone came in. The bridegroom's younger sister brought water with two hundred cowries in it and his younger brother brought the same. Kande took out the money and was going to throw the water over his sister's head, they were all joking. Malam Maigari's chief friend gave me the cowries and chased the bridegroom's sister to pour the water over her.

We went into the hut, we spread out the mats, the lamp was lit; we sat on the bed and covered our heads, Kande and I. My 'mothers' came and we put on our best clothes and arranged our head-kerchiefs. Our kinswomen were so many that they filled up the hut and overflowed into another one. Malam Maigari's kinswomen and mine, they filled up the hut *chip chip*. All my kinswomen, on my father's and my mother's side, and my friends, came in to decorate my hut and arrange the dowry while I put on my new wedding clothes. Then we spent the night chewing kola-nuts and staining our teeth with tobacco-flowers, drumming on calabashes and singing songs and calling the *bori* spirits. (6) Gude was possessed by the judge, the friend of Dangaladima—Gude was Tanko's wife from Karo; Dangaladima possessed 'Yariya, our grandmother through Rabi, my mother's co-wife. This is the song of Malam Bawa, the judge: when he comes he says 'I am the son of Inna, the judge! I am the son of Inna, the judge!' Then we sing to him:

> *There is no chief but Allah.*
> *Look at the blue blue gown of Allah!*
> *For Allah's sake do not desire anyone but me.*
> *It is friendship that takes me to Bawa's house,*
> *A promise takes me to Bawa's house,*
> *I am seeking a promise from Allah.*

They sing this song to the spirit and they sing it to the women who are talking to him. Dangaladima was sitting here and the judge was sitting there; Dangaladima the prince was turning his head like this, very haughtily, then he would laugh. There are many songs for Dangaladima, one begins:

> *You have a drummer, Daudu,*
> *Daudu, you have a drummer . . .*

Dangaladima gave the praise-singers cloths—my cloths and anyone's cloths; he is very generous. I took kolanuts and money and gave them to the spirits. Some of the children came in to watch. Then another *bori* medium was possessed by Sarkin Rafi, the chief of the stream, and his wife Nana, she possessed yet another woman. In our family there were some *bori* adepts, there was Dogo, Malam Bawa's son, he was my 'father', Amina our mother, A'i our elder sister, Rabi's mother 'Yariya and Gude. Four women and one man. Spirit possession can be inherited through your mother or your father.

Malam Maigari's senior wife was in her hut with all her kinswomen. When I arrived, her sister welcomed me. Later I set aside two kolanuts and four hundred cowries; my younger sister and my *kawa* took them to the chief wife to 'buy my position'. Later the head wife sent her younger sister to bring me four kolanuts and eight hundred cowries. After that I and my friends and kinswomen spent the night playing and drumming and *bori*-dancing, we didn't go to sleep.

In the morning everyone went home, except for my *kawa*. I took out the millet-balls that I had hidden, the food of 'the love of the two', and she carried it to the bridegroom, either in the hut of the mother of his household, his head wife, or in the entrance-hut. He gave Kande one thousand cowries. Then I swept out my hut and put the sweepings in a bowl, Kande took it to the bridegroom and his friends and they gave her four hundred cowries—then she threw it all over them and his friends chased her. After this the bride stays in her hut and the bridegroom and his friend go into the head wife's hut, then a little later his friend leaves the bridegroom there and comes to greet the bride and joke with her. After that the bridegroom gives his head wife ten kolanuts for herself and ten for the bride, with four hundred cowries and some perfume. The head wife comes and 'buys the bride's speech', she says 'There it is. I have bought your mouth!' The bride says 'Thank you', and they greet one another. Then later on in the morning, when there is no one about in the compound the bride covers her head and goes to the head wife's hut in her best clothes, to greet her. I remember Malam Maigari's head wife was cooking nice food—rice and stew—then she sent for me and I went and we ate together. We chatted, then at noon our husband's mother came and brought me ten kolanuts and six hundred cowries; she came to look at the dowry, I covered up my head like this. I used to call her 'Mother of Idirisu'. She saw the hut looking nice, she was pleased. When she had gone our husband's father—it was his father's elder brother, since his own father was dead—sent his wife with ten kolanuts and four hundred cowries. My husband's elder brother sent ten kolanuts and perfume and six hundred cowries; they all sent kolanuts and money, they greeted me.

When the bride has been married before, the chief wife makes food for four days; for those four nights the husband is in the bride's hut. Then the head wife does her own two days' cooking and he comes to sleep with her. That is six nights. Then the bride starts cooking, she cooks delicious food and it is sent to everyone in the town, his kinsfolk and her kinsfolk who are living inside the town, so that they may see the bride's cooking. After six days in Malam Maigari's compound I uncovered my head, I had become accustomed to the house, I had become a daughter of the house. At a girl's first marriage, after the bride and bridegroom have avoided one another for fourteen nights, the husband sleeps with her for the next seven nights. His head wife cooks during that time, and continues to cook for the next three months, while the bride gets used to the house. If the bride is her husband's only wife, then his mother cooks for them; she often goes on cooking for them for seven months. After this the bride has become accustomed to the house and can uncover her face.

That night Malam Maigari brought one thousand cowries and twenty kolanuts and some perfume when he came to my hut; the children were teasing him, then when everyone was asleep and I had put out the lamp and lain down, he came in. He said 'Light the lamp so that I can see your eyes'. I hid my eyes, I felt shy. When he had lit the lamp he said 'I thank you, I thank you. You have kept your promise. I thank you, I am happy.' Then we made our marriage for fifteen years, but we had no children. Then I left him. I loved him very much, I left him because I had to—I had no children. There was his head wife, she had two children when I married him, when I left she had eight; then the youngest of his wives came, she was given to him as alms, she brought forth six children, all before my eyes. She was Uwa, her father was a wealthy man in the town who gave her to Malam Maigari as a gift. Her father liked Malam Maigari, they were not kinsfolk, it was just that he admired our husband. So there were three of us. His head wife, the mother of his household, was a good-tempered woman, we were fourteen years together. Each one of us made food in turn and we all ate. Then when she was not cooking for the household, each one made cakes to sell, or other food—the maker of millet-balls made them, the maker of groundnut-cakes made them, and so on. I spun cotton, I made groundnut-cakes and bean-cakes and other sorts of cakes, I made roasted and salted groundnuts, I also wove cloth, then I made locust-bean cakes, I made a sweetmeat of rice and honey and another of sugar and groundnuts, which was very good to eat. (7) About four years after I married Malam Maigari my aunt Rabi cooled; that day she sent me her gifts for my marriage —corn, locust-bean cakes, salt, oil and rice; she sent me all those, when her anger had cooled. That is what people do.

CHAPTER VIII

A LARGE HOUSEHOLD

In Malam Maigari's compound there were two sections. (1) In the middle of our section were the cooking-hut and the granaries, and our husband and his three brothers had their huts and their wives' huts in groups, but the families were not separated by any fence. The younger married men slept in the hut of each wife in turn, the elder ones with beards had their own sleeping-hut built close to their wives' huts. Malam Maigari had a big sleeping-hut. (2) The elder brother of Malam Maigari's father, Mamman, had a separate section of the compound for his *gandu*, but the house was not completely divided, we all went to and fro within the compound. Sule, our husband's elder brother, was the head of our *gandu*. In the middle of the compound were the big *gandu* granaries, and then everyone had his own too—we women also had our own granaries. At harvest time we would buy grain and put it by; at the end of the dry season when the Cattle Fulani came we took out our grain and sold it to them and made money. Our husbands would buy the grain for us, we would give them our money and they would go to market and purchase it for us to store in our granaries.

Usuman, our eldest son, (3) gave out the *gandu* grain; we women would call to him 'Son there, get out some grain for us!' He would protest at first—'No, look at all that prickly chaff!' Then later he would go and get it out and give it to us. Usuman had been freed, he was formerly a slave of Malam Maigari's. He was married, he had two wives; he came into the kin and became the eldest son in every way—except that he would not inherit; Garba, Malam's own eldest son, would inherit if Malam died. Malam's father had owned slaves, each of his sons inherited two and each daughter one, when he died. There was Sungiji and Laraba, their children were Dancel-lelli, and Balarabe and Kande. Then Dankamuku and Madogara

119

had a daughter, Riga. Allah-kyauta and 'Yargwari had no children, and finally there was Usuman, whom Malam freed. Danbailu, Malam's father, had freed Sungiji and Dankamuku, but their wives remained slaves and so their children were slaves; if you freed the mother the children became free, if you freed the father the children were not affected. Malam's father did not study the Koran, he only worked on his farm; some of his children studied, and one was a blacksmith and one a trader. Then there were his ten slaves in their *rinji* in the forecourt of the compound. (4) When Danbailu died they were divided two and two amongst the sons, Rakia the daughter had one. The slaves used to work on the farm until the 2.30 prayer, when they finished. Danbailu himself did a little farming, but not very much. When he had died and I went to their compound I found the brothers all working very hard on the farm, they and their children and their slaves; even the slaves' wives, when they had finished making the porridge with us, would wash themselves, then they would put their hoes on their shoulders and go to the farm and take the men their food, and when they had eaten it the women would set to work too. When Azahar came, the afternoon prayer, they would stop working and the women slaves would fetch firewood. We remained there inside the compound, and in the evening they would return with the firewood and we would cook together, then they would wash themselves and take their food to their part of the compound. (5) After Sungiji and Danka-muku had been freed they stayed on in their huts in the *rinji* in the forecourt, they still worked in the *gandu*, but they could not be sold, they were sons of the house. Apart from that it was the same as before, they worked together with their old master's sons, they ate his food, he paid their tax—Sule used to pay something like twenty thousand cowries every year for the *gandu*.

My Father moves to Giwa

When I was living in Malam Maigari's compound I would go every dry season to visit my kinsfolk, for about thirty days or two months I would go visiting, to greet them all. Two years after I had married Malam, Tsoho our father left Zarewa and came to live in Old Giwa. He came because his mother Anja was living here, and he wished to be near her. When our father's father Ibrahim Dara died, his wife Anja remarried, she married Barau. Their home was

in Zarewa, and Barau had another wife besides our grandm
Anja bore him one son, her last-born, Haleru, who was th
'father'. I stayed with him before I was married to Malam,
from his compound that I was taken to my new home. Hale
elder half-brothers, his father's sons, and three of them,
Bazariya and Husaini had come to Old Giwa to farm; whei
father Barau died in Zarewa, they moved to Giwa, leavii
other brothers (there were eight sons of Barau) in Zarewa.
once when the brothers from Giwa came to visit Haleru in Z
he returned to Giwa with them and settled there. He got m
there, and after a time his brothers sent a message to his i
Anja, who was living in the compound of our father Tso
Zarewa at that time, they sent to say Haleru was not well. I
time his mother got to him he was better, and then she s
down in his compound at Giwa. Haleru had three wives, a
mother lived in his compound too. After a time Anja beca
herself, and Haleru sent for Malam Tsoho our father; whe
father got there he found his mother better, but he stayed
little with Haleru. He was walking outside Old Giwa one da
Haleru, when he saw uncleared land and he said 'Wouldn't i
good thing to farm here? Here one could eat food.' Anja had r
to go back with him to Zarewa, and Tsoho did not like to be p
from his mother. He told Haleru he would come back. (6)
my father moved to Giwa with his wife Tumbadi and hi
Kadiri, he left his brothers at Karo to farm his land and he s
down in Old Giwa, he built his compound near to Haleru's, be
of his mother; she finally died in his care. Besides his son I
our father got a client called Hasan, he came into his *ganda*
worked with him. (7) Much later, because he was a good
Father said I was to marry him. They all worked very hard.

Haleru had three wives at Old Giwa, then one day he left e
thing and went out into the world; his wife Yande followed hin
town away in Gwandu and she found him. A woman who
wandering around there saw them, but we never heard i
whether he settled down with Yande or whether he went to
other place, or whether they died, only Allah knows. V
Haleru left my father was here with his one wife and one so
and his son cleared the bush and farmed. It was because of fa
ties that he left his farms and his home at Zarewa and came to
in Giwa.

I Adopt a Son

When I had been married to Malam for two years we had a feast and our slave, called Allah-magani, Allah-the-Remedy, was freed. Malam Maigari had two little sons at that time, Danlami the third had not been born; Allah-magani was the big son of the house because the other children were young. Our son Garba was small, Malam's elder brother Sule's daughter was married, and his son was small. When he was freed Allah-magani was given his name of Usuman. (8) He was the distributor of grain, but if he wasn't there we would tell Garba to do it. We didn't say Usuman's or his wife's name, we said 'Son there!' or 'Daughter there!'; nor did we use Garba's name, we had two 'eldest sons' in the house.

When Malam decided to free Allah-magani the *malams* were assembled, a ram was killed, prayers were said and he was given his new name of Usuman. We made porridge and all kinds of food. For two nights there was playing and drumming, we women were drumming calabashes in our part of the compound and the young men were at the entrance of the compound with drummers and praise-singers. Malam Maigari gave Usuman a gown and new clothes, Usuman became his son. Usuman was there at the entrance of the compound with the young men, his friends, they were throwing away their money to the drummers. Everyone brought gifts to Malam—'reinforcements'—some brought two thousand cowries, some brought one thousand; he went to market and bought food and clothes for Usuman—a new gown, trousers and a blanket. Malam gave Usuman to me to be my son, just as if I had borne him. (9)

A year after he had been freed, we heard that a girl wanted to marry Usuman. Malam and I discussed the matter, then he gave me some money and I went to their compound, I greeted the father and I greeted the mother of the girl, I said 'Usuman wishes to marry Ladidi'. They said 'Very well, go and talk to her about it'. I went to her hut, I said 'Usuman desires you, do you want him? Do not hide your feelings, if you don't want to marry him, tell me.' She laughed, she wanted him. I poured out one thousand cowries into her little flat basket, I said 'He will come to see you to-morrow'. This was the 'money for asking'. Then her mother escorted me home and when I got back, Malam followed me into my hut. 'Does she want him?' he asked. 'Yes, she wants him,' I said. He said 'She

122

hasn't hidden anything from you?' I said 'No, she hasn't hidden anything'. He said 'Praise be to Allah'.

Next day he got some money and gave it to Usuman, two thousand cowries, Usuman and his chief friend went to the girl's compound and took it to her and talked to her. She told him that she would like to marry him. They came home and told us. We waited a little while, then I visited Ladidi's father's compound again, taking with me three thousand cowries. I went into the compound to her mother's hut, the father was there but he went away. I greeted Ladidi's mother, then I came out to the front of the compound and greeted her father, then I greeted the girl and gave her the money and told her to buy kolanuts; she got up and left the hut, she was feeling embarrassed because I was her husband's mother. She did not reply to my greeting, she just ran out.

On the following Friday morning Malam and Sule, his elder brother, took five thousand cowries. They went to greet her parents and gave them the money. They gave her father Ibrahim two thousand, her mother two thousand, and then they sent for the eldest son and gave him his share, one thousand cowries. Ladidi had been in mourning, her husband having died. Her parents said 'Make the preparations for Friday, and come in the morning to solemnize the marriage'. That is what her father said. The five thousand cowries which Malam and Sule took was for the parents of the girl and her eldest brother, they would not divide that among the kinsfolk. When the Friday arrived we bought meat, salt, kolanuts, two cloths and a kerchief; we added to these seven thousand cowries for the *sadaki*—Ladidi was a widow. I took all these things myself to her father Ibrahim's compound in the morning. They divided up the money and food inside the compound, they put the kolanuts in the entrance-hut to be given to the men after the marriage ceremony. Then they filled my hand with cowries—the gift-bearers' dues. Then Malam Maigari and Sule went to Ibrahim's entrance-hut and the marriage was solemnized, they took their kinsmen and Ibrahim and his kinsmen were there. After the ceremony everyone returned home; the bride was hiding in her hut, and Usuman was in our compound.

At night ten of us women went to Ibrahim's compound; we greeted the bride's father, we greeted the bride's mother, we said 'We have come to fetch our bride'. Her father said 'Wait until

Friday, then we will set the day for coming together'. So we returned home.

Next morning we took the *aunaka*, (10) a full bowl of millet, one of guineacorn, salt, locust-bean cakes, okras, two chickens, and peppers. We took them to the house of the bride's father. When the sun came round again, the next morning, she had ground and winnowed it all, she had cooked it, then the old ladies from her compound brought us the *aunaka* food. We divided it out to all our kinsfolk, the children took it round to their compounds, we said 'See here is the bride's porridge, the *tuwon aunaka*'.

When Friday came we were given guineacorn from the *gandu* granary; it was divided amongst us women and we pounded it to flour; about Azahar we cooked porridge and millet-balls. At La'asar (*c.* 5.30 p.m.) we ate, then we heated water and washed ourselves and our clothes. We filled a calabash with chicken, we filled ten bowls with porridge, we made four huge balls of millet-paste, three calabashes of dumplings, (11) one kind of stew for them and another kind for the porridge, and milk for the millet-balls. We took it and set it in rows, *jere*, then the women took up the loads, the children came too and helped to carry it all, and we went singing and shrilling to the bride's compound with the *jere* food. The mother of our household, Malam's senior wife, remained in our compound to get everything ready. We all went to the bride's mother's hut, we set down our loads and sat down. Her parents appeared and said 'Ah! May Allah grant she conceives, may Allah give her children!' They gave us a ball of millet-paste, a calabash of dumplings, one chicken and a calabash of porridge—the gift-bearers' dues. We went home and shared them out between us.

Later the women of the bride's kin came with mats, bowls, grinding-stones, a mortar and the pestle for it, water-pots, a curtain and a mat for the door of her hut, a pot for cooking porridge and another for cooking stew, stirring-sticks for the porridge and for the stew, and a little bowl. These form the bride's dowry. Her kins-women came in and decorated her new hut, they set out her plates and bowls, they arranged the hut and we went in and looked. Usuman was in the forecourt with the men; it was his first marriage, but as his bride was not a maiden they did not stain him with henna. When they had completed the decorations in the bride's hut, her *kawaye* dressed the bride in her new clothes.

During this I was in my hut with my friends and kinswomen,

we were there with the drummers on calabashes until the morning. You put a small calabash upside down in a larger calabash full of water and you drum on the smaller one. (12) I was the head of the marriage feast, because when Malam freed Usuman he gave him to me, so I was the bridegroom's mother. If he did anything that was not correct I spoke to him about it. Every morning he would come and greet me, and his wife also came to greet me; I would say 'Go and do such and such a thing'. Sons kneel down to greet their mothers in the same way as they do when they greet their fathers.

The morning after the feast I bought kolanuts, I added some money to them, and I sent them to Ladidi; in the evening Usuman bought kolanuts and sent them with some money to her. She came to greet me, then she ran away. The day after the feast her parents brought me the gifts due to the bridegroom's mother: rice, groundnut oil and guinea-cornflour and beanflour-cakes. We cooked the rice and sent one bowl to her father's compound, one we divided up and ate ourselves and one we sent to the other section of our own compound. The rest we sent to every compound where our kinsfolk were, even out to the villages, out to Karo; it was distributed amongst the kin. It is known as the 'bride's cooking', although the husband's mother cooked it. We put it all out into calabashes, we called the children, 'Here, you take that one; you take this one'. We set it on their heads and arranged their loads comfortably for them. They went off and took it to all the kinsfolk's compounds.

A Birth in our House

Usuman's wife, Ladidi, was with us for two months and in the third month she conceived. She had a child, we said she was not to go home to her own people, so she remained with us. She was cooking one night, then she went to her hut; I followed her and said 'Are you all right?' She said 'Yes, it's nothing'. I peeped in and saw that she was lying on her bed. Then all of us went to our huts and went to sleep. In the night I got up and listened but I didn't hear anything. At dawn I went to her hut, I heard 'A-a-a-a!' —indeed the child had already been born! There was no one in her hut with her and it was her first childbirth. I cut the cord in the middle, I washed the child seven times with warm water and soap, then I put antimony on his eyes. I looked after Ladidi, then her grandmother arrived. The people of the compound crowded into her hut when they heard the news. I took the placenta behind her hut, I buried it and covered the place with a stone; three days later when the cord fell off I buried it also in the same hole. Her grandmother came from her compound, she washed the mother with soap—you wash her thoroughly with very hot water and soap so that her inside is clean. (13) Then Ladidi returned to her hut and rubbed oil all over her body, she drank gruel until she was satisfied, she ate porridge with hot spices until she was full. A new mother doesn't put on her best clothes, but she does put antimony on her eyes and she can chew kolanuts and rub tobacco-flowers on her teeth; she lies on the bed and turns from side to side so that the heat of the fire under the bed shall get into her body. After seven days it is warmed thoroughly, the blood of childbirth has stopped flowing, her womb has gone back again into place, and she need not wear a cloth bound round her middle any more. The washing with hot water and the warmth from the fire under the bed and the hot spiced food make this happen properly. She is washed morning and evening with very hot water, the water is splashed all over her body with leaves, and it is poured into her inside so that it shall heal. Her belly is splashed with leaves dipped in the hot water. If all this is not done, the mother's inside will putrefy, it will not be good, and it will be said 'That woman did not wash properly'.(14) After the first seven days you only wash her outside, you need not wash her inside any more. Also during the first seven days she lies on her bed while her grandmother gently rubs her belly and then binds it up with cloth. The mother eats porridge with a lot of pepper, she drinks gruel mixed with honey, she is kept very warm, then her inside settles down and she feels comfortable.

I was midwife to Usuman's wife, there was no longer any shyness between us; she lay on the bed and I sat in the middle of the hut looking after my grandchild; we chatted together. I carried the babe about on my back, Ladidi gave it the breast except on the naming-day when her *kawaye* came. After a year that child died. I used to dance and play with her, Malam would take her on his knee and play 'horses' with her, and dance her up and down. But she died, the milk was not right. After that Ladidi had four miscarriages, then Usuman died. When she had finished her mourning period, Ladidi married into another compound and had two children there; they are young men now. Before he died Usuman had married a second wife, a maiden, Laminde.

Usuman's Death

Then Usuman fell ill, he kept on swelling and swelling like this, then he died. He was energetic and respected, he farmed in the *gandu* and filled his own granary besides from his own plots. He grew groundnuts, he grew sweet potatoes and pumpkins, sugarcane, several kinds of groundnuts, guineacorn, millet and *dauro*-millet. (15)

When a man dies, two *malams* wash the body. But if a woman dies two old women wash it. They should be good women, wives of *malams* or daughters of a *malam*. I often do it. The whole body is washed very thoroughly, you wash out the mouth, you close the ears, the nose and the rectum with cotton, then you wrap the body in a white cotton blanket or cloth. The prayers are recited inside the compound, then he is taken to his grave. Even if it is a woman who has died, only the men are present with the *malams* when they recite the prayers. The women are wailing in their part of the compound, the men are in the forecourt. If his wife dies when a man is old he will accompany the body to the grave, but if he is still young he will not. His dead wife's father comes the following day to greet him, and if she was not the first child of her mother, the mother will come too. If the children are young, we tell them their mother has gone to visit her relations, she will be coming back; a kinswoman takes them to her compound so that they shall not know. Then one of their father's other wives adopts them, or a kinswoman, and after some months, when they have settled down with her, the matter is explained to them. Settled Fulani don't give their children to anyone, they let them remain there in their dead mother's hut, and their father looks after them; even if they are very small the children are not given to a kinswoman. The eldest of them looks after the smaller ones. Their mother's co-wives won't look after them, and the father will refuse to give a kinswoman the care of them. You see, Fulani have no humanity. There was a settled Fulani in Mahauta near here (New Giwa), his wife died two years ago, leaving three children; a girl near to marriageable age, a little boy, and a very small girl. The eldest sister used to buy milk from the Cattle Fulani, she went to market and sold it, then she went home and ground and pounded the grain. No kin, no one to look after them, he had no other wife. Fulani have no compassion, don't have anything to do with them. (16) They arrange marriages between kinsfolk a good deal, because they don't wish to be parted from their children by marriage, but they won't look after their kinsman's child. They won't touch the child of a co-wife, either. If a Fulani woman has a child in one compound, then her husband dies and she takes the child with her when she re-marries another Fulani, then the people of his compound will drive away the child. We Habe, we adopt our co-wives' children, or a child from another compound of our kin; if its father's family do not object, a woman will bring her child to another compound when she re-marries and he is adopted there as a son. But Fulani—they've no human feelings. They only care for themselves and their own children, they aren't good people. People call the Barebare hard-hearted, but we are nothing like the Fulani. Bush Fulani, settled Fulani—they're all the same. It is true that many settled Fulani adopt children, but that is because they have married Kado (Habe) women, they have been marrying us for a long time now and it makes them a bit better, it improves their dispositions.

I Adopt More Children: some Marriages of Alms

When slaves were freed by law, I had been in Malam Maigari's household for three years. Everyone became free. (17) In our compound the slaves continued to live with us, they didn't leave or go anywhere else. Usuman, whom Malam freed before the law was made, had not been born in the house; he was bought in Zaria market when he was seven years old, but he was circumcised in our house. (18) His parents were Kamuku people. (19) I adopted him much later on, when he was grown up and Malam freed him. I also adopted Sadau, my sister Dije's child. Then when our little co-wife Uwa had a son Lawande, I adopted him when the time came to wean him. 'Lawande, Baba's son'; I was 'mother of Lawa' in the household. He is still alive now, he has three children and a compound of his own; he has built a mud-roofed hut and a two-storeyed hut, both very nice; he is very anxious that I should return to his father Maigari's compound. We gave him my younger brother's daughter Habi in marriage, Habi calls me 'Goggo', her father's sister. This is how they are related. (20) Uwa's father

Dankiawa, who disapproved of her marriage to Maigari, had a younger brother Audu. Audu had a grand-daughter called Habiba, the daughter of his son Dankurama. Her parents took Habiba and gave her to Lawa as a bride of alms. Now you see that Lawa and Habiba were brother and sister. They were also my son and daughter; Lawa, my adopted son; Habiba was the grand-daughter of Alhamdu, my father's sister, who married Audu, and thus she was my daughter. They took my daughter and married her to my son Lawa, and she was also his kinswoman through his mother Uwa, who was Dankiawa's daughter. There were two kinds of relationship involved, you see.

There was a feast, we went to the marriage ceremony at her father's compound. It was a marriage of almsgiving, but no one knew to whom they would give her. Her father Dankurama had consulted with his own father, Audu, and they had decided to give her to her kinsman. Late at night when we were all asleep we heard someone calling, 'Peace be upon you!' They asked 'Is Sule there?' Sule went to the entrance and they said 'See here is alms for Lawa, the son of Malam Maigari'. Imagine it, we had been to the marriage ceremony that morning and we didn't know she was going to come to our compound! We collected twenty thousand cowries, with salt, kolanuts and cloth to give to them, then we had the wedding-feast for the marriage of alms.

Then another night, late, someone came. 'Is Malam Maigari there?' Malam got up and went out to the entrance. 'We have brought alms for Sule.' Then we all arose, delighted. The alms was Abu. They had brought her to Sule because they liked him—he was not a *malam*. A year later 'Yartanoma was brought, the daughter of Jakinji; Jakinji's father was a wealthy man in the market, and his grandfather also was rich. They were the butchers of Zarewa, with huge compounds. There was Sarkin Pawa and Madakin Pawa, they held all the butchers' titles, (21) there must have been a hundred of them in the town and the hamlets round about. They also used to have many slaves. The butchers brought a wife to Sule— people liked him, he was quite well-off, and there was good eating, good food in his household. Every woman in the town wanted to come and live in our compound—we had beautiful women and everyone liked the men.

Then in addition to Sadau and Lawa there was Balarabe who lived in my hut; he was a pupil in Malam's school, a son of the people of Gwangwan. We took him with us on our journeys to the East and we brought him back with us. When he got older his people took him back home. All the other pupils used to return to their homes in the town every evening.

Dije's Married Life

I adopted Sadau, the daughter of my elder sister Dije, (22) I arranged her marriage and she had eight children. I adopted her after I had been living for two years with Malam Maigari. Dije was married to her kinsman Hamidu, then she broke off that marriage and left two children in Hamidu's house; she married Malam Adamu. Malam Adamu came from Kano City, he was travelling about the country teaching the Koran. He was living in a compound in the butchers' ward. Dije became pregnant and bore Sadau, but before she had weaned her she left Malam Adamu and returned to her first husband Hamidu. It happened in this way. Dije decided to leave her kinsman Hamidu, he tried and tried to prevent her but she said 'No', she was going. She liked him, he liked her, there was nothing wrong, she just left him. She stayed in our home at Karo during her *Iddah* because her parents were angry with her. Then someone saw her and told the stranger Malam Adamu about her, and Malam Adamu said he wished to marry her. Our parents discussed and discussed the matter, finally they said they agreed. Dije did not particularly like him but he wanted to marry her. She still liked Hamidu's compound. After three months she became pregnant, and when the child was born Malam Adamu said he was going to return to Kano City, and Dije said she would not go. So she left him and took the child and moved into our compound in Zarewa, where Grandmother Anja was living. When she weaned Sadau I took her, the child of the people of Kano. Hamidu came again and said he still desired her, he brought her the usual gifts for courtship. Her parents said 'Yes, we will give her to you'. The gifts were the usual ones for a woman's re-marriage, just as if they had not already been married to one another before. So Dije went back and lived with her kinsman Hamidu until he died. I went to their marriage feast with my adopted daughter Sadau. Malam Maigari also had a daughter called Sadau; his head wife left him, but he followed her home and persuaded her to come back, she was the mother of Maigari's Sadau. The two girls were born 'today

and tomorrow' they were almost twins! They were called 'Sadau
Kwarga' and 'Sadau Baba'. They used to go to market together
and they were married together, on the same day. I had three
children at the same time—Lawal and Sadau and Balarabe who
came to Malam's school; they all lived together in my hut. (23)

Malam Maigari's Teaching Expeditions

Our husband was a *malam*, he had a school with about twenty
pupils, and apart from teaching he farmed. His father had only
farmed, but his father's elder brother was a blacksmith as well. In
the rainy season Malam Maigari was at Zarewa, farming; when the
corn had been harvested and stored in the granaries, then we
would set out, Malam and I and about twenty boys, we left Malam's
two other wives and his children at home with his elder brother
Sule and his three wives, and his other elder brother Ali with two
wives. There were nine men in our compound, when their father
died the eldest brother became head of the household.

I would dress in my best clothes and we travelled in a leisurely
fashion, stopping at every walled town and putting up in the compound of the *imam*. (24) The day that we set out we slept at Beli,
in the morning we went on to Rogo, then to Danzan, then to
Karaye, then Dederi, then Godiya, then Kabu, then Beri-beri,
then Dansoshiya, then Banda, the town full of *bori* dancers, then
Kiru, Bebeji, Kura the town of stingy people, Dawaki, and many
more towns in Kano country. At Gezawa we used to stay for four
months; we would live in the *imam's* (25) compound, where all the
famous *malams* who came to the town would be entertained. The
imam's household would give us food. (26) The men who came to
study the Koran used to fill up the entrance-hut completely. They
recited and recited, students from many different places, they
would come with their writing-boards hung round their necks, and
their womenfolk would make porridge for them to bring to us as
alms. Malam Maigari was really very learned. People used to come
in from the nearby villages day after day, to study under him. At
dawn the men would get up and light the fire, then they would
study until about now (11.30 a.m.). Then they ate. Then from the
Azahar prayer until the La'asar prayer (2.30–5.30) they continued
their discussions and reading. From the sundown prayer, Man-
gariba, until far into the night they were studying. In all that

country from Kano City over towards Bornu and Hadejiya the people study a great deal, they love it. You can hear how good their Hausa is. (27) Here people can't do things like that. Both boys and girls used to come. We visited Godiya twice and Barebare twice. If we had once been to a town, the following year we would go on beyond it. We travelled on foot along the old route, to the East of Kano City. Now you see the motor road and the railway, but at that time there was only the old path.

When we arrived in a town farmers would come and bring us food—'Malam, see I have brought you some grain so that it may be cooked for you'. Once when we stopped at a certain town the people brought us twenty bundles of guineacorn, apart from all sorts of other food. I didn't have to bother with the cooking, I just sat and rested. One woman would come into the compound, another would come in—'I want you to be my *kawa*'. The day we were to leave I would be crying and they would be crying. Malam Maigari had studied in Zarewa, he had finished learning the Koran by heart; two of his sons also knew it completely. We used to spend about twenty nights on the road before we reached the town where we were going to stay; we did not hurry, we stayed one night here and one night there, sometimes we would spend seven nights in one place. We used to be away from home for about five months altogether. Once Malam took our little wife with him, she was pregnant, we all went to Maska together. When we returned home again she gave birth to her child. We went along in our best clothes, we women covered our heads and faces and peeped out at the road. Malam's head wife's hut was full of children; I don't know if she envied us, going off like that, but she couldn't leave them, she had no chance of coming. She died only last year, and her eldest son Dogara also died. The others still want me to go back to Malam Maigari's home. Then at the end of the dry season we would return home in time to clear the farms and prepare for farming. One year we went a long way eastwards, but I got tired of the wind and the dust. The following year we came here to Giwa on our way to Maska, but there was more food to the East than there was here. At that time there was no more fear of being kidnapped, the world was at peace. You could go wherever you pleased; in the past even *malams* dared not travel freely, they would be kidnapped and sold in the market. Before the world was settled, there was no travelling about. (28)

A LARGE HOUSEHOLD

When the guineacorn was harvested, Malam would say 'Good. We will set off on such-and-such a day.' I would be escorted to our hamlet, I would tell my family, 'We are setting out on such a day, we are going to travel about and teach'. I would take gifts of food to my kinsfolk, and they would give me money. On the journey we took no food with us, only money; I would set out with ten thousand cowries, Malam would take twenty thousand. The boys would have small sums, one would have two hundred, one five hundred, one a thousand, one one thousand six hundred; each one would start out with the money he had been given. It was put in a leather pouch with a small opening and tied up and wrapped in a blanket for a boy to carry. The children slung their bags round their necks, my money was in a leather bag among my things. Sometimes we would buy millet-balls and sour milk, or a chicken to eat. Whenever anyone brought us a gift we gave the bearer a small sum of money. Each boy had his writing-board, his quill and ink, and his food-bowl. The boards and the prayer-rugs and the books and pens were put in among the loads. On our return, all our kinsfolk would come to welcome us, bringing firewood and grain and rice and cotton and all sorts of things. I would come home with Bornu food which we had bought from traders—we never got as far as Bornu ourselves, we never left Kano country. Malam did not attend the markets in the towns we passed through, he never went to market while we were travelling; people would come and ask him, 'Malam, aren't you coming to market?' and he would reply, 'It was teaching that brought me here, not trade'. His boys would take up their little food-bowls and go round the market, saying 'A student greets you. Allah give you good business! Allah make it of benefit!' Everyone would put in some of the thing they were selling, then the boys would return home to the *imam's* compound and eat. They got a lot of food given to them, pumpkins, little cakes, cassava, sweet potatoes, groundnuts—all kinds of food. When they returned they brought it in to me and I took out what I wanted, the rest they kept, and ate till they were full. If there was no market that day, our boys would go into compound after compound, saying, 'Mother, if anything is left after you have eaten, give a little to Allah's students! Give us alms for the sake of Allah and His Prophet!' Then the woman would give them food or a little money, and say 'There—hard work has its reward!' They say to her 'May Allah give you good fortune'. When they came home they used to sit round the entrance-hut and eat till they were full.

When we were in Zarewa Malam held his school in the entrance-hut of our compound. After he came in from the farm at Azahar (2.30) he prayed. Then the boys would come and they would study till La'asar (5.30). They would stop then and eat their evening meal at sunset, then they would return and study a little more until he dismissed them for the day. Then the elders would come and study at night. After they had gone, you would hear him come to his sleeping-hut, he would light the lamp and continue studying far into the night. After that he would sleep a little, and at dawn he would be up. No amount of farm work could stop him from studying. At dawn you would hear the schools starting work, the children would begin reciting together, first at one then at another, then the women would begin cooking millet-paste and food for sale— the town had woken up. At night when one of us went to Malam's sleeping-hut, she would sit and spin and spin. When she was weary she would lie down to sleep. Then he would come in with the lamp and continue studying. Then when he was tired too he would come to bed and they would go to sleep. Ali, the eldest brother, with one wife and nine children, was always studying. The other elder brother, Sule, sat and traded in the market after he had finished work on the farm. Sha'ibu the blacksmith, Ali's own elder brother, lived with Ali in Mamman's section of our compound, they were sons of Malam's father's brother Mamman. When Malam Maigari's father, Danbailu, died, his sons remained in the same compound, but they formed a separate *gandu* from Danbailu's brother Mamman and his sons. Mamman was the older brother and *gandu* head, and Danbailu and his sons worked with him; when Danbailu died the *gandu* split, and his sons Sule, Maigari, Idi and Dansarki farmed in one *gandu* with Sule as its head, while Mamman's sons, Sha'ibu, Ali and Inusa, continued to farm with their father. When I first came to the household there were also nine slaves, with their wives and children.

News of my Father and Brother at Giwa

One day I heard that my father Malam Tsoho had arranged a marriage for my brother Kadiri, they lived at Old Giwa at that time. Kadiri was married to Binta. Hasan, my father's client, (29) who lived and farmed with them, was to marry Sa'a. When the dry season came I went to greet them. There they were, three men and three women in the *gandu*. First one woman made the *gandu* food, then another, they took it in turns. They were living thus, when Tumbadi, Father's wife, left him. (30) He had taken another wife, Ramatu, and Tumbadi did not like it. Ramatu's father's younger brother, a friend of our father, came to him and said, 'Malam, I have come to ask your help; Ramatu, my elder brother's daughter, went out into the world and we haven't heard a word of her since'. Her father's younger brother was like her father because her own father was dead. They were Giwa people. Ramatu had gone out into the world about seven years before this, but now her father wanted to see her, so he came and asked my father to help him. (31) Malam Tsoho looked in his book, and he said 'She is alive in the East; she is in Kano City; she will come home one morning. When she returns, will you give her to me?' Then he gave her father charms to call back his daughter, they buried them in the floor of her hut, and morning and evening her father went into the hut and called her, over the charms. 'Ho-o-o-o-o-o, Ra-ma-tu!' like that. At first her father said he did not agree that Father should marry her, 'You can't marry her,' he said, 'she is used to loose living.' Father said 'If you will not give her to me, I shall not call her'. So her father agreed. They continued there like that for about three months. Then one day she came home in the morning. There and then her father dug up the charms and took them to Malam Tsoho and told him. Her kinsfolk drummed and rejoiced, no one upbraided her, not in the least, everyone was so happy. They had charmed her back to her senses.

Two days later her father's younger brother said to her, 'Put on your best clothes, we will go and see my friend. If you like him we will give you to him in marriage.' She said 'No no, Father, I'm not going'. Then he coaxed her, he said 'Come along, now, let us go'. She followed behind him. 'Peace be upon you!' 'Upon you be peace.' 'Greetings at your coming, greetings, greetings . . .' 'Have you slept well? Are you weary? How are the people of your house? . . .' the men greeted one another, she went into the compound and Father's wife Tumbadi spread a mat for her in her hut. When Malam Tsoho and his friend came in, he saw a small woman, light and handsome—she was certainly beautiful. He took out two hundred cowries and told her to buy kolanuts, then his wife escorted

her home; 'Greet your household, greet your household for me.'
'They shall hear, they shall hear!' The women took their leave of
each other. Her father said 'You saw her, Malam?' he answered
'Yes, I saw her'. 'Do you want her?' 'Yes, I want her.' 'Can you
keep her?' 'I can.'

Next morning our father sent money to her grandmother;
Ramatu's mother had married somewhere else after her father's
death, and Ramatu lived in the hut of her father's mother. The
grandmother came and said 'Yes, she accepts it'. He said 'Thank
you'. Then he bought salt, meat, kolanuts, perfume, he tied them
up with some money in a bundle and Dada the wife of Haleru's
elder brother took them and said it was the gift for seeking a bride.
The day was set. After he married Ramatu, Mallam Tsoho brought
her to Karo and Zarewa, they spent three months visiting us all
and we all saw her. When he told his wife Tumbadi he was going
to marry Ramatu, she seemed very pleased. Then they were married, the bride came to join his household, and after seven days
Tumbadi said she could not live in the same compound with her.
Then Tumbadi left. At first she was rejoicing and it seemed as if
she was really pleased; she didn't say anything to my father until
after Ramatu came, then she left him.

Ramatu had been on her own for seven years. She was married
as a maiden, and she had a daughter. Then they brought a co-wife
into her compound and she didn't like it, so she went off on her
own. She stayed away for nearly eight years, her daughter was
seven when Ramatu went, and she was married before Ramatu
returned from Kano, she had even conceived a child. Ramatu went
off seeking pleasure, they had married her and she was not happy.
At that time the Christians had not yet arrived, but the kidnappers
did not capture her. She went to the compound of the Magajiya
at Kano—we used to gossip and she told me about it—fighting
and raiding had stopped and the world felt good. Anyone could go
into Katsina, he could go into Kano, he could go into Zaria. There
were a few prostitutes at that time, I remember Sarkin Zarewa
used to appoint a Magajiya to rule the prostitutes of the town, (32)
and the elders when they were talking used to say that there had
always been a Magajiya. When one died another was appointed.
Ramatu said a nobleman desired her, he took her and kept her in a
compound and he used to visit her regularly, but he always went
home to sleep. He came to see her continually, and he provided

her with food. For five months she lived in this way; she refused to marry him, she was independent and she preferred that. She didn't know that her father was 'calling' her, only she felt desire, desire, a longing in her heart to go home. So she took her leave and came back from Kano. Malam Tsoho and her father threw away the first charm and made another one so that she should stay, Malam Tsoho buried it in the floor of her hut at the threshold, where she would always step over it as she came in and out, he put it there so that she should settle down. My father used to keep his wives in his compound, he shut them up, Ramatu did not go out any more—she felt the difference. She lived with him for fifteen years, until he died; then two years later she died. At first when they wanted to marry her to him she said 'No, he is an old man'. Later she got used to him and then she liked him. Her kinsfolk used to come and say 'Well done, Malam. You've got her neatly tied up!' He had a plan for keeping her, she hadn't a chance.

Malam Tsoho my father was always smiling, he liked people, he was generous—all the children used to laugh with him. Perhaps he was about fifty years old when he left Zarewa and came here to Giwa. He knew how to farm, he certainly did. When Ramatu came to his compound she noticed the difference—the house of the prostitutes and the house of a *malam* are very different things. But when she got used to him she liked him, and he liked her very much—he wanted her even before he had seen her! So they lived together like that, and he didn't take another wife until he died.

CHAPTER IX

THE RITUAL OF CHILDBIRTH

We are Kado, our origin was in Bornu; this is what we do when we have children. It is a little different from the Fulani custom—their women go to their father's compound to have their children.

When you become pregnant you stay in your husband's compound. When you have brought forth your child in your husband's home, and he has been given his name seven days later, on the eighth day they take you to your parents' home. There is feasting and drumming all night, your husband remains hidden. In the morning the grandmother of the child, on the father's or the mother's side, washes the babe and ties him on her back; that is the grandmother who is the midwife. By then the child's mother is able to wash herself, but for the first seven days her cross-cousin came and did it for her, while her mother washed the baby.

But before the child is born, after you have been five months pregnant, you no longer sleep with your husband. You do all the ordinary work until the seventh month, then you do a little less. Round about the seventh month, or earlier, the husband begins to cut down wood in the bush and collect it, he and his younger brother and his joking relations. If they won't help him, his mother will. They collect a large amount of wood. Then at the eighth month the husband's mother buys ginger, potash, cloves, peppers and all kinds of hot spices. She buys them with her own money. Then she buys honey, and she helps to fetch in the wood. After nine months, one day your husband's mother comes to the door of the hut and calls you. You say 'I'm lying down. I've got a pain in my head'. The husband's mother does not come into the hut, she stays at the door and greets you. Then someone from the compound goes to your kinsfolk and tells them that you are lying down. The woman's kinswomen come—her mother's and her father's 'sisters', her own 'sisters' and her husband's 'sisters' and the wives of her husband's elder and younger 'brothers'. But her own mother doesn't come and her husband's mother stays outside the door of her hut. Her grandmothers come, one is probably her midwife when the child is born, she takes him and cuts the cord and washes him. When he is born the mother covers her head and her eyes so that she shall not see her first-born child.

If the child is a boy, he drinks only water for the first three days; if it is a girl, for four days. On the third day (for a boy) or the fourth day (for a girl) they take out the uvula and mark him with his family marks. The barber-doctor comes and does it. Then the mother's kinswomen massage her breasts to start the milk flowing, and after the child has had his family marks cut on him the midwife, the old lady who looks after the baby, brings him to his mother. But the mother refuses to look at him, she refuses to touch him, she hides her hands and covers up her head and face. It is her first child, she is very embarrassed. The father if it was also his first child, had run away to his friend's compound as soon as his wife's labour began, he stays there hiding. Then the sisters of her father and her mother come and try to make her behave sensibly. But she hides her breast and her hands, she cries and struggles and pushes away the child. They say 'Don't let the child fall, be careful, if the child falls we'll give you a dreadful whipping!' Then they hold her by the shoulders, the midwife holds the baby to its mother's breast, and it sucks the milk. After this they give him water to drink. Then they settle him down on the bed beside his mother— she moves right over to the wall, as far away from her child as she can get. After three or four days comes the naming-day. Here in her husband's home the mother won't touch the child, they try to make her but she refuses. The nurse does everything for him. After the naming day they will take the mother to her father's compound, to her mother's hut, and then she will hold her child.

On the day they remove the baby's uvula, the father of the child's father buys a chicken and porridge and stew is made. It is 'the day of eating fatness' and everyone eats well. The child's father's mother cooks and makes delicious food for the mother. The midwife grinds up peppers for her, *kimba* and she eats it. Her husband's mother won't come into the hut until after the naming-day. After you have given birth you eat a lot, rich food is made for you with meat, and a great deal of spice and pepper; you eat hot food, you are bathed with very hot water in the morning and evening, there is a fire under your bed—all because you mustn't catch cold. If this is not done you would wither and shrivel up and die with the cold. After seven days of good food and purgatives and washing, you feel strong, you can get up and go outside.

When the seventh day comes round, the naming-day, the husband's father kills a ram. The husband's mother brings out a new cloth which she gives to the child's mother, then she ties the baby on the midwife's back and they take him to have his head shaved. In the early morning they give him his name in the entrance-hut, only the *malams* and the men of the family are there. After this the husband's kinsmen distribute three calabashes of kolanuts if the child is a boy, two if it is a girl. The midwife puts him on her back and brings him out to the entrance to be given his name, then she takes him back to his mother's hut. She holds him out to his mother, but she refuses to take him. The sisters of her mother and father come and force her to take him, the mother refuses, they say 'You must give him the breast', she will not. At night, her kinswomen come and they fill up the hut. She hides on her bed, and her *kawaye* and younger sisters all sit on the bed and feel the warmth of the fire. When the midwife brings the child and says 'Here he is', the *kawaye* and friends of his mother also cover their eyes, they don't want to see the child either. They all rub their teeth with tobacco-flowers, they eat kolanuts, they put powder on their faces, they rub their arms and legs with oil, and dress themselves in their best cloths. The mother dresses up too, her friends have stained her arms and legs with henna and done her hair. If anyone says to her 'Give the babe the breast', her *kawaye* hide her so that she cannot be seen. But when there is no one about she will take her child and touch him and feed him, there is no one to see. When there are a lot of people there, as there are on the naming-day, if the baby cries one of her parents' sisters will lead the mother out of her hut to another one that is empty so that she can suckle the child. The *kawaye* are ashamed of their friend's first child now, but later they will not refuse him anything; your *kawa's* first child is your own special child. But the child's mother always remains ashamed of him.

After the naming-ceremony there is drumming all night, everyone gives away their money; the drummers drum at the entrance of the compound and the womenfolk drum on calabashes in their part of the house. There is no sleeping. When morning comes, at dawn the midwife puts the child on her back and she and the mother go alone to the compound of the mother's kinsmen. The midwife takes her to the door of her own mother's hut, and she gives the grandmother her grandchild to carry on her back. (1) The mother is washed with hot water, then her mother gives her some gruel, then she gives her her child and she takes him and gives him the breast, she does not avoid him in her own mother's hut, there is no need to. But over there in the compound of her husband it is impossible. Then she eats until she is full and she lies down and goes to sleep. Her mother puts some meat from the ram of the naming-feast into the stew, she gives her porridge and hot spices, the mother must eat good food.

Then the midwife returns to her own home, her work is finished. She is escorted to her home with her gifts, other older women of the family escort her. She receives the head of the ram, its skin, some of its internal organs, salt, locust-bean cakes, guineacorn, peppers, spices, potash and powdered spices. She takes all the child's mother's spinning things, she takes them away with her—the mother must not spin for forty days. After that her own mother will buy her some more things for spinning.

On the day that they cut out the child's uvula they give him his family marks. If it is a girl they also cut a little bit off her clitoris, a very little. When our forefathers came south from Bornu they gave up the Barebare marks that you sometimes see, the very heavy ones all over the face; the barber-doctors here can't make them. We adopted the long straight line down the forehead and nose with two little ones here under the eyes—you see the one on my nose is still there, but the others have died out. When the clitoris is clipped the little bit is put on the lintel over the door of the mother's hut. When the child is born the afterbirth is washed and put in a big fragment of a broken cooking-pot; then it is buried behind the hut with the cord. When the rest of the cord dries and falls off it is also buried behind the hut, but not in a pot. All this is the midwife's work. The barber-doctor is given spices, the ribs and liver of the ram, salt, locust-bean cakes, peppers, ginger, potash, ten kolanuts, a calabash of corn and three thousand cowries. Nowadays they give him three or four shillings instead of the cowries. Some fathers refuse to have the child's uvula cut out, then the barber-doctor gives the mother some medicine to cook and give to the baby, so that the uvula shall burst and heal and no longer be there. If they don't cut it and they don't give him medicine to drink, they may hang a piece of the root of pawpaw round his neck to heal the uvula. Sometimes if the child is a girl, the father also refuses to allow the clitoris to be cut. But the mother will never refuse to have this done, she wants her daughter to grow big and strong. If you do not clip the clitoris you will see the girl getting ill, she gets thin until she dies. If she starts to become like that, and the clitoris is clipped, and medicine put on, then she recovers.

At present I am midwife to four women, they are all pregnant, and in the coming rainy season they will be delivered. I will take the child and put him on my back and carry him about, I will wash him and make him very nice. I will be given the naming-day food to eat. There is my younger brother's wife, his mother was my father's sister, so he is my cross-cousin. There is Gude, her husband is my younger brother, he and I are the children of two brothers. There is Almajara, her husband is also my younger brother, he and I are the children of brothers; and it is the same with 'Yardada. You see, if your father's elder brother has children, they are your brothers and sisters, but slightly different from your own brothers and sisters. But you call them 'elder brother' and 'younger brother' according to whether they are older or younger than you are; if they are younger they are your younger brothers, even though their father was your father's elder brother. Settled Fulani are different, they would call all the children of their father's elder brother 'elder brother', whether the children are really older or younger than themselves. We are Habe, we are different. Then too Fulani won't let their children be adopted, they don't like their laughter taken away to another compound; the child is their laughter and pleasure. We give children to our kinsmen, if they have none of their own we cannot refuse them.

If the child is your first, you remain in your mother's hut for six months, you lie on the bed over the fire, your mother washes you with hot water morning and evening for forty days. On the fortieth day after the birth, alms are distributed to the nearby compounds; porridge is made and a food made from millet-flour and sugar, and about this time (9.30 a.m.) alms are taken to the compounds round about and everyone says 'Are the forty days over? Allah be praised! May Allah preserve the child!' The food is taken to the compounds of the kinsfolk, and everyone is given a little; the children take it round. There is no drumming or dancing, only the distribution of the food. About five or six *mudu* of grain would be used for the porridge; people with a lot of grain might use ten. The child's mother adorns herself, the baby is dressed up and one of the little girls ties him on her back and takes him round the compounds of all his kinsfolk. Everyone takes up the child and plays with him and sings to him like this:

> *Child here, I don't want to hear you crying,*
> *When you cry, my mind is upset,*
> *My heart is broken.*
> *Child here, I don't like to hear you crying.*
> *Mother too, she doesn't like to hear you crying,*
> *Father's sister too, she doesn't like to hear you crying,*
> *Mother's sister too, she doesn't like to hear you crying . . .*

We sing the song for all the kinswomen. Then we sing to him:

> *This child is the father's sister's child,*
> *This child is the mother's sister's child,*
> *You are goggo's child,*
> *You are inna's child,*
> > *You are children of Habe people.*

If a settled Fulani has married a Kado, then we mix up Fulani and Hausa and sing the song with the Fulani names for the Fulani kinswomen and the Hausa ones for the Hausa. You know we're Kado, Habe, we Barebare, people of the country; we didn't come from another country like the Fulani.

Then when the baby cries the little girl who brought him picks him up and ties him on her back and takes him home to suck. It is on the fortieth day that she takes him to the compound of his father's kin, the next day she takes him to his mother's kin. If the little girl gets tired of sitting there while they play with him, she runs off home, and if the baby cries one of the kinswomen puts him on her back and takes him home to his mother. They collect about two thousand cowries for him and take him back with his money. Next day he goes to his mother's kin to be seen, they sing to him and play with him and send him home with two thousand cowries.

The child's grandmother, his mother's mother, is his foster-mother, she washes him and carries him about on her back. When

143

she is tired his grandfather takes him and plays with him, he says 'Hallo ugly one—Oh but you're ugly!' or 'You with the great big head, the huge head!' Your grandparents give you your nickname and sometimes everyone calls you by it all your life, you can't stop them.

After forty days the mother only washes in the morning; altogether she goes on washing for five months. When the sixth month comes, or the seventh, the mother's kinsfolk collect presents for her as they did for her dowry. They get two sacks of rice and two of guineacorn—one from her father's and one from her mother's kin; salt and locust-bean cakes and ten or twenty bottles of oil, groundnut oil or palm-oil or butter. Five cloths are given to her by her mother's side and five by her father's side. Except for the two cloths they gave her on the child's naming-day, her husband's family don't have to give the mother anything. In the husband's compound they cook porridge and stew, millet-paste, and chickens, they buy sour milk; when the mother's kinsfolk have eaten the midday meal they collect together her 'dowry', some other woman ties the baby on her back and the mother covers her face and head and goes along with her kinswomen. The drummers go with them all the way to the husband's compound. The settled Fulani make a procession round the market to show everyone the 'dowry', but we go straight to the husband's home. When they arrive the praise-singers call out 'Here is the daughter of so-and-so, the grand-daughter of so-and-so, see she has returned home safely!' The drummers and praise-singers are given money. Her hut has been swept out and whe she comes in the mother goes straight to her hut. The child has returned to his father's house. The mother will no longer refuse him the breast when her husband's kinswomen bring him. But even when he is grown up his parents will not talk to him if there is anyone there, only if they are alone privately with him. They never use his name, they address him 'You, son', 'You, daughter', or 'That son', 'Son there'. When he is old enough to understand he learns that his parents are ashamed of him. With the second child there is some shame, but after that there is none with the others. But you never look directly at your first child. No one must be able to say 'They pick up their first child, they fondle him, they have no shame, they look straight at their eldest child!' If the mother is alone with him she picks him up, she fondles him, she talks to him.

THE RITUAL OF CHILDBIRTH

There are other relatives whose names we never use: the husband's 'mothers' are called 'Mother of . . .' one of their other children. You must not utter your husband's name, either. Your husband's father is 'Maigida'—'Master of the house'—unless the marriage is between kin, when he is already your father, so you go on calling him 'Baba', 'Father'. Your husband's elder brothers and their wives you call 'Yaya', his elder sister and her husband are 'Yaya' too, like your own elder brothers and sisters. But you joke with his younger brother, and you joke with all your husband's joking relations—his grandparents and cross-cousins. Your husband's mother will say 'Daughter there, do so-and-so', you will reply 'Yes, Mother of Mairo', or 'Yes, Mother of Abubakar'. If she has no other child besides your husband, so there is no name you can use, you may say 'Mother'. You may sit and talk with her. My first husband's mother, Duma's mother, was my father's sister, so I just kept on calling her *Goggo*, father's sister. You don't chat with your husband's father, you just kneel down and greet him.

Two years after the child's birth, one of the child's grandmothers, usually his father's mother who often lives in the same compound, comes at dawn and knocks on the mother's hut door; she goes in and picks up the child and takes him or her off to her own hut. The child's mother runs off to her own mother's home. In the morning the child bursts out crying, he cries bitterly. Then his grandfather, the father of his father, writes a text on his board and washes off the ink of the text to drink, (2) then the womenfolk make gruel and he drinks it. He keeps running to his mother's hut, but he doesn't see her there and he bursts out crying. After three or four days he forgets about the breast. His grandmother has him in her hut and she looks after him. After fourteen days the mother's kinsfolk collect 'dowry' for her at their compound, basketfuls of rice, millet, guineacorn, salt, bean-cakes, locust-bean cakes, and her kinswomen bring her to her husband's home. When she arrives everyone says 'Allah give us the bird on the back!', 'Allah give us all health!' Everyone comes to rejoice, the mother dips in to the food they have brought and gives everyone a little, both the people of the compound and any visitors who may come. When her child sees her he rushes to her and she pushes him away and says 'Go on, run off to your own hut!', his grandmother picks him up and comforts him, then he comes back to his mother, and the grandmother carries him off to her own hut. Here is the father's mother's hut, here is the child's mother's hut, quite close to one another. Some children put up with it and stay in their grandmother's hut, some don't and come back to their mother's hut and stay there. Sometimes the child is adopted into another compound, a father's sister or a mother's sister, or one of the grandparents, adopt him. The child's own parents give him to her and she carries him on her back. The kinsfolk of the child's father usually take the first child, and the kinsfolk of the mother take the second. Sometimes the third child is also adopted, but the rest usually stay in their mother's hut. It is we Habe who do that, we give our child as a gift to someone to carry on their back. Fulani won't give him to anyone. Fulani won't give their child to a brother, they don't want their laughter taken to another compound. They laugh and are happy with the child, they won't let him go to another house. If they marry a Habe woman perhaps they will give away a child, but they wouldn't do so on their own. Even if the mother dies, they leave the children in her hut and the father looks after them.

Before a wife has borne a child her own kin send her gifts at the two annual feasts—rice, guineacorn, salt, locust-bean cakes—at every feast they send her these gifts. (3) When she has a child they give her all the 'dowry' for a birth, and after that they make no more gifts to her at the feasts. As I never had a child, my parents always sent me things every feast—sweetmeats, guineacorn, rice, salt, locust-bean cakes, my father and my parents sent them, even after Father had moved to Giwa. My husband rested from taking grain out of his granary, he bought no salt or things for stew, the food they sent would last us for about twenty days. Your family does that because you have not brought forth your child, and yet they want you to feel happy and stay in your hut, and not get up and leave your husband. You see, the husband has paid them a great deal of money, so the wife's family keep on returning the gifts until there is a child. The husband rests from providing food. They don't want their daughter to see her hut bare and go off on her own; if she has a child she will not want to go away.

If a lot of children have died and then one lives, they take her and lay her down at a place where paths meet, near the compound. Whoever comes along and sees the baby on the road says 'Look, there's my slave—lost property!' Then he would bring a leather lead like they used to use for slaves when they travelled about, and a ring, he would tie the lead round her neck with a ring in front and one behind, and it wouldn't be removed until she married. They put on the lead, she was a 'slave who had been found', but she stayed in her father's compound. She would be called 'Ba'i' and the man who had found her always called her 'Slave'. When it was time to marry her, her 'master' would come and claim his ransom money. One would ask for five shillings, one would ask for ten shillings. The father's and mother's kin collected the money and ransomed their daughter. It was just the same for boys, they were called 'Bawa'.

Mother's Milk

We call mother's milk the 'child's judge'—it always silences him; if he cries, give him the breast, he sucks and is satisfied and then he is quiet! When a child is seven days old we rub the soles of his feet with his mother's milk to kill the flesh there, then even in the dry season he won't feel the heat of the path. If the mother's milk gets onto the child's genitals it will kill them too; you know Sankira, the man who sweeps up the market here in Giwa, he also dances and is a praise-singer—he's not well. The thing that causes a person to be ill in this way is that his mother has not been careful when she is suckling him; she should always cover her other breast with her cloth, so that no milk shall fall on her child's genitals. If milk falls on them they will die. If the child is a boy he won't be able to do anything with women; if a girl, there will be no entrance, it will be blocked up, or her genitals will die. Her husband will send her away, she won't be able to bear children. If it is a man he will not seek after women. Some of these people are hard-working, they make money and put it by. Some of them work very hard at farming, we had one in our *rinji* at Karo, he worked very hard indeed, but he did not go after women, he had no power. He was one of our slaves and he worked a lot, he was very hard-working. Then there was a girl who was not healthy, she came here to New Giwa, she came from the south; her name was Shekara. She was beautiful with light reddish skin. She said she wished to be a *jakadiya*—to Fagaci. He desired her, she was very beautiful with her firm round breasts, but after a short time she left his compound. The children kept on singing at her,

> She's blocked up, she's only looked at,
> Without a door, without a path. (4)

147

It was a pitiful thing. They kept on and on, we told them 'For shame, to behave so unkindly to her!' At first it was said to be a lie, but indeed it was true. Closed up, who would touch her? She stayed here for about six months, she was Fagaci's *jakadiya* but since there was no entrance he sent her away. She used to come to our house to grind grain for us, the children were plaguing her. I drove them away, I said 'If Allah has willed this on her, will you also ridicule her like that?' She said 'Indeed, you are right'. She came and ground grain in our house, later she went away but I don't know where she went. A lovely girl. There was Danzuma, too, when he was circumcised it putrefied and fell off, then they gave him medicine and it healed. But he was not able to do anything with women.

A mother should not go to her husband while she has a child she is suckling. If she does, the child gets thin, he dries up, he won't get strong, he won't be healthy. If she goes after a year, the child won't get strong; but if she goes after two years it is nothing, he is already strong before that, it does not matter if she conceives again after two years. If she only sleeps with her husband and does not become pregnant, it will not hurt her child, it will not spoil her milk. But if another child enters in, her milk will make the first one ill. If she must go to her husband, she should take a kolanut and sew it up in leather into a charm and wear it round her waist; when she weans her child that is that, she throws away the charm and does as she wishes, then there is another child. It is not sleeping with the husband that spoils her milk, it is the pregnancy that does that. But if her husband desires her, then in the day she carries her child, at night she carries her husband—this is what pleases Allah. He does not like argumentative women. But it is not right that she should sleep with her husband for two years; if he insists she should wear the kolanut charm. As you know, there is medicine to make the pregnancy 'go to sleep', but that is not a good thing.

There was my grand-daughter Dantambai, her mother was the grand-daughter of my father Malam Buhari; Dantambai was Musa's head wife. When she came to wash, after she had given birth to a child, her mother who bore her came to wash her at her husband's compound. Her mother slept in the hut with Dantambai and the baby. Before five months had elapsed her husband desired her, he crept up to the hut when her mother was asleep and beckoned to her—like this. She got up and went out to him, she also wanted him. Her mother woke up while she was away with him. In the morning her husband came to the hut to greet his mother-in-law. Dantambai's mother was angry, she scolded him, she said 'What is the reason for this work? You have three other wives.' He was silent. Again he came, she slipped out, and they did as they pleased. Her mother was very angry and said she would return to her own home. When people asked her why, she said it was nothing. But her kinswomen said 'Ap. She is going to her husband's hut!' She was spreading scandal. Dantambai's husband had his sleeping-hut in the middle and the huts of his four wives round it, it was quite easy to go from her hut to his. Her husband Musa was the son of my *kawa* Kande; Dantambai was my grand-daughter. Her mother went to Musa's mother Kande, and told her she was going home. She told her the reason. Kande said 'At five months one goes to the husband's hut? (5) Doesn't she want the child to be healthy?' She sent for Musa, her eldest child, she said 'Of the South Gate, have you no shame?' She lectured him. (6)

Dantambai became pregnant eight months after the first child was born; for seven months he drank milk, then he drank 'pregnant milk' until when she was near to her time they weaned him. When Dantambai knew she was pregnant they sent for her mother, but she was angry and said she would not come. Dantambai and her husband were delighted, but their parents were angry. They said they would give her medicine so that the pregnancy should lie down but he refused, he said 'Here is one child, let's have the other one too!' If you go back to your husband's hut, what do you expect? The second child was born after a year, there was already a child on her back, then there was the infant, they were both being suckled. They sent for me and I said the elder child must be taken to the market in the very early morning, and when the butchers killed a bull they must get the stomach of the bull while it was still warm and rub the child's whole body with it, then the woman who took him must tie him on her back and bring him back to the compound at once. Then she must wash him all over with warm water, and get some butter and rub him with it. Every market-day at Zarewa for two weeks, that is seven market-days, they did this. Then he was all right; he ate food—gruel and *tuwo* and *fura* and sour milk, he was weaned after a year. He grew strong and well, the children are both alive and healthy now. The new pregnancy spoils the milk and the child ails. But when his body was rubbed with the bull's stomach, then he passed a lot of urine, then his body became strong. (7) Those two brothers are young men now, they have both been married recently. She went back to her husband because he desired her very much and she desired him; she was his head wife, he had three others, but she was the one he preferred.

CHAPTER X

TROUBLE OVER A MARRIAGE OF ALMS

One evening when I had been with Malam Maigari for about seven years, we women were sitting eating our evening meal when we heard someone at the entrance, 'Peace be upon you!' Our husband's elder brother said 'Ap. Who's that?' He called out 'Upon you be peace!' and he went out to the entrance. He saw Dankiawa's younger brother, Audu and Dankiawa's wife Tsohuwa and daughter Uwa, whose head and face were covered, they were there at the door of our compound. I said 'What, have they brought us a bride of alms?' and everyone laughed. Uwa's mother had said one day to Malam that he must build a two-storeyed room like the ones the Arabs build, (1) and she would give him a bride as a gift. But he was certain she would not be able to do it, because the girl's father did not agree, so when he had built the new hut I went into it and left my old hut. Uwa was my *kawa*. Then, when they had come to the entrance, Audu the younger brother of Uwa's father said to Sule 'Give her to Malam Maigari as alms'. Sule took her hand and gave her to me, I took her hand and led her to my hut—we were delighted. Then Sule went and told Malam, he came out and he was glad indeed. Then Audu and Tsohuwa went home.

We tidied the hut, we put on our best things, then we played and drummed on calabashes and celebrated. Uwa's father knew nothing about all this; his younger brother Audu had held the ceremony for her marriage to one of the Prophet's representatives that morning, and brought her over with her mother at night. Their compound was next but one to ours, so when her father Dankiawa heard our drumming he asked in his squeaky voice, 'What is the meaning of all that drumming?' Tsohuwa, Uwa's mother's co-wife said 'There is a marriage in Danbailu's house, they have married Maigari and Uwa'. He said nothing and returned to his

151

hut. He was angry. Before this he had married her off to his brother (in the household of his brother?) in Beli, she was taken there and when she had been there for three months she ran away; after they took her back she ran away again. Her mother didn't approve of the marriage but her father wished to marry her to his kinsman. Finally she broke it off, she went away into Kano country and got a divorce. When she came back she and her own mother, Giwa, put their heads together. Tsohuwa was Giwa's co-wife. Uwa wanted Maigari and he wanted Uwa very much indeed. Very well, Giwa consulted with her husband's younger brother Audu, she coaxed him, she persuaded her joking relation, they talked the matter over until he agreed. So they brought Uwa to our compound as a bride of alms. (2) Next morning we sent twenty thousand cowries as a gift to the bringers of alms. Her father was hot with anger, he said to his wife Giwa 'Pick up your belongings and clear out!' She replied 'Very well', she departed and went to live in her son's compound; she paid her money and had a hut built for herself in the forecourt of his compound and there she lived, she never remarried. Dankiawa drove away her children too, he didn't want them, he didn't like them at all after that. They went to live with their mother and her kin.

In the morning before they brought Uwa, they had performed a marriage ceremony between her representative and a man who acted as representative of the Prophet Mohammed, then they gave her to the servant of the Prophet as alms. In the evening after they had brought her we passed the night in drumming and celebration. In the morning we pounded the grain and ground it, we worked at the preparing of food. In the afternoon we bought a small goat, some chickens and meat, we cooked that and we sent it to her mother, who was in her son's house; we did not send any to her father because he disapproved of the marriage. That night we held the feast, her mother's kin came but her father forbade his kinsfolk to come, except for his younger brother Audu, who came together with his wives and children. Dankiawa was angry with his younger brother for a full year; Audu lived in a hamlet and Dankiawa did not go to the hamlet, nor did Audu visit Dankiawa's compound. But we spent the night rejoicing, all the women of the household in every hut were celebrating and feasting; for two nights we didn't sleep. Malam and the other *malams* of the town all filled up the entrance-hut, they spent the night reading the Ishiriniya (3) and

giving thanks to Allah. We were rejoicing and drumming on calabashes. You don't have the ordinary drums for an alms marriage,
you only have drumming on calabashes. We were singing a song
of thanksgiving.

> *Calabash-drummers, what is the news?*
> *The news is of Allah the Ruler,*
> *Allah has received a gift,*
> *Allah gives thanks for the gift,*
> > *The mouth that eats and drinks*
> > *Will certainly return thanks;*
> > *He who neither eats nor drinks,*
> > *If he gives thanks he does so uselessly.*
> *Allah accepts the gift,*
> *Allah gives thanks for the gift.*
> *We give thanks, we are grateful.*
> *Allah accepts the gift.*
> *We give thanks for the gift of a handmaid,*
> *We give thanks, we are grateful.*

And there is much more of that song. We gave Gude, the chief
calabash-drummer, a blouse, a head-scarf, money, kolanuts—she
sang their thanks for these gifts, too, in a different song. We had
been given a daughter, we had been given marriage gifts, they had
made us a gift indeed. Malam was overjoyed, we were happy too.
We knew Uwa well—their compound was very close, there was
only one in between theirs and ours.

Another Marriage of Alms which annoyed Aunt Rabi

Then came Afiruwa. She had been the wife of my elder brother
Nasamai, the son of my father's sister Rabi—the one who rescued
her from the king's palace at Abuja. Afiruwa was my *kawa*, we
were always visiting one another. Then she ended her marriage
with Nasamai, and when she had finished Iddah, Sule, our husband's elder brother, began courting her. He and Alarama, her
father's younger brother, were friends, they put their heads together then they told me and said I was not to be angry. I said
'Very well. Has it got anything to do with me? My sister has left
my brother—well, may Allah give him another wife!' Afiruwa was
angry with Nasamai because he was courting a wealthy woman of

Makarfi, she heard the story and said she would not live with a rich woman, so she left him. She wanted Sule, she had known him and he had wanted her ever since she was a maiden, he used to meet her in the market and give her money, but my elder brother married her first. Sule had her in the end, though, the rich woman drove her out before she had even arrived! I was happy, here was my hut and there was hers right beside it, my *kawa* had come to our compound. Sule had three wives, he had Iyami and Ajuma, then he married Afiruwa, but she had no children.

Aunt Rabi, who was rescued from Abuja, married our kinsman Mamman in our compound in Zarewa. She was confined to his compound, he secluded his wives. When her anger had cooled she used to come to Malam's compound to visit me in the evenings. Then after they brought her son's wife Afiruwa to our household, she never came any more. (4) Her son's wife left him and came to our compound—wasn't that enough to make Aunt Rabi angry with us? Then Nasamai married Abu Rogo, he also married Abu Zarewa, then he married Maria, then he married Matan Dodo, the wealthy woman from Makarfi; after five months he got rid of her. Matan Dodo was the one who drove out Afiruwa. She was not an amiable woman, she did not like her co-wives: when she was leaving she threatened to break up her hut, because Nasamai had built it for her with her money, and she wouldn't have another woman living in it. (5) After she walked out she went to the Chief of Zarewa and told him that Nasamai was eating up all her wealth, he was taking her money and wasting it. Yet before she came she had given it to him, she wanted him to build her a hut, she desired him.

The Chief who went Mad

The chief of Zarewa at that time was Aliyu, his praise-song ran 'Daudu's man, not to be fooled with—Those who play with you soon learn toughness!' Aliyu was a friend of Nasamai. If anyone annoyed him he seized hold of him like a wrestler, he would throw him on the ground and throttle him. His elder brother the former Sarkin Zarewa, Usuman, hadn't a hot temper, but when Aliyu succeeded—then there was trouble. His elder brother Usuman Daudu (6) was the Galadima of the town, Usuman was the Galadima, Aliyu was formerly the Ciroma. When their father died Galadima Usuman became Chief. Then he went mad; he was travelling to Kano City and he went off wandering in the bush on his horse, and when he arrived at Kano he was muttering mad words. The King of Kano ordered him to be bound and taken home, they brought him back to Zarewa and gave him medicine, he was removed from office. He was kept there in his compound, he smashed all the pottery to bits and he attacked anyone who came near him until a man of the Maguzawa (7) was found who gave him medicine; he got better, and his four wives returned to him. After a year the madness returned, and he had to be bound again. Then every year at harvest time he would go mad for two or three months, then he would recover and come back to his senses and see people and exchange greetings with them. So it was, until the next dry season. It often happens that when the harmattan blows madness seizes people, either the madness of violence or the madness of muttering. An old lady came to Giwa last harmattan season, she was here for seven days, and she babbled away all the time. The year before last there was a madman, it took four men to hold him, they brought him and put him in the gaol here and then they took him to the asylum in Zaria. That was in the beginning of the dry season, too. (8) The wind brings the spirits from their city in the East, we call them 'Children of the East', the spirits, the *bori*, the jinns. Daudu Sarkin Zarewa refused to give them alms, the *bori*-adepts told him he should give alms to the spirits, a bull and chickens, but he did not do it. So the spirits were angry and caught him. He trembled all over, as they shook him. If he had given them alms, or if his kinsmen had done so, the spirits would not have troubled him. But his father was dead and his mother was not wealthy, Daudu and his brothers had no money, he had gone mad and spent his money. A compound was built for him over at the North Gate, and he was kept there alone; his mother's people would put food there for him, when he saw it he would take it and eat and he would throw it about. For three years they were making remedies and medicine for him, they went on and on, the medicine of the Maguzawa. They put pepper and perfumed wood and some kind of medicine with fire, they put it in a potsherd, they opened the door of his hut and pushed it in. The spirits inhaled the smoke, they smelt the smoke, then when Usuman was coughing the Bamaguje (9) went in and gave him medicine to drink. When he was quieter the Bamaguje would lead him out of the hut and wash him with the medicine, then he told him to sit down there and he sat down. He inhaled the perfumed smoke, then he returned to his hut and the door was shut. When the spirits started up again you would hear him banging on the door, *dim, dim*; when they were tired, then they would begin to talk. After the Bamaguje had given him medicine in this way every day for three months, the spirits left him and he recovered. He would come out to see people, he was shaved, he got new clothes to put on. But when the fit was on him he would burn his clothes in the fire. When he was better his kinsfolk said to him 'You may go where you please'. He went about and abused no one. His mother gave the Bamaguje about twenty thousand cowries. He might go on for two years without any trouble, then when his mind was disturbed she went quickly to the hamlet and called the Bamaguje. I heard that he died last year. Every dry season, at harvest time, it would return.

We have a fable about the madness caused by jealousy between a man's wives. There was a wife who went to a *malam*. She asked him to give her medicine so that her co-wife would go mad and leave her in the compound alone. He said 'Here it is. If you call her and she doesn't answer, you will go mad. If she answers, she will go mad. Do you understand?' She said she understood. The next day she returned to him and he gave her the medicine. He said 'It is not my responsibility'. She said 'I will find her'. She returned home and called her co-wife. Silence. Then she began to dance in the open space of the compound, then madness seized her. The co-wife's father was a *malam* also, and he had told her 'Don't take anything she gives you, don't reply if she calls you'. When she heard the other wife calling her name she remained quite quiet. When the jealous wife went mad she went off into the bush. That is a tale of long ago; they still do that sort of thing, but not in the same way as they did in the past; nowadays women get charms, but only to drive out their co-wives. They don't use medicine for madness now, they are afraid of you—they don't want to be caught and taken before the Christians and killed. (10) It is the same with all the bad things of the past—they are finished, people are afraid to do them. Now life is peaceful.

Nasamai's Rich Wife

To return to Nasamai's wife, the rich one from Makarfi. Audu Nasamai was a great farmer, there was a long song about him, it called him 'the slave of the hoe'; if you went to stay with him you *ate* farming, he worked so hard. (11) Nasamai was circumcised at the same time as Sarkin Zarewa Aliyu of whom his song said 'whoever plays with you will feel your strength'. (12) Matan Dodo, the rich woman from Makarfi, sold her possessions and collected a great deal of money, she took the money to Sarkin Zarewa and she said 'Here you are, eat some kolanuts and give me a divorce from him!' He ate kolanuts, and he granted her the divorce. When he sent for Nasamai to discuss it with him, Nasamai said 'Yes, she can go; I don't want her'. Nasamai drank farming at the breast, he inherited it from his mother's father, Ibrahim Dara. He used to harvest a hundred bundles of grain singlehanded.

My Adopted Daughter is Married

I arranged a kinship marriage for my adopted daughter Sadau, the child of my sister Dije; I married her to Aunt Rabi's grandson, the son of her son Mijiniya. Sadau had seven children and her co-wife had three; all ten are alive still. There were four men, all her kinsmen, who wished to marry her; I told her to choose from amongst them the one she liked best. When I asked my sister Dije about it, she said we should give her to a man in the compound of Dije's husband Hamidu, to a son of his elder brother. I said the girl preferred someone else in our family, she did not wish to go to that compound. So I came here to Giwa and discussed it with our father Tsoho. I went to Malam Buhari at Karo and he said 'May Allah bless you for this act of kinship'. Malam Maigari had said to me 'Go and see your parents about the matter'. So I went to Karo and spent the day there and told them; then Sadau and I came to Giwa for seven days, and when I returned I went to the house of Nasamai, who was the younger brother of the young man's father. His own father was away to the eastward. Nasamai collected twenty shillings, which he gave me, the bride's mother. I gave five shillings of it to Maigari's household, ten shillings to our kinsmen at Karo, and five shillings to Sadau's own mother Dije. It was distributed to everyone so that they should know. Everybody was very pleased. On each market-day in Zarewa he would give her a shilling, on Fridays and Sundays he would give her sixpence. Then when the Great Feast came his kinsfolk brought

157

ten shillings and a cloth, a basket of rice, one of guineacorn and one of millet, four chickens, and some oil; they brought all these gifts to our compound. Sadau visited all the compounds accompanied by three children whom she had chosen. She did this seven days before the feast. We call these the 'children of putting on henna'. Henna was prepared and they were stained with henna, and given very nice food. On the day of the festival after we had watched the horsemen gallop to greet the Chief of Zarewa, everyone went home and ate till he was satisfied, then the girls and youths played their games. The three children accompanied Sadau to her husband's home, it was her first marriage; they played with her *kawaye*, then they stayed with her for three months so that she had someone to run errands for her.

I remember they used to call Malam Maigari's house 'The house of the beautiful women at the South Gate'.

Aunt Rabi breaks up my Marriage

For fifteen years I was in Malam Maigari's compound, then my father's sister Rabi (13) came and said 'Look at everyone bearing children, look at everyone else bearing children; leave that compound and you will bear children too'. I said 'I will not leave him, I am not going anywhere else'. My *kawa* Tine had been married five times, then when she married the Chief of Kilu, a big town in Kano country, she had her first child, a son. My mother Rabi (14) knew this. 'Yarbala had been married three times, then when she went to Garaje and married, at last she had a daughter. My father's sister said 'Leave him and you will have children'. I refused and said I would not leave his compound. From the very first she had not liked this marriage; then when she had cooled down there had been Afiruwa's marriage, and when she was annoyed about that she kept on saying that I should leave, she did not want me to stay in their compound since they had taken the wife of her son.

When I was going to leave I did not tell anyone. I went to the compound of the Chief of Zarewa, the mad one, but he was well then. He sent for Malam Maigari, he said 'See the daughter of the people at Karo has come to break off her marriage'. We went home, Malam came into my hut, he talked to me and asked me to be patient. I said 'It's my mother, she wants me to leave you'. We returned to Sarkin Zarewa. Malam's elder brother said 'They must not be separated. Ask her where is the fault, no one has ever annoyed her, neither child nor man.' Sarki said 'Think it over, go back and make up your marriage'. I said 'My mother says I must leave, she says I must leave him, she does not want me to remain here in this compound with Afiruwa'. We were there for some time, then Malam Maigari said 'I am in love'. I said 'It is not anyone's fault, my mother wants me to leave'. The chief gave me my divorce paper, he gave Malam his, Malam said he did not wish me to return the *sadaki*, I was to keep it, he would prefer it so. I went to Aunt Rabi's compound and stayed there. Malam Maigari sent a message to say that if I ceased being angry would I please come back and we would re-make the marriage. Aunt Rabi was rejoicing over me, she was happy, so I said I would not go back.

Even now I love him and he loves me. When I go to Zarewa to see my kin, I stay for three months in his house; he and his wives are always asking me to come back. When my last husband, Yari Malam Hasan, died, they wanted me to go back but my younger brother Kadiri married me off here to Ibrahim. Ai, my younger brother is here, I am living in his house, I eat his porridge, I don't have to do any work; his wife Gwamma makes porridge for me. At Malam Maigari's house they said they would like me to go back and just live there, they would do the work for me. But, you see, I can always lecture Kadiri and he has to listen; this month I was annoyed with him, I told him off and he listened and did what I said. I like my younger brother. Sadau's household too, they keep asking me to go to their compound and live. Later perhaps I may return to Malam Maigari's house and live with him; if Kadiri was at Zarewa I should go at once. There are kinsfolk here, there are kinsfolk there—at Zarewa and in the hamlets—in every compound there are kinsfolk of mine, more than a hundred of my grand-children and grandchildren's children. I am feeling annoyed just now because the children have not come over to greet me. They say they want me to go so that they can see me; I say 'Very well, you can come here and see me'. Perhaps later in the dry season I will visit our town. The mother of our household, Malam Maigari's head wife, died last year, and also his eldest son Dogara; he sent to say he wanted me to return—but here I am with my husband Ibrahim, I go and greet him, I take him some kolanuts, he brings me kolanuts. He has no hut in his compound and I say I will not live in the hut of his wife who has gone wandering off, because she may return; also I prefer my brother's house. Also there are my adopted children here, there are kinsfolk here. I said that just now I will not go back.

Cowives and Children in Their Compound

Family at Home

Baba at Home

Spinning and Weaving

Farming Bee

Giwa Market

Fagaci Muhammadu, District He[ad of]
Giwa in 1950

Warder and Prisoners

PART FOUR

CHAPTER XI

c. 1922–1943
THIRD MARRIAGE

My Father arranges my Marriage

After I had left Malam Maigari, my elder sister Mati (we were children of two brothers) came to visit her kinsfolk round Zarewa, and when she was going back to her husband's home I escorted her and stayed with her for seven days, then I returned. She wanted me to come to their compound and marry her husband's kinsman. Their hamlet was Jiba near Surruwaje, not far from Funtua in Katsina. They had a nice home, a large pleasant compound with many children. The head of the household was Sarkin Yaki, the chief of war, (1) and they farmed as a *gandu*. They were Giwa people, but Mai Sudan had driven them from Giwa and they had gone to a Funtua hamlet. (2) Sarkin Yaki's job in war-time was to remain in the compound in the hamlet, he did not take refuge in the walled town.

The son of Mati's husband, called Danmasugida, desired me; he had four wives but he put away one of them and was going to marry me. (3) But my father Malam Tsoho heard the news as Mati's husband's folk were Giwa people and their kinsfolk came and went and knew all that was going on. One day about noon my brother Kadiri arrived unexpectedly with his younger sister Hawwa, and another man and an old lady, they came and greeted the people of the compound and said 'Is Baba here?' They had met the one who wanted to marry me, he was on his way to market, he said to them 'Go to our compound, be patient and wait till I return'. When they arrived they enquired for me from the men of the household. They said they would not wait; I said 'Wait till he returns and I will give him back his money, and in the morning

163

we will set out'. I was feeling angry, I desired him and he desired me, even my hut was ready—he had divorced one of his wives so that I could come at once. His kinsfolk gave my people chicken and porridge, but Kadiri and the others were annoyed and said they would not eat, they were cross because we were not going to start out that evening. When the owners of the compound had talked to them they relented and ate. In the morning Danmasugida brought money and gave it to them, he asked them to give it to my father and say to him that Danmasugida wanted my father to give me to him. When we got home Father refused to accept it, it was put by until Danmasugida came, and returned to him then.

When I got to Father's home in Giwa I said 'Here I am', he said 'Welcome, welcome, and bless you'. He said 'I want you to be married here; there is a boy here' (but he was a grown man), 'he came to learn the Koran'. My father liked him because of his uprightness; I agreed to marry him because he was a good man.

My new husband's name was Danbiyu, Hasan—he was a farmer and he worked at the prison; his title was *Yari*, Keeper of the Prison to Fagaci Ahmadu who ruled Giwa district. (4) The Warder's compound at Old Giwa was our home. They always seem to have twins as warders—when Danbiyu died they had another Hasan, and now Fagaci Muhammadu's warder is Hasan, Fagaci's younger full brother. (5)

After I had been three days in my father's compound, Malam Hasan came back from their village, Ma'aji, where he had been to tell his father about the marriage. Hasan was tall, a son of the Sokoto people; his father had been the Sultan of Sokoto's messenger in the past. Hasan already had two wives, Juma and Ladi, both *bori* dancers; every Friday they would be *bori* dancing. Juma's father had no son, she was his only child; she had had three children by a previous husband, but they were all blind and died. When she was a girl she was possessed by so many *bori* spirits that she went mad and wandered about in the bush; then her father paid money and she was initiated. (6) Then she married and had the three children who died, so they 'cooked' her again. After that she married Malam Hasan and was possessed very well. Before that they were all over the place. She used to be possessed by Sarkin Aljannu, the king of the spirits; when he really comes, you put mats on the floor of the hut like a chief's court, and when you have done that, then his medium speaks and everyone prostrates themselves and listens. In another compound she had two children, a boy and a girl, with perfectly good eyes and straight noses. Then she broke up that marriage and came to Malam Hasan but she left the children with their father, he kept his own children. After a year she left our compound and married a drummer who had come to Giwa and stayed at our compound, he played for an evening at the entrance of our compound. After that Ladi also left Malam Hasan, and I lived there with his wife Sa'a at Old Giwa. We were together for two years, Sa'a and I, and then she left, her time there had come to an end. (7) Then Malam Hasan went and married Salamatu, she gave me plenty of trouble; one day we had cooked beans, she refused to give me any. He came in and said to me 'Haven't you any food?' I said 'She has refused to give me any'. There they were, plenty of them, she had put them aside. Then when he picked up some to give them to me, she knocked them over. Then he said 'Get out!' She said 'Very well, it is best that way'. She went to the judge Sa'idu. He said 'Look at you, you've had twenty marriages. You come to live with a patient girl, then you plague her.' Then he put an end to the marriage. (8)

My Husband and his Twin Sister Hasana

When his other wives had gone away and left me alone, I stayed a long time alone with Malam Hasan. He was a reasonable man. His father had been a courtier of the Sultan of Sokoto, he was called Dogon Jakada, 'the tall messenger'. He died ten years ago. His work was to bring horses to the King of Zaria; in return he got slaves from the King of Zaria and took them to the Sultan. One day when he was in Zaria City there was a young woman who had just finished mourning for her husband, her name was Hawwa. She had a child on her back. The Sokoto man desired her, so he went to the King of Zaria and said 'I have seen a beautiful girl in your city; I would like to marry her'. The king ordered the head of her compound to be called, Dogon Jakada went to her compound, and they arranged it. She desired him and she said she would go to Sokoto with him. Her mother wept. When they went to Sokoto she became pregnant, and she bore Garba; she had Mamman, and the twins, my husband Hasan and Hasana, and when the youngest of her children had been weaned she died. Hasan and Hasana were small children of about seven years old. Dogon Jakada picked them up and tied them onto his horse with a turban, they weren't strong enough to hold on. He left three children behind at home and he put these two on his horse and led the horse all the way to Zaria, to bring them to their grandparents so that the kinsfolk of his dead wife could see what kind of children their daughter bore. He had taken away their daughter and she had died; was it not fitting that he should bring her children to show them? When Dogon Jakada married her, Hawwa's mother had divorced her father because she did not agree to her daughter's going to Sokoto; her father agreed but her mother did not. Dogon Jakada took Hasan and Hasana out from the City to a hamlet to see their grandmother, but she was angry and would not receive them. Dogon Jakada spent the night at a village called Ma'aji; it was raining, and when the morning came Hasan played at planting guineacorn on the floor of the hut. Dogon Jakada said 'Come, it's time to go home'. Hasan said 'Father, look at the rain; let's stay here and farm. We're tired of travelling. Our mother's kinsfolk don't want us—let's farm here.' Hasana said 'Give me a grinding-stone, I'll make porridge so that we can eat'. Then the Sultan of Sokoto's messenger said 'Very well, we will stay here then. When the dry season comes we will go home.' So they cleared some land and farmed, Dogon Jakada sold his horse and they bought food to eat. When the dry season came, he said he would buy a horse and they would go home. Hasan said 'Father, buy a goat and I will look after it'. He bought Hasan a goat, he built a house, the rest of the money he put by till he married. Then he married Matan Baba. They lived like that, the goats multiplied and the granaries were full. He separated the twins and sent Hasan to school with a *malam*, and he sent Hasana to another but she refused to study and ran home. Hasan was four years in the *malam's* school at Ricifa in Makarfi, when he returned home they farmed. Then he married Kaji, a woman with a black nature, she left him; then his father married him off to Kande; after a year he dismissed her. Dogon Jakada washed Hasana and gave her as a bride of alms to Maiyadia; they took her to him but she ran away, they took her again and she ran away, finally she ran off to Zaria City. Then her father filled a basket with cowries, he gave it to the *malam* and said 'The bride that I gave you as alms refuses to stay; see this; buy salt for your household with it'. (9)

Then a friend of Dogon Jakada saw Hasana in Zaria; she was wandering from house to house, living in the hut of an old lady, a distant kinswoman. He brought her back to her father, Dogon Jakada was angry and said 'Take her away, I give her to you'. When he got back to Zaria her father's friend married her off to someone who took her to Bada, away over near Ilorin. There she conceived but she miscarried, then the husband died. Hasana's elder brother by her mother Hawwa, born when she was married before she met Dogon Jakada, went away to Bada on foot on a trading expedition; there were no motors or trains then, he walked. He found her and brought her back and married her off to Kamuku in his own house. But she walked out and married Sali. Then she left Sali, who lived in Tudun Wada near Zaria. Before this I had married Malam Hasan, her twin brother; when I married him he sent to Tudun Wada to Sali's house to tell her, but she replied 'I'm on my way to Minna, I'll see you when I come back'. Then she went to Minna for two years.

Two years after I had married Malam Hasan she came home, but Hasan found a place for her to stay some way away from our compound. When she came back from Minna she took her father a gown, trousers and a turban, with twenty thousand cowries, she said she repented. He accepted her repentance and forgave her and he married her to Malam Zakari who was in charge of the railway work on the new Zaria railway, he worked with the Company who built the railway. (10) We had the feast at the Company near Ma'aji. Malam Zakari came and greeted her younger brother with two shillings, he greeted her father with three shillings, but Dogon Jakada said he did not want the money and gave it to Hasana; he said he was not going to take any money for her, he would just marry her off. She was given five shillings and the *sadaki* was ten shillings. Then they brought the marriage-gifts of a calabash of kolanuts, salt, meat, two cloths, a kerchief and a blouse. She knew Zakari well, their compound was here and the Company's compound there, about as far away as the school is from here. He was a fighter; when she began quarrelling he picked up a knife and said 'Right. Come here and let me kill you!' She was silent. He said 'Get up and come and kill me!' Silence. Then 'May Allah make you patient, Malam!' She left him four times, then when she had come home for her Iddah and no one sought her, she went back to him. He got a new bride, I remember; we went, one of his friends had given him his daughter. We were away for three days, we fetched the bride from Danmahawaye on a horse and took her to the Company compound. He gave them money and he gave them money, she was the daughter of his friend's elder brother. We took her from her father's house, they had bathed the bride, they had washed her all over then they gave her to us—'The big hunt was good, the big hunt brought luck!' There were three drummers with big drums, there were people from Zaria, from Giwa and from Ma'aji. Malam Zakari was a Kano man, from Kano City. His new bride found him with two wives, Hasana and Lami, great big women and both quarrelsome. Malam was an amiable man, he laughed a lot and liked fine clothes, he was generous; he was also hot-tempered. If his temper rose, that was that, everyone fled. They were clearing the way and building the railway line, the labourers liked him. When he had married that wife he didn't wait long before he took another bride from Zaria and that was his fourth wife. Now they have all left and he has others.

At that time my husband Hasan had a wife Adama in our compound who was three months pregnant. When her son was born Dogon Jakada had just died. Hasana was ill, she sent a cloth for the naming. Hasan gave me his daughter; when she was weaned Hasana wanted to have her but Malam refused, he said nothing should part me from her but her marriage. Hasana was cross, she wept and she went off to their village, to Ma'aji. Hasan left her alone for two days, then when she had calmed down he went and told her to be patient. Then she came back and said there was another child coming, we should give her that one to adopt. Later Adama produced A'i, Malam Hasan gave A'i to Hasana, she is with her now. Adama objected and she and Hasana fought, *kichi-kichi-kichi*. I watched the fight, Adama broke Hasana's arm; Kantoma broke one and Adama broke the other. That quarrel went on for three years. Hasana got A'i and tied her on her back —then off she went to Minna. For three years we didn't see her. She went ten times to Minna but she always came back to Malam Zakari. Poor A'i drank trouble in Hasana's care. When Hasana came back she married Malam Zakari's retainer Musa; Musa later married another of Zakari's wives when he dismissed her too. His compound was not joined to Zakari's—Malam Zakari didn't care. When she married Musa, Hasana moved with him across the road to her father's compound after her father had died; there was a well inside that compound. When she broke off that marriage, Musa remained in the compound and married another of Malam Zakari's divorced wives, and to this day he is in the compound, the well is there and even at the end of the dry season it does not dry up; everyone in the village uses it. Hasan inherited the house, but he and Musa merely greet one another. Hasan also inherited the locust-bean trees and the farms, but he lent them out because he was working for Fagaci.

After she had left Musa, Hasana came back to Giwa and married Tafarki; they spent forty nights together, then there was fighting and beating, the marriage went to pieces. When he had divorced her she married Kantoma, Fagaci's retainer; when they had been thirty nights together they started quarrelling, we watched while he beat her on the road—we laughed very much. When that marriage was finished she made another, with Tula at Giwa. It didn't last a year, after four months there was a fight and he drove her away. She married Balarabe and in two weeks that marriage was broken. When she and Kantoma had that fight they were down in the marsh; we all watched, they wrestled and she seized him by the throat, but he won. He broke her arm and they carried Hasana to our compound and bandaged it to a piece of wood so that it should heal. Kantoma went straight back to Fagaci's compound, he didn't come near her. Fagaci had heard the story, so when he saw him he said 'Come come, haven't you been to greet her? Go at once!' Kantoma had to go, so he came in and said to his wife 'Hallo!' then he stuck out his tongue like this. He never came back.

Next there was Maiturmi, a trader who was staying at Na Arewa's compound. Soon after he had arrived Na Arewa said to him 'Look here, this woman is seeking marriage'. Maiturmi said 'Oh no, she's quarrelsome—I've heard the tale'. Na Arewa argued with him and persuaded him, then he made enquiries and was told 'Keep away from her, she is very bad-tempered'. But Na Arewa went on and on, and finally Maitrumi brought sixpence and twenty kolanuts and her gift of a shilling; no cloth, no salt, no grain, nothing. After ten days he bought guineacorn, he did not buy any salt or locust-bean cakes or things for stew as he ought to do, so she made him plain porridge without stew. She made a lovely stew for herself with the ingredients which she had bought with her own money. Wasn't that her nature showing itself? If he said anything to her she would start a fight. She is a huge woman and he was an enormous man. In the night he took up all his loads and his cloth that he was selling and he fled—we never saw him again. That was the year before last. The reason he did not buy things for soup was that he saw she had them already by her. He came back to Giwa the day before yesterday and went round and greeted people, but he avoided meeting Hasana, he kept his visit quiet. She didn't even know he was there, then when he had gone they told her and she said 'Ap. Didn't he come to greet me?' We all laughed.

When Hasana got married in Minna she took her daughter with her, she had adopted the girl when she was about six years old from amongst her mother's people in Zaria City. Her name was Lauretu. When Hasana got to Minna she married Lauretu to a Nupe man, and when the girl's family heard they were very angry and refused to accept the marriage money; Hasana came back to us and told her brother about it, Malam Hasan told her to go to Minna and fetch Lauretu home. When she got to Minna Hasana picked up all the girl's things and they went to the judge. Lauretu's husband said that his wife's mother had come to put an end to the marriage. Then the judge at Minna asked him 'Do you still want her?' and the Nupe man answered 'Yes, I want her'. The judge asked Lauretu 'Do you still want him?' she said 'May Allah forgive you, Malam, I want him'. Then Hasana said Lauretu's mother was angry and her kinsfolk were angry, and she must leave her husband and return to Zaria. They spent ten days in the judge's court, he refused to end the marriage. Then Hasana took the girl to her hut and beat her, she said 'I'm tired of your mother's upbraidings, you are to come home'. When they returned to the judge the girl said 'Allah forgive you, Malam, I don't wish the marriage. Here is my mother who wishes me to go back to Zaria; I will go back.' The judge was very annoyed but he divorced them, and Lauretu returned to Zaria. When they arrived in Zaria at her mother's compound, my husband Hasan said Hasana was to bring Lauretu back to Giwa. Lauretu was the daughter of an elder brother of Hasan and Hasana.

When she had been in Old Giwa for a few days I said I liked Lauretu, I would like her to be given to my younger brother Kadiri, she was a very nice girl. We were happy, my younger sister went to the market, I gave her a shilling and she bought kolanuts and perfume. Hasana lived in the ward of the Kano people, we lived in Fagaci's ward. I sent for Kadiri, I said 'Bring a shilling and buy kolanuts and perfume for their arrival, there is a very nice girl for you'. He said 'You wouldn't let me have that beautiful one before, now you want me to marry this ugly one?' I said Ladi was full of quarrels like Hasana, Lauretu was not quarrelsome. He said 'Very well', he brought a shilling, we put it to mine and we bought kolanuts, perfume, millet-balls and milk, threepence each, we added a shilling with them and sent them over to Hasana's compound. We swept out the hut and when Hasana and Lauretu arrived we sent my younger sister with the gifts for welcoming them. When they saw them they said 'Whose work is this?' We said 'It is ours'. They said 'That's not all; what do you want?' We said 'Indeed, we want your daughter, we hear she is no longer married'. Hasana said 'I forbid it'. Everyone laughed. When Lauretu had finished her Iddah, her father's kin agreed and we went to Zaria for the marriage ceremony. Before that Kadiri had given her gifts. He took two cloths and a kerchief, ten shillings *sadaki*, thirty shillings money of seeking, and salt and meat. When the marriage was made we returned to Giwa and sent the *aunaka*. At that time she was only a young girl of fourteen years. She had been married at Minna when she was thirteen, when she had been there five months Hasana arose and went and fetched her back because of the upbraidings of her kin in Zaria, who refused to accept the marriage money. Well, we set out the *aunaka* in my father Malam Tsoho's house, he was still alive then; I was present as one of the bride's kin and one of the bridegroom's too. The drummers and singers from Yakawada and Gangara came, they kept up their drumming until it was morning; the women in the compound were drumming their calabashes, we were in Kadiri's section of our father Tsoho's compound. When I had arranged this marriage I went and told my father and he was glad and gave it his blessing, 'May Allah grant that they live in peace'. Gwamma was already married to Kadiri, she has been married to him now for about twenty years and she always stays. Lauretu had two children, the boy died but the girl is here, she is Yelwa, the young girl who lives with me now. Lauretu was eight years in Kadiri's house, then her mother Hasana saw the chance for them to live together in Sankira's house, so she persuaded her to come away. (11) Hasana lives in Sankira's house now, she just lives there, she isn't married; when Maiturmi fled she lived in someone else's compound, there was swearing and quarrelling, then the owners of the compound threw out her belongings and drove her out. This was after Malam Hasan's death. Sankira's wife felt compassion for her and said 'There's an old woman and they have thrown out her things, shouldn't we give her a hut?' They were not related to her. Sankira the brothel-keeper used to be a retainer of Mainasara but the wives of Maina-sara and Sankira argued and fought until a complaint was taken to the district judge, and the judge ordered Sankira to live in the fore-court of the compound, he and his wife were not to live close to Mainasara's wife. When the dry season came Sankira said Kadiri should build Hasana a hut in his own compound, but Kadiri refused, he was afraid of fights. During the first year that Hasana spent in Sankira's compound they had behaved very well to her, she ate good porridge and stew; then she made Lauretu break up her marriage with Kadiri, 'Break up that marriage,' she said, 'and come and marry Sankira'. Lauretu was living happily, her husband loved her and she had children. But her mother upbraided her and bothered her until she said 'Very well', and she ended the marriage. Kadiri complained to the court because his marriage had been broken up by a third person, and the judge forbade Sankira to marry Lauretu because he had enticed her out of Kadiri's house before she had left of her own will. Then Sankira went to Zaria, he greeted her father, he greeted her mother, he greeted her kin; finally they agreed. Lauretu said she wanted to marry Sankira. She really wanted Kadiri, but her mother forbade it. Even today, four years later, Kadiri and Hasana do not speak to one another— she broke up his marriage for him. Hasana and Lauretu went to Zaria, they greeted her family; they went in the motor lorry and came back again together. Sankira had gone first and arranged the marriage in Zaria, Hasana and Lauretu were not present then. Before she married Sankira, Lauretu was there in his compound, living in her mother Hasana's hut, she used to make the food with Sankira's wife; Sankira and she used to go out and talk in another compound, his wife heard and saw them. When he got married secretly to her, everyone in the town heard the gossip—'Sankira is seeking Lauretu, 'Yanbiyu (Hasana) has given her to him'. Hasana was quarrelling with Sankira's other wife too—'Get out of this house and leave me my daughter!' So she ran away to Anguwan Shehu where her kinsfolk live; when she appealed to the judge for a divorce he told her to put up with it and go back, so she did. Hasana drove her out with her abuse four times, then the judge was weary and he broke up the marriage, he said 'It's this wretched woman who has prevented you from staying'. When Sankira got another wife, Gude from Gangara, Hasana drove her out too after five months. Hasana had paid her money and had her hut built; when Sankira went travelling as a praise-singer, he left them their compound, Hasana, Lauretu and the eight prostitutes. Sankira is not happy at all. There is his mother-in-law with her daughter, he gets up and leaves his home to them and goes off on his own. This year he hasn't done any farming, people are saying that he is getting ready to run away like Maiturmi. He says he'll leave with Lauretu and change his town—he is from Kano country—he's tired of nagging and he will leave Hasana her house. Then people ask him to be patient, they don't want him to go. He can't get rid of Hasana, she has paid her money and had her hut built in his compound. (12) She makes her own porridge and stew with her own oil and meat; she tells the prostitutes they can give her a halfpenny and she will give them oil, if they give her another she will give them stew, after they have bought the porridge from her. Then they take it out into the compound to eat, no one goes into her hut except Lauretu, and Hasana scolds her too, Lauretu does not find her easy.

Hasana always went to men when she saw the chance, whether she was married or not, it made no difference. She is too old now. When she was a young girl she didn't like her father's wife Kadi. She said she was going to take out some guineacorn from the granary and when Kadi told her not to, Hasana hit her. When her father Dogon Jakada heard, he came, he saw they were quarrelling and hitting one another and crying, his wife told him that he didn't like her, he preferred his daughter, and Hasana told him he didn't like her, he liked his wife—then Dogon Jakada said he was tired of this quarrelling, and he took Hasana to Zaria to a *malam* and said she was to study. But she kept on running away. Between her marriages she used to come back to our compound, Malam Hasan her twin brother said we were to give her her food separately in her hut, so that she couldn't start quarrelling with us. Whenever Hasan heard her start up, he fled! She never had any more children after her miscarriage at Minna. She adopted Lauretu, and now she has A'i, the daughter of Malam Hasan and my co-wife Adama, she will be marrying her off next year. (13)

CHAPTER XII

MY HUSBAND MARRIES MY FRIEND ADAMA

When we had lived together, Hasan and I, for about seven years, Danfangi, (1) the chief of Giwa town, died, leaving his wife Adama pregnant. She and I put our heads together—she used to visit our compound—and I said 'Won't you marry my husband? We can have a son and live happily together.' (2) Four months after she had had her child we started to seek her in marriage. An old man was also courting her, but she was young and did not want him, so Malam Hasan repaid him his gifts. I said to Malam, 'Look at Adama, she wants to marry you'. Malam said 'Oh, you! She doesn't want me. Look at her mother, she doesn't agree.' Then I took Malam's gifts to Adama, she and I used to discuss our affairs together; she used to come to our compound and we would have a talk, I would go to their hamlet and gossip to her. After five months, on the day she finished her ablutions, Malam gave Malam Akilu his friend thirty shillings to take to her, so that her family should divide it. Her mother forbade the marriage, she said she would not agree. The daughter said she did agree. That was that, they accepted our gift. The child's father's kin—Danfangi's younger brother—bothered her and bothered her, they said they would not agree to her joining Malam Hasan till the following year. So then she picked up her things and absconded to the village where the younger brother of Danfangi lived, and she coaxed him and argued with him until he agreed to the marriage. Her mother just wanted money to be given to her so that she could spend it.

The Day of Coming Together was a Friday, we were all ready, then at dawn Fagaci sent Malam Hasan to Birnin Gwari. (3) He was needed suddenly on official business. In those days we had no bicycles, he went on foot. Adama came but her bridegroom wasn't there. We had a great feast, there was porridge and chickens, rice and sweetmeats from all the kin in the hamlets round about. At night we took the *jere* food to the bride's compound and everybody ate it. At night, too, we filled up the compound with visitors, and then the bride was brought. The drummers of the big and small drums, the players of stringed instruments and Fagaci's pipe-players, (4) they all came to the front of our compound—but the bridegroom wasn't at home! We spent the night enjoying ourselves, the *bori* came, Giwa, Dangaladiman Busa's mother, was possessed. The menfolk were throwing away their money, the womenfolk were throwing away their money, but the bridegroom wasn't there. When he had been four days in Birnin Gwari he returned. We had set out her dowry in rows in the bride's hut, like the ridges on a farm. The bride with her baby on her back. Her kinsfolk all crowded to the wedding, my kinsfolk from Zarewa came too. We swept the house clean.

I took Adama's child Audi, I carried him on my back. Until she weaned him he only lived with us, we were her guardians. Then when she had weaned Audi she had her first daughter by Malam, they gave her to me and I carried her about on my back—Hawwa, she is married to Sarkin Yelwa's son now. Hawwa became my daughter. I carried her about on my back, I washed her, I carried her and I washed her and Allah preserved her. Later there was some dispute about her, our husband said he would not agree to her being taken away, she must remain with me. He knew I loved her, he did not want my heart to be broken. Just before he died he called us and he said to Adama, 'I shall not get up again. Do not cause her sorrow on account of that daughter; Baba is to keep her.' I loved Hawwa, my husband gave her to me in that way.

Adama had seven children in our compound; the girls 'Yardada, Safia, A'i, Goma and the boys, Wada, Garba and Audi. I took 'Yardada (Hawwa) and Wada when they were weaned, they are mine; if they went into Adama's hut she would say 'Run away to your own hut!' and they would run off. Garba and Safia died. Goma died last year. Four of Adama's children are alive now. Ten days after our husband died she brought forth Audi; it is six years now since Malam Hasan died. Our husband died leaving Adama pregnant, and her first husband had done the same thing.

Wada, Adama's son, is living in the compound of Malam Tanimu now, the District Scribe; (5) when Malam Hasan died

Malam Idi was District Scribe, and he took Wada; then Malam
Idi was posted somewhere else and Malam Tanimu came as District
Scribe, so Wada stayed on in his compound. Malam Idi went away
with four retainers, (6) Adamu, Lawal, Umaru and Abba, he set
out with his four young men, but they all left him and returned
home. He had given them wives here in this town, and they went
off with their wives and left him. They said here he did them well,
with plenty of good food and oil, but when he left he gave them
work and no food, so they ran away. Lawal was the son of Danfangi
and my co-wife Adama; at first after his father's death he stayed
in a hamlet with some of his father's kinsmen; then he came to our
compound to be with his mother; then when our husband Hasan
died (Lawal was happy living with us) Lawal went to the District
Scribe. Then when the District Scribe gave him a wife and a home
of his own, he settled in his own compound and farmed.

Abba's father had been angry with him, when he was a young
man, so he became a client. Adamu came from Kano, he was
wandering about on his own, his people lived in Kiru; then the
District Scribe saw him and said he could come and fetch his
horse's grass for him (14)—that was that, the scribe had got a son.
Umaru was the son of Katsina people, he too was wandering about
on his own, a handsome boy with light skin, the scribe liked him
and persuaded him to become his client. Malam Idi had sons of
his own, but they were very young. I washed them myself when
they were born, I was called in. Three of Malam Idi's sons died
and there are four left now, but at that time he had no one old
enough to help with the work, so he looked out for retainers and
gave them gowns and whatever they needed. When he was transferred to another town he took his young men to Zaria for the
celebrations at the feast, and when it was over he asked them if
they were returning with him. They said 'No', they all refused and
came back here to Giwa. Apart from fetching the horse's grass his
retainers farmed for the District Scribe; and they went errands for
him wherever he sent them. Adamu is in the compound of the
district judge now, Lawal is here farming, Abba is doing metalwork
with the well-diggers, (15) they strengthen the wells and they use
a bellows to heat the metal. At the end of each month he is paid
thirty-five shillings. His wife lives here in his compound. Umaru
went off into the world.

MY HUSBAND MARRIES MY FRIEND ADAMA

More about my Adopted Children and about Boys and Girls

I adopted Adama's first child by Malam Hasan, 'Yardada (Hawwa); she and I carried 'Yardada on our backs and washed her and looked after her. When she had been suckled for two years I took her and she lived in my hut. She always ran away from her mother and came to me. I washed her, I put her antimony on her eyes, I bought her cloths with my own money, I bathed her and brought her up. If her mother came for her she would say 'Hide me, Baba, hide me, Baba, I'll swear at her!' Adama would come to the door of my hut and say 'Where is that daughter there?' I would say 'Oh, she isn't here'. 'Yardada was hiding behind me like this. She would start cursing her mother, 'Your mother! Your father!' Adama would say 'Ap. You're even hiding her while she abuses me!' We were joking. When 'Yardada's younger brother Wada was weaned, he also kept coming to my hut, he said he was going to live there. 'Yardada didn't approve, she said 'Get rid of Wada, Baba, so that he leaves us alone in our hut—don't let him eat up our porridge for us, don't let him get our millet-paste!' But he wouldn't go back to Adama's hut, he said 'You are my mother, this is where I shall live'. I had plenty of trouble at night, there they were, the two of them on my bed, fighting one another; one would lie behind me and one in front, then the one lying behind would want to come in front—'Baba, turn over, turn over!' They squashed me, I suffered a lot, indeed I did! Adama said Wada was to go back to her hut, but he refused. When he had sense we sent him away and he slept in his mother's hut. But if I went anywhere, he and 'Yardada followed me; our husband would say 'You're very patient, the children give you a lot of bother'.

Malam Hasan did not build a sleeping-hut for himself, he said he didn't like it; he came to our huts—in mine there were two beds, his and mine. If there are a lot of children one makes a separate hut for the husband, he eats his food there and then there is a different hut for the children. If it is like our compound was, with no husband's hut, when the children get sense—about three or four years old—then you turn them out and they go and sleep somewhere else when the husband comes to your hut. When they get older and go out playing in the evening, they go to the hut of some old lady and sleep, and in the morning they come home. The boys too sleep in the hut in the forecourt of someone's compound, they gather together and spend the night. Old people are the friends of children. Yelwa, my adopted daughter, and the girls with whom she is playing often come into my hut, they fill up the hut and sleep; they bring their boys with them. When the old woman is tired of them she drives them out, 'Run off to the boys' hut, run off to the boys' hut!' Then they all go off to the hut at the front of some compound, the boys and girls all go and they light a lamp, they talk and tell stories and laugh. When the girls get older, some of them become pregnant, but not many; they laugh and joke but they don't lie together a great deal. (7) Also, when they are thirteen or fourteen years old you marry them at once and they get a husband—some of them conceive after five months, some of them wait five years and are not pregnant. If the girl has been with men, her husband will be angry when he marries her; some will drive her out, some will put up with it. If she should become pregnant before she is married her lover, if he is a good man, will say he wishes to marry her. There is a feast and everyone rejoices. If it is not like that, she will say 'It is his' and he will say 'No', some men even run away and go out into the world. Then the girl's family marry her off quickly. If her husband sees that she is pregnant he may go to the judge and say the child is not his; then there is quarrelling and arguing, sometimes he will divorce the girl, sometimes he will stay with her. If he divorces her her family wail. Some girls like that run away and live on their own. Some even kill the child, they say they don't want it, but some put their own thing on their back, they wash their child and carry him about so that he shall be strong. There was a girl in our town who had a child before she was married, she said 'It belongs to so-and-so', and he said it was not his. When the child grew up she was lovely, then the man said it was his, he married the mother and accepted his own child. 'A child born before the beginning' we call it, a child born before his mother is married, that is a bastard. There were not many in Old Giwa, and I have only heard of three since we came here to New Giwa six years ago —they were people from the hamlets, not living in the town. If that happens the *kawaye* of the girl make songs and the girl feels very ashamed, she drinks medicine.

What have you been eating, you're swelling up like an okra!
Perhaps it's sweet potatoes you've been eating.

MY HUSBAND MARRIES MY FRIEND ADAMA

Allah preserve us till harvest
And let us see how the okra swells up! (8)

After nine months, indeed she'll bring it forth, you'll see the okra
emerge! They sing songs at her everywhere—where's the pleasure
of it? The parents of girls forbid them to go with young men, but
some do it. There was a girl called Karimatu, she used to go into
the sleeping-hut of a certain man who had one wife carrying her
child on her back. (9) Karimatu went in to him, she kept going,
and she became pregnant. Tsohuwa, from Fatika, had adopted her,
the girl was from Fatika too; they lived in the same compound as
the man, in a different section. When they took the man before the
judge the judge said he was to pay the man to whom she was
betrothed; he paid up, and she was married. Three months later
she had a child, a boy.

Those sort of girls sleep in an old woman's hut, then when the
old woman is asleep they slip out quietly, no one knows. A clever
one may go off and pay money and get a charm, then she goes to
ruin. If they get pregnant some of them drink henna, they vomit
and they get diarrhœa and they usually miscarry. If they take
indigo, they get very ill indeed. Some tie a kolanut round their
waist so that they can sleep with a man and not become pregnant.
Then there is writing-medicine, the ink of a text; if a *malam* wants
money, then won't he give it to you? Of course he will. But not all
malams do it. Some old women don't care, they say the girls can
go and do what they like, they let them go and sleep with the
young men. Others scold the girls. But if you have adopted a girl
you will not permit it.

An Adoption Dispute

When Adama had Wada they offered him to Hasana but she
wouldn't accept him, she wanted a girl. Then when A'i was born
our husband said she was to be given to Hasana; Adama refused,
she said the girl would die. She and Hasana fought and struggled,
I separated them. Nine months after she had weaned A'i, Hasana
came but Adama refused to give her A'i until she had borne Goma.
Hasana was carrying out her Iddah in their village, Ma'aji; our
husband sent for her, then when she came he took A'i and gave her
to Hasana outside the compound, then he escorted Hasana home.

When Hasana came to visit us Adama swore at her and abused her. Hasan said to Adama 'You are not going to have the child while I am alive'. They quarrelled and quarrelled until Hasana got up in a huff and went off. Malam Hasan knew what she was like, but look at her, with no children; she wanted a child and he couldn't refuse her. (10) He had many children himself. She and Adama were both crying with rage, Adama said 'Black woman with a black nature, may Allah be niggardly to you!' Goma remained with her mother Adama, she died last year when she was nine years old. Dije, Audi—she is still here with her mother.

What Happened to my Adopted Children

I have brought up many children; at our home in Zarewa I looked after my younger brother Tanko and my younger sister Maimuna, I used to carry them about on my back when I was a little girl, but I didn't arrange their marriages for them. The three children I had in Malam Maigari's compound returned to their parents before it was time to marry them, but I arranged Usuman's marriage. Sadau I married off, too. Here in Old Giwa I had Ali, the son of my younger brother Danbaba—Danbaba and I were true cross-cousins, his mother and my father had the same mother and father, he was Hawwa's son. When I had weaned him I had him for two years, then he died. After him I was given Ali, the son of Shera my younger brother by the woman whom you met in the Prison Warder's compound the day you were there—she left my brother Shera and married the present warder, Fagaci's younger brother. She is a friend of mine, that is why I took you to their compound so that you could meet her. Shera and I are children of brothers, he is Malam Shehu's son, of grandmother Anja's kin. There were several of her kinsfolk living at Old Giwa. I didn't keep Ali for long, I just weaned him and after two weeks I took him back to their compound. But Sadau and Yelwa I kept until I married them off. I married 'Yardada in Sarkin Yelwa's compound, she has been there for four years now and last year she had a child. Yelwa who is with me now is the daughter of Kadiri and Lauretu. I was the midwife when she was born, I washed her and looked after her, then when she was weaned I adopted her. When Hasana enticed Lauretu away from my brother's compound I kept Yelwa.

MY HUSBAND MARRIES MY FRIEND ADAMA

The Warder's Work

I had been married to Malam Hasan, Yarin Giwa, for about ten years when a boy was sent by a woman kolanut seller to buy £7-worth of kolanuts at Maska. He bought them, then he sold them at Funtua and ran away with the money. For a year she didn't see him. Then she heard someone had seen him at Funtua. From there he went to Kaya, and at that time the woman trader was at Kaya too. A policeman caught him, and he was brought to the prison at Giwa, followed by six women. He was taken before the judge and with great difficulty they extracted twenty shillings from him; he swore on the Koran that he had only taken £1, not £7. The judge dismissed them and he went home. (11) The following Monday seven men returned with him, raving mad—he had sworn to a lie. He was biting people and hitting them, and singing a song,

> I am a wanderer,
> I have broken trust, I ate it,
> I am a wanderer.

Then he would start cursing people. He was there in our gaol for fourteen days, when Malam Hasan gave him his porridge he would attack him and try to hurt him. He went on and on, he beat on the door, finally he got out. We fled. Malam Hasan was in the entrance-hut of Fagaci's house, when he spied him outside he rose up, he beat him and said 'Go back to your hut!' He beat him and beat him, then he got him back to his hut and they secured him with leg irons. Seven days later my younger sister had twin children; before they were born the madman was saying to me, 'You, see the two children in that compound over there, see the two children there in your sister's house, grandmother, grandmother'. Then he abused me and he said 'You'll never have any children, see your younger sister over there, she's brought forth two children'. We knew nothing about it then. He was fettered hand and foot but he snapped the irons and broke down the door and got out. Malam came and said 'Go back to your hut'. He closed the door on him. I went over to my sister's compound and said to her 'The madman in our house says you have brought forth twins'. She was just sitting there, nothing had happened. We both had a good laugh. After I had gone back to my compound and before I

181

had finished making the porridge, she had brought forth twins! He was abusing me, he kept saying to me 'Grandmother, you won't have any children, you'll never bear children—get over there to the children!' When the twins were born I went over there, I often went to her compound. On the naming-day I made maize porridge for the feast. That day Fagaci sent Malam Hasan out on some official business; some Bornu people going from Zaria to Funtua with their camels had had a fight and killed a man; Fagaci said 'Warriors, go, bring me back that man!' They pursued them and they caught them some way away; the two camels were not theirs, they were violent robbers who had killed the owner of the camels and taken his beasts. Malam Hasan left us with the madman in the compound; he kept on at me, 'Grandmother, give me some porridge!' I got a boy to push the porridge in to him and shut the door quickly. He called out 'Grandmother, your porridge is delicious'. Then we went to the naming feast. I refused to go back to our compound that night, I slept in my sister's home. In the night the madman got out and came to the front of the compound: 'Come and give me some of your porridge, Grandmother, come and give me my porridge!' I wouldn't go back. At dawn Malam returned and drove him back to the prison. Then he came to my sister's compound and fetched me home. After he had been with us fourteen days he was taken by four men to the Asylum in Zaria. When they reached the gate of Zaria City he said, 'Leave me to say my prayers. In thirty days I shall die.' That was that, thirty days later he died. He used to keep saying 'I broke trust, I broke it. I broke faith. I stole seven pounds, I only gave you one pound, I stole six pounds. I broke trust, then I lied.' When he was about to swear on the Koran the judge said to him, 'Did you take one pound or seven?' He answered 'One pound'. The judge said 'Tell the truth, or you will die or go mad'. Then he swore to one pound. He swore falsely, that is what caused him to go mad. If he had said 'Yes, I did take seven pounds. I will try and pay it back slowly', that would have been all right, nothing would have happened. That is the madness of breaking faith, or perjury.

Malam Hasan had his compound and three farms at Old Giwa; he farmed grain, cotton and groundnuts. We grew millet and ate, we grew guineacorn and ate it—in all the years I lived with him we never bought grain. He farmed and he performed his official duties as Yari, warder of the district gaol. He worked for Fagaci. 'Yari, you are to go to such-and-such a place . . .' He did not pay tax. When we had a prisoner, Fagaci would send his food from his own compound. If a prisoner stayed for several months, money for his food was sent from Zaria; then Fagaci would say to Malam Hasan, 'Go and buy the ingredients for stew', and he would give him ten or twelve shillings. (12) If prisoners were in the gaol for three months, it was quite a lot of money at a penny a day each, and the best white guineacorn costing only a halfpenny a *mudu* while the heavy red kind was three-tenths of a penny. When the money had mounted up, Fagaci Ahmadu would say 'Take it, Yari, buy yourself salt and locust-bean cakes or a gown'. Fagaci Ahmadu was generous. Sometimes we would have ten prisoners, sometimes twenty, sometimes five. If there had been a fight and the Bush Fulani had been using their staves on a farm, our prison would be full. Bush Fulani were terrified of being imprisoned. One day they caught a whole lot, men and women, and we couldn't get to sleep for their wailing. They refused to eat, they refused to drink, irons had been put on their arms and legs and they were wailing. In the morning the prisoners would be taken out to sweep the open space outside the entrance of Fagaci's compound; some of them swept it while others hoed it until it was absolutely tidy. The Bush Fulani would rather pay a great deal of money than be imprisoned or taken to Zaria—that was like death to them. All their kinsfolk would gather, the Fulani in the prison would not want to be seen, then when they were brought outside to sweep up they would start their wailing. (13)

Then there were thieves; they were not beaten, except when they refused to confess. If they would not confess to the judge for three days, then they were whipped in the prison. Then if they kept on telling the judge that they were not guilty, the judge would say 'Wash his eyes for him, Yari, wash his eyes for him'. Then Yari would beat them there, in the judge's court, until they confessed— 'May Allah forgive you, Malam, it was I'. The judge sat on his chair like this, waiting. Malam Hasan beat them until they confessed. For instance, if you caught a man and you were certain he was the thief, but he wasn't: first Yari would give him a hiding, he would say 'Yari, it isn't me, spare my life, Yari, it was not me!' When Yari took him before the judge, if he still said it was not him the judge would say 'Wash his eyes for him, Yari, improve his character'. Then if they beat him and he still said it was not he, the judge would say he was to swear on the Koran; then if he swore, that was that, you could be certain he was not the thief.

There was a certain Fulani who had been stealing in seven towns, he was called 'Aeroplane'. He swallowed charms sewn up in leather covers, they were there inside him; if he was caught he said that he wanted water, if he was given water to drink, that was that—he vanished, you looked for him but you couldn't see him. He had vanished. Another time he would say he wanted tobacco, if you gave him tobacco he waved his hand like this, and became a crow. (14) At last they caught him, four men held him so that he shouldn't vanish or become a crow. If he felt like it he would turn into water, if he saw fit he would turn into a crow. They brought him to Fagaci's compound, with the goods he had stolen from seven towns—you should have seen the clothes! They opened up his loads, everyone was staring and staring. They said, 'Aeroplane, where did you get these things?' He said 'They are the goods from twenty towns'. All the people were summoned to inspect his goods and claim their possessions; everyone said 'Aeroplane has been caught', they said 'Praise be to Allah!' He used to go into a hut in the daytime, nobody could see him. There were people from Iyatawa, Fatika, Turawa—all the surrounding towns. He said 'You won't see me, I shall go into a hut like water, I shall go into a hut like milk, I shall go into a hut like a rat—you won't see me'. He was fourteen days in our compound, then they took him to Zaria, he was sentenced to a year in prison because he didn't deny the charges. If someone came and said that a thing was his, Aeroplane would say 'No, I didn't take it from your town—that belongs to the people of Fatika'. When he had been in our house for twelve days, everyone had claimed back his possessions, he was let out of the prison hut. He sat down, he sang and we all laughed; he was of a pleasant disposition apart from the stealing.

> *Aeroplane going on a long journey,*
> *If he goes far, it's till next year—I'll return!*

If you caught him the charm was finished, it would not help him. Before you had caught him the charm was effective; if he was given water and he didn't drink it, he vanished. When he was caught they wouldn't give him any water that day. Our husband Yari Malam Hasan destroyed the power of the charms; he took a winnowing-basket, a broom and some water; he fanned the broom and the water with the basket, then the charm Aeroplane had swallowed was finished, it was no good. That was what he did to thieves who had swallowed charms. Then they could only sit in the mud-roofed gaol in our compound, that was all. When they took Aeroplane to Zaria they convicted him, but because he didn't argue they only gave him a year. Aeroplane—aye, he made us laugh!

Another Kind of Madness

Our husband worked as prison warder for Fagaci Ahmadu in Old Giwa for about twenty years. When I first used to come to Giwa I remember Madaki Yero, the son of Aliyu, king of Zaria, ruled Giwa district. People liked him, he was generous, but then they took away his father Aliyu, the Christians were angry with him because he committed some fault against them, and we heard that they had taken him to farm tobacco in a town called Yankwa, they said it was beyond the water, a long way away; we call him 'the *Sarki* who went to Yankwa, Aliyu who went to Yankwa'. I was still living in Malam Maigari's compound when we heard that they had seized the King of Zaria, and later we heard that he had died. When he heard about this, after a little while the Madaki began to behave as if he were mad; he would talk to himself, he would sit like this and keep on saying, 'My father, Sarki Aliyu . . .' He kept on talking, he was afraid, and he was unhappy because he couldn't see his father. A little later he went mad, he went off into the bush. Then he was removed from the position. (15) He went to another town, and he died there. When he heard that they had dismissed his father, and he did not see him because they had taken him away, he was miserable, his life was ruined, until he went mad. If you are there and your father is a king you feel good; then they take him away, and where is your pleasure? If they had left him in his own country it would have been all right, but they took him far away to some strange place.

Fagaci Ahmadu and his Household

Then when I came to live in Old Giwa I found that Aminu's father, Fagaci Ahmadu, had been Fagaci for a year. (16) When I first came he was tall and slim like Aminu; then he ate and ate until he was full, and he became an enormous man—fatter than our judge is. He farmed, his farms lay near the Gangara road. His retainers ate up the food. There was a granary in his compound as large as this hut, porridge was made in the morning from twenty *mudu* of grain and in the evening from twenty *mudu* if there were not too many visitors; if there were many guests, thirty *mudu* of grain would be used. (17) Ten *mudu* would be brought to us, and we would grind the flour to help them. They would bring fifteen bowls of porridge out to Fagaci's entrance-hut, some would be taken to the compounds where guests were lodged, and the retainers at the door of his compound would eat the rest. Inside the compound his four wives would prepare food separately for his household, while the wives of his retainers cooked theirs separately. Fagaci had two concubines, (18) Kande and Ramatu, and his wives were called Jika, Kumbu, Laminde and Gude. His head wife, Jika, he had married as a maiden when he was a young man, she had remained with him a long time. When Aminu's mother, a concubine, died twenty days after Aminu was born, Jika suckled him, thus she is Aminu's mother; she is still alive now, in Zaria City. Kumbu also was with Fagaci a long time. Fagaci Ahmadu married two girls in Zaria, then he divorced them; then he took a daughter of the Fatika people, she bore him a daughter, then he divorced her; he took a daughter of the Kakangi people and he divorced her. When he died he left four wives to mourn him.

When Fagaci went on tour through his District (19) he used to take his wife Gude with him. She would go on horseback, she wore long full trousers which cost a hundred shillings, a long woman's blouse, a cloth, a head-kerchief, and then over it all a nobleman's mantle with a hood. She would go along like this, peeping out— she was handsome. The wives of his retainers walked in front of her and behind her. After they left Giwa they would sleep two nights at Gangara; two nights at Kaya, two nights at Fatika; then they went round by Iyatawa, Murai, Galadimawa, Kakangi, Bajimi, Tsibiri, Mutumbarkai, Garinyashi, Shika, and so by Ma'aji and Guga station and home. That was how Fagaci went on tour, with his wife on a mare. There would be the pipe-players and drummers in front—Magajin Busa and Dangaladiman Busa and Sarkin Makada and the rest of them, together with some who have died now; (20) then the attendants, Galadiman Zagi, Dangaladiman Zagi, Madakin Zagi, Sarkin Zagi and Lando; two in front and one on each side of his horse, when Fagaci was going to mount his horse he would lean on the shoulder of one of them, when he was going to dismount he would lean on him. The grooms and the retainers on foot followed behind, and lastly the wives and the loads. Gude went on ahead with her women, she went to their resting-place and settled down, she and the *jakadiya* and the women who cooked the food. Fagaci could not go with her, she was his wife. (21) She went ahead on her mare, a beautiful mare beautifully caparisoned. She rode in her fine trousers and blouse and cloth and the golden-yellow mantle with silver tassels. Fagaci wouldn't leave her at home—desire, desire, desire. She remained with him for sixteen years, she had no children, then she committed adultery with Haba. Now she is married at Funtua, she is still beautiful. Fagaci had four wives and his concubines, but it was only Gude he thought of.

The Story of Fagaci Ahmadu

Fagaci Ahmadu's father was Malam Baba, Magtakardan Kano, the King of Kano's scribe. Something angered him in Kano and he came back to Zaria. Ahmadu was at school in Kano, (22) and one day he came home to Zaria to see his father. At that time the King of Zaria had collected a great many *malams* but they failed to understand the calculations of the Zaria taxes; they all tried and tried, they failed; the business was all tied up in knots—then they would argue. When the king heard that the son of the Magatakardan Kano had come, and that he had attended your sort of school in Kano, he sent for him.

'You, boy.'

'May Allah give you the victory, may your life be prolonged.'

'Approach me, boy.'

'Allah grant the king long life.'

'Look at this money, it is all muddled up. I hear you have learnt the Christians' arithmetic. Come and figure out the wealth of Zaria for us.'

Then they spread mats on the floor for Ahmadu and he sat down with the books, all at once he cleared it up, he calculated it, he said 'It is thus, it is thus and thus'. They gave him the Treasurer's compound, they put him in charge of the Treasury, he was appointed Ma'ajin Zazzau. After that he held another office which I have forgotten. The King of Kano sent messengers, he sent messengers to Malam Baba, but Malam Baba was annoyed with Kano and he said he was not going back. There was Ahmadu, too, with the wealth of learning. Then when they sent him to rule Giwa he farmed a good deal, he filled up his granaries. I was twenty-seven years in Malam Hasan's hand, or rather I married him twenty-seven years ago; this Fagaci has been here seven years; that is, we were twenty years with Fagaci Ahmadu. (23)

Old Giwa and its Market

Soon after Fagaci Ahmadu came to Giwa they sent letters and said he was to choose a new place for the town. He assembled the *malams* and they discussed the matter, that was all; nothing was done about it. They went on like that, Fagaci said 'Very well'. It was just for the sake of change—there was no reason why we should leave—no illness, nothing. (24) There were twenty silk-cotton trees, thirty baobab-trees, mangoes *tim*, ficus-trees, they were all there; there was masses of guineacorn, it was very fine farmland. It was a big town, Old Yelwa was only a small town but Old Giwa was very broad. They simply wanted to move us. But water was difficult, there was a stream near the town but it had no water in it—the animals drank thirst, the people drank thirst, water was very hard to get. Aye, here we have no trouble in getting water, they have certainly helped us. In Old Giwa there were wells everywhere, in the rains there would be water, then at this season (January) there would be none. We women used to go to a stream away to the east of Giwa, about this time in the morning we would return—it must have been as far as from here to Old Yelwa. When we came here to New Giwa everyone rejoiced at the water. Also we are farming here now, there is bush. Over at Old Giwa there was health, there was farming—but there was no water.

There was also no market at Old Giwa. The market refused to take; (25) the *bori* adepts danced for fourteen days, and it looked as though the market might settle, but since there was no water it did not take. *Bori*-dancers and drummers and players on stringed instruments were assembled, they all worked. In the middle of the day they rested, then at Azahar (2.30) they went to the front of Fagaci's compound, the *bori*-dancers leapt up and fell down again. When it was decided to try to build up the market, Fagaci sent over near Danmahawaye to call some powerful *bori*-dancers, the ones who have medicine for madness. Fagaci sent for them because the market was a failure. In the Madaki's time the market at Old Giwa used to be full, and when we came it was going well, but after the Madaki died it refused to go. 'They' (26) said they were to be given a black bull and black goats and black cloth, but Fagaci would not give them their things. After that they were here, they went on living here, but the market wouldn't go. They didn't go anywhere else, they were here, they just put a stop to the market. All the villagers picked up their produce and set out for Gangara or Dundubus or Anguwan Shehu, and we heard nothing at Old Giwa, no drumming, nothing, just silence. Both the *malams* and the *bori*-dancers were always going to Fagaci and saying 'This is what you should do if the market is to do well', and he always replied, 'Yes, *quite* so', but he never did anything. Now this present one, when they told him to give a white cloth and four bowls of milk, he gave them; and you see the market is here at New Giwa. (27)

When Fagaci Ahmadu sent for the *bori*-dancers to Old Giwa, they worked in the day at this time (11.30) then they rested, then at Azahar (2.30) they started again. Then at La'asar (5.30) they rested, then they made *bori* again; then they ate their evening food, and after that they were at it until the middle of the night. Every day it was the same, no other work was done. The girls' drummer would be playing in one place, and the fiddlers (28) and *bori*-drummers would be in the market or at the front of Fagaci's compound. People gave them gifts of money, kolanuts, clothes. Everyone who came gave them gifts, each person would give something to the spirit he liked best. That is how you build a market, you establish a market; you collect all the spirits and you attend to their affairs, then the market settles. But that market at Old Giwa didn't settle down, it came for the *bori*, there were people there like a whole country, but when the *bori*-dancers left, the market left too.

They tried and they tried to get Old Giwa moved, but Fagaci Ahmadu did nothing. Then when this Fagaci came it was arranged, the place was chosen and we were told to make ready. The new town was to be built near the place where Abdulkarim, the King of Zaria, had died, the place where he foretold that one day there would be many people. (29) The people did not wish to come here but they were afraid (to refuse). When they were assembled and asked, they said they agreed. But we didn't want it. Now you see we find the place pleasant, there is plenty of water, no sickness, and farmland. At Old Giwa there was guineaworm—oh dear, oh dear. There was a great deal of guineaworm, and it was a trouble to get water.

CHAPTER XIII

FORMAL FRIENDSHIPS

I have two *kawaye* here at Giwa, you remember there were five of us at Zarewa when we were young girls. (1) These are different. One woman says to the other 'My desire' and the other answers 'Good faith'. I have had my *kawa* 'Yargoggo, the wife of Tanko, for about ten years, Laraba has been my *kawa* for fifteen years; we have exchanged gifts together. Laraba sent a message to say she liked me, then I bought gifts of friendship and sent them to her—a bottle of perfume, twenty kolanuts, and powder. When I had been living in Giwa for about four years she sent the wife of her younger brother, who came to our compound and said 'I am to tell you that Laraba likes you'. I said 'Yes, I like her'. I bought gifts of liking, I gave them to my co-wife Adama to take to Laraba. On the Friday Laraba came. I spread mats, I spread more mats on the floor of my hut, we greeted one another, we rejoiced and gave thanks, a friendship had been made. Laraba divided the kolanuts of friendship among the people of her compound, and she sent some to a great many other compounds to the men and women of her kin and anyone who knew us; you distribute the kolanuts of friendship and everyone who receives one says 'May Allah increase friendship and agreement!' We were there thus until seven days before the feast when Laraba bought two chickens, a calabash full of rice, salt, onions, locust-bean cakes, a calabash of kolanuts, a bottle of oil—she sent it all to me so that I should eat good food. The day before the feast I got about four shillings, and I sent her money for hairdressing so that she could buy some henna and stain her arms and legs and have her hairdresser to do her hair. The following festival she bought a young she-goat and chickens and two calabashes of kolanuts, salt, locust-bean cakes, and oil, and sent it all to me. Then her co-wife had a child, so I bought a big

191

cloth, I put £1 with it and a huge bowl full of guineacorn; the cloth was for her to tie her co-wife's child on her back, the guineacorn so that she could make gruel, and the money so that she could pay the barber-doctor. That is, I completed the ceremony—there would be no further gifts to cement the friendship, it was made and thenceforth we would exchange ceremonial gifts with one another, if she had a ceremony in her compound or among her kinsfolk I would take her a little florin, if I had a ceremony she would bring me four shillings, next time she had one I would take her eight shillings—ceremony after ceremony, at each one you do that. When the money reaches ten or twelve shillings we divide; if I am due to give her twelve shillings and we are going to divide, I bring the twelve shillings and give it to her, she keeps six shillings and returns six to me, then I take out threepence and give it to her in addition, I say 'We will start again'. Next time one of us has a ceremony we start again at sixpence. We consult one another and discuss our affairs, her daughter is my daughter, her son is my son.

Then I have an adopted younger brother, I have adopted Shera my kinsman as my younger brother. (2) I gave him thirty kolanuts. Once when I came over to Giwa from Zarewa to visit my father, Shera was a little boy who couldn't talk properly. I said 'Goodness, who is that ugly boy, haven't they washed him properly?' He ran away to his mother and said 'Come and wash me, there is a visitor at the house of the Father-of-goats, we must go and see her, please put antimony on my eyes'. (3) Then he dragged her round to Malam Tsoho's compound, he said 'Malam, malam, where is your visitor?' He replied 'She is there in Ramatu's hut'. (3) Then he went to her hut, pulling his mother along and when she saw me she said 'Oh, it's you! Welcome, welcome—welcome to Baba! Listen, this child has been plaguing me, he said some stranger said he hadn't been washed, then he made me draw water and wash him and put on his antimony, then he brought me here.' Then Shera went to Malam Tsoho, the children called him Father-of-the-Goat. They were very fond of him, they used to come and eat their food with him—his own grandchildren and the other children in the town. They would say 'Babantakwiya, give us a goat and we'll kill it and eat it!' He would say 'Right, choose the one you want'. Then they would choose a huge one and he would say 'Where's the knife?' Then they wouldn't be able to find a knife, or if they found one he would seize it and hide it, and you would hear them crying, 'Babantakwiya has taken away our knife!' One day the goat butted one of them, he went crying to Malam Tsoho and Father went and slapped the goat, then they all chanted 'Babantakwiya has revenged us!' One day when a goat had been killed and distributed as alms Shera came, 'Babantakwiya, Babantakwiya, they've killed a goat and only given me a tiny little bone like this!' Then he went to the hut of Father's wife Ramatu and she gave him his share, then when he wanted a lot more she drove him out—off he ran to Father's hut, 'Babantakwiya, hide me in your hut, sit by the door and if they come in you beat them'. So Father hid him.

Our father liked good food; he reared goats at that time, he was getting too old to farm, and he sold his goats to the butchers, they paid him for them and gave him the head, which he would give to his wife to cook. Then Shera would come along, 'Look at Babantakwiya eating. Look at Ramatu eating. Look at Kadiri eating. And they've only given me a few bones. Give me some meat!' Then the children would come singing 'Babantakwiya who has *fura* and meat, Babantakwiya the owner of *fura* and meat!' then he would call 'Ramatu!' she would answer 'Yes?' and he would say 'Buy some sour milk and mix me some millet-paste'. Then the children, there were usually five or six of them, would say 'What's in that calabash?' He used to put his millet-balls and his meat in calabashes and hang them up on the wall out of reach. Then he would reach down one of them and give them millet-paste to eat until they were full.

When I came from Zarewa to Father's compound I used to see Shera, I noticed he was sensible. Then he grew up, by the time I came to marry Malam Hasan he was a young man. Whenever he came back from Zaria he brought me kolanuts and perfume and soap. Then he saw a girl whom he desired; he and his friends used to come to our compound, Muhammadu and Shera, Danbaba and Sha'ibu, they would come in the evenings and spend the time talking and telling stories with the young girls. Then he told me he wanted to marry Lami, and he gave me money to take to her mother. Her mother told me, 'Indeed, I can't accept it; you see the chief wants her. You know, if a chief wants a commoner and he is courting her—well, that boy will have to leave it.' When that one failed he went to Zaria and saw a girl in the compound of one of the king's policemen, (4) he came back and told me he wanted

her, she was a good discreet girl. I said 'But it's a long way away—
will they give her to you?' He used to go into Zaria to buy cloth
and other things to sell here. After three months, their work brought
them here to our town, the girl and her mother and her mother's
husband Dogari—he wasn't her father, her father had gone out
into the world and her mother had re-married and taken the children with her. When they came Shera gave her gifts, he gave the
girl hers and I took the money of seeking to her parents. Shera's
father was dead, but his mother was alive. I presided over the
marriage. Ever since he had first begun coming to spend the evenings in my hut, he had been my adopted younger brother; whenever
he went to Zaria he brought me soap and perfume. The four young
men used to come, with lots of girls from our ward, and they would
fill up the hut; each one chose his own girl. We lit the lamp, we
talked about the world and we told stories, then when they had
talked their fill and were tired the boys went off to their compound
and the girls slept in my hut; if my husband came in they went to
my co-wife's hut. Some girls went and spent the night with the
young men, in the morning they would go back to their own
homes. (5) They used to come from time to time, then one day I
bought thirty kolanuts and I gave them to Shera with some money,
I told him to go to the dancing and get the drummer to drum to the
girl he liked best. He puts his gift down for her, the praise-singer
calls out, 'So-and-so has put down a shilling for you'. Then when
Shera farmed and harvested a huge bundle, he would bring it to
me. At the feast I would give him money, about a shilling, to give
to the girls, and he would bring me meat.

For the ceremony of 'setting the day' for Shera's marriage, we
took to the bride's compound eight shillings and grain, salt, eight
mats, rice, kolanuts, flour and sugar. There was also a shilling for
the grandparents, with stew-ingredients. It took ten people to
carry the gifts, we took them to her parents' compound. They
spread mats for me to sit on. Everyone took their own share, then
the bride's *kawa* and her 'slave', the younger sister of the bridegroom, went and fetched the drummers and they all danced. Meanwhile they spread mats for me in the shade at the centre of the
compound and the bride's father's younger sister and her mother's
younger sister came to 'despise the gifts'. They looked at them and
said 'Look at those small gifts, that isn't much—we won't accept
it!' We were all laughing, and they went on, 'Take up your loads

and go away, we shan't give you our daughter'. At last they were persuaded, but they accepted them unwillingly. Then the younger sisters of the bride's father and mother, they have no shame, they pronounce judgment, they say 'You must bring five cloths and a blouse and a head-cloth, and if you don't bring them we will not give you our daughter!' They are the grasping ones, quite shameless—the girl's parents only look on, everyone is laughing and shrilling and jeering, 'a-hai-ye!' They look at the cloth and say it is not strong. They find fault with the gifts and reject them. Later the mother's younger sister will act as *mawankiya*. The bride's mother's younger sister and her father's younger sister can joke together, they do not have to avoid one another.

Then one feast Shera bought me a huge cloth, he sent his wife to bring it to me; I bought a fine gown and sent it to him. Aye, we've been friends a long time—is it twenty years? A long time. He has three wives; three have left him, now he has three here. They all had children, they left the children and separated from him; he has ten children alive now, and some have died. After his first marriage I was not responsible for any other of his marriages. That is an 'adopted younger brother', a *kanen rana*. His elder brother Malam Akilu is Kadiri's *kanen rana*. I call Shera Danmori, (6) the son of enjoyment, and he calls me Hanazullumi, Prevent-worry. Nothing in the world can worry him, he sees me and he likes me. We enjoy things, we are satisfied, I stop him from worrying. Even now when he has a beard, if some matter needing discussion arises, he comes and we discuss it together. I go to his entrance-hut, he bows down—I am like his mother—then I sit in the entrance-hut, or we go inside the compound and we talk. If I go into the compound his wives kneel down to greet me, they call me *Yayan rana* or *Yaya*, because I am like their husband's elder sister, it is not really like a mother-in-law. There is real relationship by marriage between me and Gwamma, my younger brother's wife.

Lami is my 'adopted younger sister', *Kanwar rana*, I call her Katifa. I began to like her here in Giwa when I was in Malam Hasan's compound. When I came to Giwa to Malam Hasan's house, her family lived next door. Once when I went to Zarewa for a month she arranged with someone to come and whitewash my hut, so that it looked very nice. When I returned and saw it, I bought a very nice cloth, a big one costing ten shillings, and soap and perfume, with ten shillings in money. She gave the money to the women and children who had helped to whitewash the hut, and the cloth and the soap, the perfume and the henna were hers. She sent me kolanuts of liking, 'kola to sweep the path'—the path of friendship—she sent thirty kolanuts and some soap and a small mat. Her co-wife brought them. She said 'Here are kolanuts of liking, kola to sweep the path, kola to spread the news'. Everyone saw that we liked one another. I divided the kolas amongst the people of the compound, my kinsfolk and friends, so that they should all see. Then at the feast she sent me rice, honey, two chickens, a bottle of oil, some salt and some locust-bean cakes, she sent it all to me. The day before the feast I sent her ten shillings for dressing her hair. On the day of the feast she came to greet me. I arranged the mats on the floor, I got very beautiful cloth and put it for her to sit on and one for her co-wife. My co-wife Adama fanned them as they sat there. When she had fanned them suffici- ently I told her to leave them thus to rest. Then I took out three- pence and gave it to Adama for fanning them. Then she and her co-wife covered their heads, they bent low and greeted me, they did not say anything. I said 'Flatterers, flatterers', they then rose up and sat down again. They don't say anything at all from the time they come in, and they do not stand up straight inside your hut, they kneel down. I gave Adama, who escorted them home, perfume, ten kolanuts and a shilling, which she gave to them.

For five months your adopted younger sister *kanwar rana* feels shy, if she sees you she kneels to greet you and says nothing, you say 'Flatterer, flatterer!' Every Friday she came to greet me, her elder sister, her *Yaya*. (7) A *Yaya* does not go to the compound of her *kanwar rana* except to attend a feast or a naming-ceremony. (8) Every Friday when she comes you must give her things—perfume, kolanuts, a shilling and henna. She divides it with the woman who escorts her. If you have a ceremony she will bring you gifts, but apart from that the *kanwa* does not bring gifts to you. If however you have a ceremony, your *kanwa* goes to a lot of trouble; she must bring two calabashes of kolanuts, oil, chicken, a large bowl of rice and one of guineacorn flour. At her *yaya's* feast she sits apart, the *yaya's kawaye* are sitting beside her, the *kanwa* kneels down before them like this. She is her *yaya's* servant. She fans the *kawaye* and they give her threepence or sixpence. (9) Then the *kawaye* say 'We are sitting here idly—bring the calabash drummers!'

Then one takes off her blouse and gives it to the drummer, one takes off her cloth and gives it. When one of Adama's children was born my hut was full, my *kawaye* were giving the drummers cloth and money; I took off my blouse, I took off my cloth, I gave them money, until the drummer said 'Baba is worth a lot more than her *kawaye*, they ought to call her *Yaya*'. The drummer sang a song about it, she made my friends angry—*kawaye* are equals, they do not call one another *yaya*. Then one got up and went out, she was angry; I followed her and brought her back and she calmed down. I couldn't stop the drummers—can you stop praise-singers? The other *kawaye* knew it was only joking. I said 'I haven't sent anyone away, you calabash-drummers, continue to drum, when you are tired you keep on drumming until the day dawns'. The drummer was shouting 'By Allah, you women, you must call Baba *Yaya*, by the Name of Allah she is worth a lot more than you are!' They said 'No she is not, you shameless drummer'. My *kanwa* did not stand up, a *kanwa* remains on her knees; the wife of Shera, my *kanen rana*, was there with Katifa my own *kanwa*, they sat together and waited on my *kawaye*. Everyone comes to a ceremony like this bringing a lamp; you put kolanuts and tobacco-flowers and perfume in front of each one—the kolanuts are those which your *kanwa* brought 'for the *kawaye* to eat'.

After five months the shame ceases and your *kanwa* comes to see you and may talk, there is friendship between you. You would not eat food in her compound, though; if she has a ceremony she sends food to you in your own compound; she sends her *yaya* cooked rice, cooked meat, chicken, honey, millet-balls and small cakes of flour. The *yaya* divides it up among the people of her compound and she eats her own share, then she gets up and washes her hands and goes to her *kanwa's* hut, where she finds they have spread mats and cloths, she sits down. There are cigarettes, there is chewing-tobacco, there are kolanuts and tobacco-flowers and perfume and lamps. Her *kanwa* has provided it all. I know one woman who has six *yayas*, and she does this for all of them, but most people do not have as many as that. If I need something done like pounding or grinding corn, then I send it to my *kanwa* and she does it for me; that is because of respect, I don't pay her. If I see that there is something she wants, I get it and give it to her. She is not shy or ashamed after the first five months, but if I have a ceremony the shame returns and she acts as my servant. Your own younger sister, in the family, does not do all this—only your *kanwar rana*, your adopted one.

The *yaya* first sends 'gifts of liking' to a younger woman whom she wishes as her *kanwa*, but if the younger one wants to have her as a *yaya* she can say 'I should like to be *kanwa* to so-and-so', and then the elder woman will hear about it.

I have two *kawaye* here in Giwa now, and I sometimes hear from my old ones in Zarewa too. I have one adopted younger brother, my *kanen rana*, Shera, whom I call Danmori, and one adopted sister, my *kanwar rana* Katifa. Some people have a great many friends of different kinds, *kawaye* and *yaya* and *kanwa*, but that is not good, you cannot really like so many people. Fagaci Ahmadu's head wife Jika had too many, whoever wished to be her *kawa*, she agreed. Even Hasana. One day Jika sent me *kawa*-gifts and said she liked me. At that time my own *kawa's* daughter said she liked Fagaci's wife and the child sent *kawa*-gifts to Jika. That was that, Jika accepted the gifts. When I heard that she had accepted gifts of liking from this little girl, then I was annoyed. (10) The next morning was Friday (we were secluded so I couldn't go out myself) I called my younger sister Kande, I said she was to go into Fagaci's compound and sit down and say nothing, she was to sit silent. If they questioned her she was to say 'The grand-daughter of Ibrahim sent me'. I said she was to tell them to give her part of the 'gift of liking' which that child had sent to Jika. She went and she said I had sent her, 'She says you are to give me fifty kolanuts and the mat and the bottle of perfume, she wants to see the things of mutual respect and good fortune; she says it is not fitting to hide from a *kawa* any gifts of liking'. They took out ten kolanuts and a little perfume and the small mat—Jika had distributed the rest round the people of her compound. Then I sent for Matansarki and Kande—Kande was my 'younger sister' but *kanwar rana*, not a relative—and 'Yarsoba. I cut up the kolanuts like this in little bits, I put them in a particularly nice bowl and wrapped it up in a Fatika mat. Then I sent for a woman praise-singer and I told her to go into Fagaci's compound and say 'Ibrahim's grand-daughter says "May Allah increase liking and agreement, may Allah multiply your *kawaye*!" ' Kande my *kanwar rana* was *kawa* with Gwanja, the child who had sent the gifts to Fagaci's wife. I said 'Go and abuse your *kawa* Gwanja, it is I who am sending you'. I told her to say 'Haven't you any shame, being *kawa* with women old enough to be your parents? You certainly have no shame. With older women, your mothers, are you going to share the ceremonies of life, are you going to share in the ceremonies of older women, (11) you impudent shameless girl?' My *kanwa* Kande went and told her off.

On the Friday they were drumming calabashes in Fagaci's compound; we went in and sat down at the door of the head wife's hut and refused to go in; we said they could come and drum outside, we were not going to enter. Jika's co-wives came round and whispered 'Welcome, Ibrahim's grand-daughter!', they crawled, they came and knelt down. I took out sixpence, I called the woman praise-singer, she came and said 'May your life be prolonged, grand-daughter of Ibrahim'. I gave her the sixpence. Jika the head wife came out of her hut and went and sat in the cooking-hut, she said 'Ap'. Before we had spoken to one another Fagaci sent in to say we must leave, they were going to shut the entrance of the compound. The women said 'This commoner's wife is angry, indeed!'

Fagaci's chief wife Jika had too many *kawaye*; there were about ten of them in Zaria apart from the ones in Giwa. When her daughter was married about thirty of them came, and they quarrelled—if you have too many *kawaye* don't you expect quarrelling between them? The girl, too, Gwanja—I gave her medicine for her impudence. She came to the door of our compound and said she felt ashamed, she would not come in. Then I came out and she greeted me and said 'May Allah make you patient!' I replied 'I have forgotten it, that is that'. My *kawa's* daughter!

Then the daughter of Fagaci's concubine was married in Zaria to a son of the Madaki Yero who went mad. The marriage money was about three hundred shillings, there were fifteen marriage cloths, then when they were collecting the dowry Fagaci added more as a gift, and he gave his daughter two silver anklets and two silver bracelets, two necklaces and four lengths of cloth. Sambo who had adopted her—he's an old man now but he used to be Chief of Kaduna—gave her bracelets and anklets, four full lengths of cloth and two necklaces. (12) Then Fagaci gave the bridegroom a horse and fifty shillings and an embroidered gown and embroidered trousers and a turban. Then look at Jika with her twenty *kawaye*! We were going, Adama and I, then Malam said 'Oh no, you aren't going, where you go there's quarrelling, you'll go and quarrel with the women'. We were preparing and preparing, then he came and forbade it. 'You're not going, you daughter of quarrels!' So we didn't go. The girl's own mother stayed at home and the rest of Fagaci's wives went in a motor to Zaria on the day of the feast.

For two years I was angry with Jika, then we made it up, and then Fagaci divorced her. After two years had passed I said 'If you want me then you must reduce the number of your *kawaye* that are all over the place—don't be *kawa* with everyone, young and old. Then we will have friendship, we will be partners in the affairs of life.' When we had arranged this, Fagaci divorced her, he gave her the money for the train and said she could go to Kano. When she went home to Kano and stayed there two years without getting married, he told her to come back to his compound in Zaria City, he gave her five shillings every month for food and she just lived in his house. (13) She is still there in his house—Aminu's mother—and Aminu looks after her food now.

The Obligations of Bond Friendship

Some *kawaye* deceive one another, there are those who will sleep with their *kawa's* husband in the hut in the forecourt.

> *The* kawa *broke faith,*
> *The useless* kawa, *the worthless* kawa,
> *I shall never be* yaya *again,*
> *I shall never take another* kanwar rana,
> *You women, don't you have another* yaya,
> *Don't you have another* kanwar rana,
> Yaya *broke trust,*
> *Useless* yaya, *worthless* yaya.

It happened here in New Giwa three years ago at a naming-day feast. There was a young woman here who had a *yaya*, there was friendship between them, the *kanwa* would take a valuable gift to her *yaya*, and if she did anything wrong her *yaya* reprimanded her; the *kanwa's* husband showed her *yaya* respect, he bowed down to his wife's *yaya*. When the feast was being held the young woman was in the hut of the chief wife, then she went outside for some fresh air and she looked for her *yaya*; she searched and searched, then she went to the hut in the forecourt of the compound, and she saw two people inside—she peeped in and she saw her husband and her *yaya*. They were lying together. Then there was fighting and struggling, the husband fled, the *yaya* fled. They were covered with shame. The girl returned to the hut where they were drumming, everyone knew; they made that song that I've just sung. The next morning she went off and broke up her marriage, then her *yaya* broke up hers also and married the husband of her *kanwar rana*. That is what people do. The *yaya* even told the *kanwar rana* that she should come back to her husband and be her co-wife, they would have *yaya* and *kanwar rana* together in the same compound! The girl refused. Then the *yaya* and the husband disagreed and later he got rid of the *yaya* and brought back the *kanwar rana* to his compound. People behave like that a good deal, but a true *kawa* does not do that. Only a treacherous husband and a treacherous *kawa* do it, they break faith.

I still exchange gifts with my *kawaye* in Zarewa; some years ago when Sadau's daughter was married, she came to tell me, and her father also came to tell me. I took out some gifts, small mats and a sack of cotton, some plates and bowls and a few things for stew. Then I went to Zarewa and all my *kawaye* came to my granddaughter's feast, they came to my ceremony. We remained there for a month. If I have a ceremony I send to tell them and they come and if any of them cannot come she sends her gift. You never forget your exchange-gifts. Now three of them have died, Kande, Zaila and Lami. Matan Sarki is alive with her husband Danmakarfi. Here in Giwa 'Yargoggo and Laraba are my *kawaye*. Then there is my Danmori and Katifa and Kande. If those *kanen rana* have a ceremony I send them five shillings. If I have a ceremony they bring me what they can. Katifa and I do not keep it up so much now, she is older, but Danmori and I always do. But *kanwa* and *yaya* lasts till you die.

Between different *kawaye* of the same woman, there is jealousy and quarrelling as there is between co-wives. If I go to a ceremony of Matan Sarki's, some of her *kawaye* smile at me and I smile at them. If one of them turns her back on you, then you turn your back on her—she is jealous, she doesn't like you. You spit at her. If the owner of the hut, like Matan Sarki, sees that happening she turns away and pretends not to notice, but she will not try to stop them. The owner of the hut is pleased; they like her, her *kawaye* are quarrelling because of her, she is liked. She does not really feel cross about it. A husband, if his wives are jealous but they don't fight or quarrel, is pleased because he knows he is desired. *Kanwar rana* and *kanen rana* are also jealous of their *yaya*.

You will not touch the first child of your *kawa*; (14) you know 'Yarjaba—she and 'Yardada are *kawaye*, so 'Yarjaba will not touch my grandchild Maikumata. If she is playing with a stone and it falls near me when I am carrying the child on my back, she will ask me to push it over to her, she won't come near him. She will sit over there, she will come no closer. His mother will suckle him when no one is there, but her *kawa* will never touch him. The mother's *kanwar rana* will take the child on her back and look after him. *Yaya*, too, will take up the first child of her *kanwar rana*.

A man's principal woman friend, *babbar kawa*, gives him gifts for his feast when he gets married; then when she gets married, he repays her. They play and joke in the market before they each get married, but they are not related. (15) The bridegroom's real younger sister, his kinswoman, is the bride's 'slave' at the time of the marriage. Then there is also a 'slave of the bride of the bridegroom'; the bridegroom's parents send money to the compound of a girl with a message that they want her to be this kind of 'slave'. (16) She is the bridegroom's *kanwar rana*, but it only lasts for a day.

The kind of *kanwar rana* that I have told you about is the kind we have in Kano country; they have that kind everywhere, but it may be a little different in Zaria. You know we are cleverer than they are—we Kano people know more than the Zaria people.

Another Faithless Bond Friend

Once at Old Giwa we had a new school teacher. He was called Malam Haba. (17) Fagaci Ahmadu's *jakadiya* went to welcome his wife when they arrived and she saw that Malam Haba's wife was very beautiful, she had light reddish-tinted skin like Fagaci's favourite wife Gude. The *jakadiya* went back to the compound and said to Gude, 'I have seen the stranger's wife; she is beautiful like you, you ought to be *kawa* with her'. Friday came, then Gude bought ten white kolanuts and ten red ones and perfume, she put them in a bowl and the *jakadiya* took them to Haba's wife, she said 'Gude welcomes you on your arrival'. Her husband came in and asked 'Who brought you this thing of fortune?' The kolanuts of liking were accepted, she distributed them; Haba did not forbid it. When Friday came round again Haba's wife went to Fagaci's compound and she greeted Gude; Haba said she could go to Gude's compound and see her, so at night she put on her best clothes and went. When she arrived at Fagaci's compound she called out 'Ahuwo!'—no one there knew her. Giwa the *jakadiya* came out and took her in to Gude's hut. Haba's wife stayed at a distance and covered her eyes while Gude welcomed her and all the women of the household welcomed her. She sat quite silent and Gude the owner of the hut sat silent, they said nothing; everyone came in and said 'Welcome!' and the visitor clapped her hands gently together and said 'M-hm, m-hm'. Then Gude called Giwa and told her to escort her visitor home. She left the gifts she had brought— rice, a bottle of oil and sweetmeats, the gifts of liking. She put them down in the hut without saying anything. The next morning Gude gave Giwa and Doguwa, who had taken her home, sixpence for their errand, and they took back her bowls to Haba's wife and greeted her—'How did you get home last night? Did you sleep well? How are the people of your household?' She answered 'Very well, thank you, we are all very well. How is Majidadi?' She called Gude Majidadi and Gude called her Ma'aji. (18) When Haba's wife visited Gude for the second time she talked to her. Then when the feast was near Gude sent her five shillings hairdressing money, and that day also Giwa the *jakadiya* had a child in her husband's compound; Haba's wife brought a gift to Gude. At the naming-day feast Gude gave her *kawa* kolanuts and tobacco-flowers and a lamp and some perfume, that was to 'buy her mouth'. (19) Haba's wife looked at all the things, everyone laughed and was happy, then she greeted the owner of the hut and said 'Indeed you have gone to a lot of trouble; I thank you, I thank you, praise be to Allah'.

Things went on like that for some time, then one day Fagaci Ahmadu went to Zaria. Then one night Gude went to her *kawa's* compound to visit her. Haba was in the entrance-hut when she arrived, he couldn't see her in the dark, but her perfume over-powered him. He seized her and wouldn't let her go into the compound, he couldn't see her but he could smell the scent of her perfume, so he caught her and carried her off to the hut in the fore-court, they lay down together there and did what they pleased. When they were tired Gude did not go into the women's quarters of the compound to see her *kawa*, she slipped quietly back into Fagaci's compound—as you know, noblemen's wives are never allowed to go out. It was said he had been sending her gifts in

secret, and her *kawa*, his wife, did not know about it. When Fagaci
returned there was no one who would say anything to him, they
were afraid. Everyone saw and knew, but they dared not tell
Fagaci. Gude continued to go to Haba's compound at night whenever she had the chance. One day someone told Fagaci, 'Gude is
going out at night'. They told him the scandal. Then Fagaci took
a whip and beat her, he told her she was to tell him what she had
been doing. He whipped her in her hut, he said she was to tell
him what she had done—he knew perfectly well what she had done
—she refused, she said 'There is the well at the door of the compound, kill me'. He was going to Kaya on tour—he used to take
her with him on her mare because he desired her, he had married
her as a young girl; she said 'I will tell you at Kaya'. When they
reached Kaya she refused to tell him; she ran away for fourteen
days, when he had her brought back she wouldn't listen to him;
he gave her a choice this time, he didn't beat her. Then she ran
away to Kano to her kinsmen, she was away for three months, then
Fagaci sent his servants to fetch her home in the train. He was
angry with anyone who spoke to him. He desired her. She went and
got charms so that they should be divorced, but Fagaci did not
want to divorce her, he wanted to keep her. She was not happy.
Then the king ordered Fagaci to divorce her so that she could
marry whom she pleased, so Fagaci had to divorce her. She went
to Funtua and married a rich man there.

Gude did not want to live in Fagaci's compound, he was very
jealous of her. From the first she had wanted to stay with her own
folk at Kakangi, but Fagaci saw her and wanted her, so they had
to give her to him. Since he was a nobleman with everything she
could want, she said she liked him—she didn't desire him, but
there was his rank and position. He had given her father the
chieftainship of Kakangi village before she was born, then he made
her brother the Chief of Kakangi because he desired the daughter
in his house. (20)

Fagaci also knew that it was Haba—the men of the town had
told him. When Fagaci had divorced Gude he said that Haba was
to leave the town; as Haba was the schoolmaster Fagaci wrote a
letter and had him transferred somewhere else. When he had first
arrived, Fagaci had sent him a sack of guineacorn, a sack of rice
and stew-ingredients; long ago he had been a boy with Haba's
father in Zaria. It was not right of Haba, he betrayed the con-

fidence of an important older man, and he was not much more than a boy. She used to get out, you see, after they had eaten the evening meal, when everyone was chatting and telling tales; then quietly, very quietly she would cover her head and face and slip out, then off to Haba's compound. Before they had shut up the entrance of Fagaci's compound she would return. He deceived Fagaci, she deceived her *kawa*. Gude wanted Haba's wife to be her *kawa* before she had met her, because she had heard from the *jakadiya* that she was a beautiful girl, so she wanted her as her friend. Haba also had not seen Gude, but he had heard about her; everyone in the household liked her, she was very popular. When he heard that, he sent her gifts in secret; I don't know who took them, his wife knew nothing about what her *kawa* was doing.

More Formal Friendships: Adopted 'Mothers' and 'Fathers'

If an older woman sees a younger woman, she may decide that she would like her to become her daughter; she looks at her and likes her. Then she gives her something valuable, she will send something like rice and other foods, and she calls the younger woman 'daughter of fortune', *'yar arziki*. Or it may be a man, she will call him 'son of fortune', *dan arziki*. Then after about ten days, supposing you are the younger woman, you pound millet-paste, you buy sour milk, you fill up a bowl with it and you add a lot of guineacorn flour so that your new mother can drink millet-paste and sour milk, and make herself gruel with the flour. You send someone to take it to her and she gives the bearer of the gift two-pence or threepence. That is that, until there is a ceremony; if you have one you send to tell her, if she has one she sends to tell you. You give one another whatever you can, you do not have fixed gifts; the 'mother-of-the-hut' may give her new daughter a bowl of grain, a bottle of oil and a bowl of salt; the 'daughter of fortune' may do a little pounding of grain and she gives her mother some flour, then she buys firewood for her. Then when she visits her mother the daughter of fortune will be given a little cotton or a bottle of oil. There is no shyness between a mother-of-the-hut and her daughter of fortune, it is not like *yaya* and *kanwa*—with them there is shame like that between husband and wife at a first marriage, until they become accustomed to it, then there is friendship and they share the ceremonies of life. A mother-of-the-hut and her daughter of fortune (she is also called '*yar rana*, adopted daughter) consult and talk together and the mother advises the daughter and corrects her if she does anything she shouldn't.

These different kinds of friends are all of different ages; for instance, if a girl sees another woman whom she wants as a friend, if she is old, as I am, then the girl will say 'I should like her to be my mother-of-the-hut, my adopted mother'. If the old lady hears of it and likes the girl, she will send her a little gift and call her 'daughter of fortune' or adopted daughter. If the girl sees a woman she likes and the woman has been married for about ten years, while the girl has been married for about four years, then they will be *yaya* and *kanwa* with one another—adopted elder and younger sisters. If the two are about the same age, they become *kawaye*.

An adopted father, *uban daki* or *uban rana*, is rather different; if your kinsmen take you to a compound to be married and it is far from your own home, then they will find a reliable man, the head of a compound, aged about fifty years, who will watch over you in your new home; they say to you 'Here is your father'. You make some very nice millet-balls with millet, you make enough to fill three large calabashes, you buy sour milk and you send it all to your father to greet him. When the feast comes he has some guineacorn ground and fills up a basket with flour, he takes a calabash of rice, a bottle of oil, some salt and some locust-bean cakes and he sends it all to you in your husband's compound. You take the grain and grind it, you make porridge and you divide it among the people of the household, you say 'See what my father-of-the-hut has sent me'.

CHAPTER XIV

FAGACI AHMADU'S DEATH AND HIS SUCCESSOR

We had been many years in Old Giwa, when at the time of the feast all Fagaci's followers mounted their horses to accompany him to Zaria to greet the king. The drummers and pipe-players were playing,

> *Father of Aminu, return in safety,*
> *Grandson of Gando, return in health,*
> *Son of Malam Baba, return in safety . . .*

Fagaci Ahmadu was not well but he went in to Zaria. When he got there they told the king that he could not mount his horse, and they gave his son Aminu his father's horse so that he went and rode in the procession in his place. The day after the feast the king went in the early morning to greet Fagaci, but he could hardly rise from his bed; after the king had left he died. When we heard the news I wailed, I wept, we went in to his wives and concubines and they wept and wailed too. Aminu's mother, Amina, died twenty days after he was born, and his father's head-wife Jika gave him her breast and suckled him; he was the eldest son. It was said that Aminu was only a boy, and so he wasn't given his father's title; they say he may get it in future. Everyone in the district likes him.

When Fagaci Ahmadu died in Zaria his wives and his retainers were at Giwa in his compound; in Zaria his property was divided up among his children, his farms and horses and cattle. But the farm at Giwa was not amongst them, it would be inherited by the next holder of the office. His drummers and musicians and retainers waited by his compound in Giwa for about seven months, each one in his own compound, farming and waiting. His wives mourned him for one hundred and thirty days, then when they had washed they went to their own homes. When we heard that the new Fagaci, Muhammadu, had been appointed, the musicians and followers made ready and went to Zaria to escort him to Giwa. That day there was celebrating, the women were drumming calabashes in the compounds, in the open there was drumming everywhere, there was dancing and celebration—the country had a chief again. We were no longer living in the prison compound at that time; when Malam Hasan became ill he had said he could not manage the work and he was retired, then another warder called Hasan was appointed—the one who made that little mistake —and after he had been dismissed this one was appointed, Fagaci Muhammadu's younger brother Hasan.

When Fagaci Muhammadu arrived he entered Fagaci Ahmadu's compound and he inherited some of the retainers; (1) others of them had gone to Aminu and attached themselves to him. But when Fagaci Muhammadu went into Fagaci Ahmadu's sleeping-hut that night, he went to go to sleep, he saw the room was full of snakes, he saw black kids everywhere and he was terrified; he saw a lot of other unpleasant things too. (2) He came outside and there he saw a woman sitting, she was very fair, at the centre of the compound; she was sitting on a chair and she had a lamp. She was called Maifitilla, the one with the lamp; the previous Fagaci used to talk to her, they would sit at the centre of his house, she in her iron chair with her iron lamp—she would come to greet him. Then she would pick up her chair and go back to her home in the river in the house of her husband Maidaru, in the stream behind Fagaci's compound.

That kind of spirit is inherited in the way of the compound, in the way of the house—even common people have them, everyone has his own. (3) When one dies they take to his son or his grand-children, they don't leave the house. Maifitilla is only a spirit, she isn't an ancestor—she is a spirit of inheritance. The bush spirits are different, if they come then we talk to them and try to drive them out; some of them stay. Maifitilla followed Fagaci Ahmadu from his compound in Zaria City, he used to give his spirits their things—he didn't care about the market spirits, only those of his house. Not a week would pass without his killing a ram and giving them alms. There was a song about Fagaci Ahmadu, 'Mother who prevents crying, He who never fails anyone's trust'. His son

Aminu doesn't look after 'them', that is why 'they' don't look after him. He has no importance now, perhaps if he took care of 'them', 'they' would give him the title. (4)

When Fagaci had seen the things in Fagaci Ahmadu's hut, he called his wife and she came and saw them too, she said 'Come away, shut up that hut'. Fagaci sent for Aminu, Ahmadu's son, and told him 'You are to sleep in here and tell me what you see'. Aminu spent the night in the hut; in the morning Fagaci asked him 'What did you see?' Aminu said 'I didn't see anything'. He was a son of that house, they wouldn't trouble him. In the morning he said 'I didn't see anything', and Fagaci said 'Very well'. But Muhammadu never went into Fagaci Ahmadu's sleeping-hut again. They say he kept on seeing Maifitilla in the night, sitting in the middle of the compound. You know how it is, someone who is in someone else's place, it isn't his inheritance, always feels afraid of the other's inheritance; everyone has his own inheritance, his own things don't frighten him, but another's inheritance terrifies him.

It wasn't any kind of medicine, it was just them—the spirits that one doesn't see. They are here in the compound, they are here in the town. But they liked Ahmadu, he always gave them alms; every Friday and Sunday he caused rams to be killed for them and kids, he gave them chickens and porridge; they were taken outside the door of his compound, and anyone could come and eat. The alms were given to the people and they, the ones we don't see, they felt good when they saw it, they knew it was meant for them. All village chiefs, too, ought to do this—they ought to give the spirits the things that they like, and all will be well with the people. When this one came he was much too clever, he refused to give them what they should have, he didn't give them alms. Then he saw something terrifying in his compound—only he saw it—but he refused to give them alms and he ran away. He appealed to the king, he appealed to the Europeans, he said he wanted to build a new town. When we moved here to New Giwa the spirits filled the town, the European spirits began to come too. The *malams* advised that it would be right to give these strangers alms so that they should dwell at peace in the town. Whether he gave it to them in secret, I don't know; but he never gave them alms at the front of his compound. Now you see there is illness, there is meningitis, there is trouble. This is the cause of it. 'They' have been here since the creation of the world, at every birthday they are here but we can't see them. (5)

There is medicine for titles, it can be put in the compound of a chief; if a stranger succeeds to the title and not a son of the dead chief's house, the stranger will be terrified. It isn't good that a stranger should inherit the title. But the things that Fagaci saw were different.

The Death of my Husband, Malam Hasan the Warder; we move to New Giwa

We lived happily in Malam Hasan's compound; if I asked Adama to do something she said 'Yes, certainly', if she asked me to do something I agreed. There was no jealousy over the children. Our husband gave us sufficient food, we were happy. Even now I visit Adama's compound, she is married to Ibrahim the praise-singer, and we talk. In the dry season when we were preparing to come here to New Giwa, the men cut down trees and cleared the place and laid out the sites for the compounds. Everyone harvested his guineacorn, then everyone was shown his new house-site and he put in the fence-poles, in the dry season everyone worked and worked and all the huts were built. For two weeks we went back and forth, taking all our belongings and our goats and everything to the new town. When we had settled down, there was a celebration at the front of Fagaci's new compound, there was drumming and sport and dancing and *bori* for two days.

But before we left Old Giwa Malam Hasan fell ill; the cold caught him. He worked hard in the prison, then he would be sent off here, he would be sent off there, he was always going away on business, always on foot, even in the rains. When age came upon him the cold caught him, that kind of illness in your body—when you move you feel it in your legs, in your arms, in your back, in your neck. He moved about slowly with a stick. He was relieved of his work and he rested; when Adama had had four of her children we moved from the warder's compound. We lived in a compound near the river, but the river was dried up, the water would not flow. We used to go out at night to draw water from a well near the compound, but that water was not good, it was bitter. We used it for washing clothes, and went to the stream far away to fetch drinking-water when our own river dried up. When our husband became ill we were no longer confined to the compound, we went out; when he had been well, he paid boys to fetch us wood and water, but when we saw that he was in pain we went and fetched the wood and water ourselves. When Malam Hasan told Fagaci Ahmadu that he wasn't well, Fagaci sent to Ma'aji for some herbs and Hasan drank the medicine; he felt better, but then his head started to ache and his body ached. Then one day he lay down and said 'I shan't get up from this illness'. We said, 'Be patient and bear it, may Allah heal you'. Two days later he died. He hadn't been strong for some time, he couldn't eat, he only drank a little gruel. We were there together, I and my co-wife and our children, she had been pregnant for a long time and ten days later she bore Audi. We wailed, we threw ourselves down on the ground, we wailed and wept. The next morning we sent a boy to tell Hasana, when she came she wailed and wailed, her brother was dead. Everyone in the town collected and all the *malams*. Adama and I remained together in one hut in the interior of the compound and the women all came to greet us. After three days his kinsfolk and our kinsfolk and the townspeople came to greet us, after seven days they came and distributed alms to the *malams*. (6) Adama's son by Danfangi received all the alms and gave it to the *malams*, they prayed for the dead man. Some people brought a penny, some threepence, some sixpence; Hasana gave five shillings. Adama's gift, with that of her kinsfolk, was five shillings too. All the grain that people brought was distributed amongst the *malams*, it was not for us; we ate the grain from our granary. After forty days they gave alms again; in the morning people brought us guineacorn in calabashes, we pounded five mortars of grain, Adama and I and the children and grandchildren. One portion of flour was made up with milk, one with sugar, and a third with honey, all as alms. It is not cooked, it is called *cuge*. Men and women kept coming all that morning, they brought alms, they poured out guineacorn, sixpence, a shilling—we gave them the *cuge* to eat, and we sent the children to take it to the other compounds and to the *malams*. The *malams* came too, to recite the prayers; they were given our husband's clothes, and alms of food and money. But we gave them the clothes on the seventh day, that is what is done. On the fortieth day the alms are finished. We remained in mourning for a hundred and thirty days. Adama couldn't carry it out, because Audi was born so soon after Malam died. You say your five daily prayers and you pray for your husband. Adama had her child in our compound. I went into her hut but I could not be the midwife because I was in mourning. I went into her hut and I sat down there and I took the child. Adama's own mother looked after the little girl and was midwife; Adama was washing for five months after the birth. I wasn't feeling well at that time and I didn't cook any food, but if I had been well I could have done it. Dije and Sanda, who lived in another part of the compound, made porridge for us. They were the wives of two of Fagaci's followers, their husbands had farms and ran errands for Fagaci. (7)

When you are in mourning you boil water every Friday morning, you make it very hot, and you go behind your hut and wash your body; you come in and massage your body with oil. Every day you do your ordinary ablutions before you say your prayers, you wash your face, your feet, your underneath and your hands. The cloth and blouse and kerchief that you wore at the beginning of your mourning are not changed until the end of it. There is no Friday when you don't wash all over, but on the other days of the week you only do your ablutions. You wash your head thoroughly but you cannot cut your hair. You may go out in the daytime, quietly, to greet someone or to do some work. You don't have your hair dressed, every Friday you wash it and leave it as it is. You cannot go to feasts or naming-feasts or any ceremonies. You cannot rub tobacco-flowers on your teeth, but you can eat kolanuts—they are food, they aren't forbidden. You may put on antimony and you may shave round the edge of your hair to tidy it. When your husband dies, you must wail; if you loved him, then you are sad at heart also, he isn't there. If you didn't particularly like him, you wail because of compassion, you had got used to him and now he isn't here. Ah, Allah preserve us in health!

Our husband died three years after Fagaci Ahmadu died. When he was retired from his work as Warder, another man came to do his work, Hasan a Barebare. My kinswoman Gambo was wandering on her own near Kaduna and there she met Hasan, this Barebare and he married her. When they brought him here to work and I saw her, I said 'Ap! And they said you had gone to the bad, you were just living on your own!' Her mother was my father's sister, we were joking relations. Her husband made some mistake and they dismissed him—it was said that he accepted money from prisoners and then left the door open so that they escaped. He went away to

Likoro, his own town, and farmed. They took their daughter 'Yarbaba with them; they are there to this day. Adama married a praise-singer, and she is living here in New Giwa; he is called Ibrahim Roko. Her co-wife is a *bori*-dancer who also does hair-dressing; her *bori* is very good. Later I married Ibrahim Dantsoho, he farms but he has no hut for me in his compound, so I live in my younger brother's compound. (8) There are four of us, Dantsoho's wives. He gives me no food, I am here in my own compound.

PART FIVE

CHAPTER XV

1943–1950
LAST YEARS AND FOURTH
MARRIAGE

I go to live with my Brother Kadiri

After a hundred and thirty days a widow comes out of mourning. That night she does not sleep, there is drumming on calabashes until the morning. The morning comes and she bathes herself, she dresses in a new blouse, a new cloth, a new head-kerchief. She takes off her old clothes and gives them as alms to an old woman. Everyone in your kin and in your husband's kin comes with alms —guineacorn, rice, millet, money. You prepare porridge and *cuge*, the *malams* come and recite the prayers, and you distribute food to them and send it round the compounds. (1) At Azahar everyone who has come for the prayers and greetings gets up and goes home. If the woman is young, not an old lady like me, that same day that the *malams* have recited the last prayers they also recite the marriage verses and she is married again. As I was old I went to the compound of my younger brother Kadiri, taking Yelwa and 'Yardada with me; I left Adama there in our compound with her baby and Wada and Goma and Lawal. Kadiri's compound was some way away in the ward of the Kano people; there were about twenty compounds of Kano people there. I was always going to the other side of the town to visit Adama, and she would come to our compound; her mother's home was near ours. When I left she was sad and upset, she wanted me to stay with her but I said I couldn't do so. Over by the ford there weren't many people, but in the Kano ward there were kinsmen and lots of people and the compounds were close together. I prefer a place with plenty of people, you feel cheerful. It was just the same at Karo when I left the hamlet to go back into the town. (2) But Adama and I were always meeting on the path, she would be going to my home and I would be going to hers.

When I came to Kadiri's household he had three wives, Gwamma and Lauretu and another Gwamma. We moved to New Giwa with them. I went into my father's hut, he had died two years before. His wife Ramatu had also died, there were seven months between her death and Malam Hasan's. When our father Malam Tsoho was alive, he lived in one section of the compound and Kadiri had another. I did not inherit anything, Father was not rich. There was some grain, which we divided, and when Malam Hasan died he left us grain, too. A year after Malam Hasan died we moved to New Giwa, we took all our possessions, the houses were built, and we all came here.

I haven't been ill much in my life, but when Malam Hasan died I had the itch, scabies, all my body itched with it and I scratched until I bled. Then I got an enormous cake of soap and I washed and washed, then it bled, then water came out of it, then it healed up. I had scabies for five months. The sores don't come out on your face and legs, only on your body. When I had washed myself thoroughly I used to rub in oil, then I lit the fire and rested while the warmth made the oil sink into my skin. Everyone who touches a person with scabies catches it. I was carrying Yelwa on my back, she got it; then I returned her to her mother Adama and she got it too. Once when I was a girl I had something wrong with my eyes, they kept on running, and got red. We got a little herb called *pitilli*. (3) It is a little fruit, you bite it and you find the red seeds inside, like cotton-seeds. You get them out and crush them to powder and you put the powder on your eyes and lie down. Later you get up and wash your eyes and they heal. I have never been pregnant with a child; Kadiri only has one, yet my younger sister has lots of children, her hut is full. I drank *malams'* medicine, I drank *bori* medicine, but I never had one. You can only have that which Allah gives you—isn't that so? That is your destiny. (4)

More about the move to New Giwa and the Spirits

In the time of Aminu's father, Fagaci Ahmadu, it was said that we should move from Old Giwa; he was told to choose Fatika or Kaya or Guga or Bakori, (5) whichever he preferred; they even began to prepare a place at Guga, then he died. But here where we are now, a certain King of Zaria called Audu, (6) who died a long time ago, said there would be people, he said that here they would seek for food. But the *bori*, who know everything, say that we shall go back to Old Giwa. You know there are the stranger *bori*, the European spirits here, but the old ones of the North are over there in the old place. Ever since Mai Sudan came Old Giwa had been spoilt, everyone fled—like Fatika and Old Yelwa— although at Old Giwa there was a stream nearby, and they farmed sugar and all kinds of marsh crops; it was a good place, but you see it now with three compounds. The people all went to live in the bush.

Not all the spirits from Old Giwa have come here with us; when we were going to move, four of the chief spirits refused to come. There was one called Dauko in the ficus-tree at the front of our compound; there was Malam Alhaji whose home was in the silk-cotton tree; Gajere-mai-baka lived at the base of a baobab tree; Mashi bako lived in a white-ants' nest. Those four refused to come. When we held the *bori* dance here at New Giwa, Inna, the Fulani woman, came, she was coaxed and persuaded to come. (7) Two *bori*-dancers, Garban Tsundu and Tata, went to her tree in the middle of the night and fetched her. When they asked her to come she said 'Very well, if they want me to come let them give me a white cloth and some milk, let them build fifteen market-stalls; then I shall come'. Inna is lame, so they went to fetch her with something to carry her back in. Perhaps they took a big box with a lid, then they opened it and left it there for her to enter. Then they brought the box and put it down at the foot of the tamarind tree in the market here, they opened it. She came out and settled down in that tree. They can see her, the children of *bori*, but one who is never possessed doesn't see them, not one. *Bori*-dancers see their own things, but we see nothing. Before Inna was brought the market would not go properly, the mother of the market was not there. Then at the foot of her tamarind tree, when they had brought her, they gave her milk and they gave alms in the market, the children of the townspeople came and drank milk. The *bori*-dancing lasted for fourteen days, the prostitutes came and there was *bori*-dancing at the edge of the market and in front of Fagaci's compound. There was an old market at the crossroads, but there was none here in New Giwa before we came. That is why there was no mother of the market. Fagaci sent to a village near Zarewa for

Tata, the son of my *kawa*; I had accompanied his mother to her husband's home when she was married; Tata has medicine for madness. They sent for him when they were going to found the market. There were thirty *bori*-dancers, there were a thousand onlookers, there were ten big drums and many other smaller ones. For three years the market would not fill up. Ever since Mai Sudan ruined Giwa there have been no people—they all dispersed. At Old Giwa the market would not go, then when we came here there was no proper market for three years. We were wondering what to do, then Fagaci sent and called the expert *bori*-dancers to come. When the Fulani woman, Inna, came she said 'The market is here at the foot of the tamarind. Come!' Everyone swept the place and cut down the other trees and built the market-stalls. The men of Anguwan Shehu, the men of Giwa and the men of Anguwan Mahauta did it. The Fulani woman said she wanted fifteen more stalls besides the ten they had already built. When they had built them and she was there, the market got going and it has been going ever since; you see what a thriving market it is. The *bori*-dancers who came to found this market were Tata and Garban Tsundu from the borders of Zaria, Katsina and Kano. The *bori* said there must be thirty market-stalls, but now there are forty. The spirits like lots of people. They said a black bull must be killed, but he refused. When he refused, some of the spirits said they would leave. The market is the people's, but it belongs to the spirits also. If you give them alms you please their hearts, then they settle down and cause men to come with their loads, they draw people and draw people—lots of people. When Fagaci came here he brought them secretly, they helped him to build the town. Now you see he is against them, he is afraid. Formerly they used to have *bori*-dancing at the door of his compound, there was drumming and *bori* came, he gave them money. Now he refuses to allow it, perhaps he is afraid of the king? (8)

Damau, a *bori* expert, died a few years ago. He said that the lord of the land, if he was going to build this town, if he was going to found the market, must give a black bull and black kids to the spirits. They would build a big market and bring many people. If now he was to build the market with the spirits, you would see that everyone would come and build his house here. Even now the market is not quite right. (9) If he agreed with them, and he killed a black bull, the spirits would drink the blood and the people would eat the meat, if he killed black kids the spirits would drink the blood, the people would eat the meat, and the town would grow to a great size, also he should build market-stalls. But if he only builds stalls and does not give them what is theirs, the town will not become great. If Tata and Garban Tsundu and Kwara from Kuringi came, and called the *bori*, then you would see the town become big. They are the principal *bori* experts, with a hundred spirits each. If they came you would see men from the hamlets, men from Kaya and Guga and Gangara, even from Tudun Wada Zaria—they would come and fill up our town. It was like that during the fourteen days that they spent here. In our village they had medicine for madness, they carried out the work of the *bori*, and people assembled in crowds. That is their work, building markets. They built Fillata and Makarfi. (10) If they were called here, they would come and do their work and go home. When they left and the onlookers had gone home, the market would thrive because it would have become the house of the spirits. The best of the *bori* experts would have brought them and put them here, and then every market-day people would keep on coming with things to sell. If he was to give them alms only once, they would stay.

Fagaci Ahmadu's alms were not for the market spirits, he didn't care about the market. They were for men. He was popular, everyone liked him; the king liked him, the noblemen of Zaria liked him, the people of his district all liked him. If he mounted his horse crowds of people would come, they wanted to see him. This was his praise-song:

> *Allah preserve for us the owner of the land,*
> *Allah preserve Fagacin Zaria,*
> *Grandson of Gando, grandson of Gando,*
> *Fagacin Zazzau,*
> *Grandson of Gando, Kantomati's son.*

Kantomati was a European, he and Fagaci Ahmadu liked one another; he often came to see Fagaci. (11) Fagaci Ahmadu was certainly well liked. Everyone could see his good nature, so they liked him. People were not afraid of him, anyone could approach and come near him; they used to bring him gifts because of his amiable personality, even the common people brought him gifts because they liked him, not because they had to. This present Fagaci is popular, also, he does not trouble anybody. You see he laughs and is good-natured. He likes the *bori*, but only in private, because he is afraid. He left the old town because he was afraid of the other one. (12) All the rulers like the *bori*—if they didn't, would their work be any good? Of course they all agree with them. So do the *malams*, secretly. The *malams* call on the *bori* in private, in the darkness at night. Everyone wants the spirits, kings and noblemen want them, *malams* and wives shut away in their compounds—it is with them that we work in this world, without them would our labour be any use? The work of *malams* is one thing, the work of *bori* experts is another, each has his own kind of work and they must not be mixed up. There is the work of *malams*, of *bori*, of magicians, of witches; they are all different but at heart everyone loves the spirits. There are spirits of the bush animals, there are spirits of the bush trees, there are spirits of the springs, there are spirits of the streams, there are spirits of the rocks, there are spirits of the paths, there are spirits of men inside the town. There are inherited spirits like Dangaladima and Nana and Sarkin Rafi, if one *bori*-dancer dies they follow someone else in his kin. But there is always someone in the mother's or father's kin to inherit them. (13) There are black spirits also; you get black kids, black cloth, black chickens, if they trouble you you give them these things, you go away into the bush and separate yourself from them. If they come into the town and possess a man, morning and evening he shouts wildly, then you have to make medicine to drive them out, and take them their gifts out there. Spirits bear children, but they do not die. If a man does something wrong they come and tell. When people do wrong or oppress, they are very frightened of them; they spread the news, they tell, they make public the crime.

Prostitutes and Bori *in Giwa and Zarewa*

All the *bori* adepts in Giwa now are women, there are no men. There was a man, Damau, but he died the year before last. There is Maidaji's wife and Kande in one compound; at Tanko's house there are two wives who are possessed. There is a prostitute, Ba'i, her husband is a farmer in a village; she hasn't broken off the marriage and he hasn't divorced her, if he comes into Giwa and fetches her home, she may stay with him two nights and then she leaves again. (14) There is also Ladi, Ibrahim Maroki's wife, Adama's co-wife. You know Kande in Maidaji's house? Her husband was the Cotton Malam at Kaya market, he embezzled all the cotton money and ran away from the European two years ago, she doesn't know where he is. She lives in Maidaji's house and does her spinning, if a man comes and fetches her at night she goes out with him and doesn't come in again. Then there is 'Yar Shehu the wife of Kwando the drummer. She came down here on her wanderings from Kano, a prostitute, she was married to Madakin Danfangi at Gangara (15) for seven years; then she left him and came here and married Kwando last year. Malam Akilu who trades in the market has a wife, Gwaji, whom he married as a maiden, now she has seven children; she is possessed by *bori*. There is also Habi, the wife of Dangaladiman Busa who plays the pipe for Fagaci. Dangaladima is frightened of *bori*, he won't go near anyone while they are possessed; if Rabi is possessed he leaves the compound. Rabi had many *bori* on her for a long time, but after they 'cooked' her the spirits were better. Dangaladima's mother, Fatsuma, has *bori* too. Her daughters, Gwaje and Gambo, both have *bori*, they are married. Sharu, the wife of Fagaci's Sarkin Fada, (16) was given eye-medicine and is no longer possessed. Matan Malam, the wife of the chief blacksmith, had medicine and her spirits are less now. Cigoro has them and the wife of Ibrahim the leather-worker. There are a lot of *bori*-dancers in Giwa and they are good ones.

Twenty days ago Fagaci forbade *bori*-dancing in the town. (17) Then Tanko's wife went to Fagaci's compound to greet his wives, and as she came out from the women's quarters she had to pass through the room where he was sitting. She and her three co-wives knelt down to greet him, and as she was kneeling down the *bori* came and possessed her—it was Baturen Gwari, the European from Gwari country. 'Imprison me, bind me, call the police and lock me up! Isn't there an order forbidding *bori*? Very well, look at me, I have come. Lock me up then!' When the spirit was quiet for a little the women pushed her out and took her home—she went on and on. She sang this 'praise-song' right before Fagaci.

> *We are the end,*
> *We are meningitis,*
> *We are all the other illness,*
> *We own the bit of earth behind the hut,*
> *Laughing one, there's no cure for this illness,*
> *Reveller, there is no rejoicing without us.*

Fagaci said 'I have forbidden that; call the policeman!' But they led her out of his presence and took her home. The night before last Ba'i was dancing *bori* with drumming in the entrance-hut near our compound. Last night they were possessed in Sankira's house. The town is theirs, they went to Fagaci's compound and appeared; they aren't afraid of him.

When we came here there were the spirits of the place, then the Old Giwa spirits came and they joined them. At first they refused to come, they said there was grain and guineacorn at the old town. They say that one day we shall go back. Inna the Fulani woman refused to come, but they persuaded her and brought her. The chief ones are still over there, though—Malam Alhaji and Babban Inuwa, Maibaka and Sarkin Aljannu. Spirits are everywhere, but these ones prefer to remain in Old Giwa. They only come here and visit us. Dangaladima comes, he feels ashamed before his father and avoids him, he is Sarkin Aljannu's eldest son; the Gwari Woman adopted him but she is not his real mother, Inna the Fulani bore him. Malam Alhaji is Sarki's slave, and his slave the Gwari Woman adopted the firstborn son. (18)

None of us in Malam Maigari's house were possessed by *bori*; there was *bori* in Karo and Zarewa, and we used to go and watch it from the time we were children; then some of our kinsmen married *bori* adepts and we used to see them calling the spirits in our kinsmen's homes. There were four compounds of *bori* in Zarewa, the compounds of the prostitutes. They would sweep a space and lay down mats inside the compound, in the shade of a tree, then they would dance and call the spirits, we watched it all. They used to do it in the daytime, then they would become tired and eat their midday food; at night they lit the lamps and started again—that was the prostitutes' work. They did that every day, in the rains or in the dry season. Hadn't the Chief of Zarewa appointed them? He appointed Magajiya, Lemo, Auta, Dandaudu—all of them. If a prostitute arrived and was seeking the compound of Lemo or Magajiya, someone would direct her there. In the evenings first one would be possessed, then when she was tired another would take her place; the young men and older men and the children of the town filled up the compound. At night there would be *bori*-dancing, they leapt up and fell down, they leapt in the air and fell to the ground. It is their craft. When a man wanted a prostitute he would throw away his money to the drummers. Here in Giwa a few nights ago they were doing it. The Tobacco Malam took a cloth of his wife's and gave it to a prostitute who was dancing *bori*, he wanted her. His wife heard about it and went off home to her kinsmen. Fagaci ordered the Tobacco Malam to follow her, he said she was to return. She did return, the Tobacco Malam brought her two very beautiful cloths and she came back. The Farming Malam threw away ten shillings and the Forest Guard one pound that same night. (19) The man who wants a prostitute gives her his money, he puts the money before her on the mat on which she is sitting, and she gives it away to the drummers and praise-singers. He gives her gifts and he gives her gifts—she won't refuse him. If a stranger comes to a town and goes to the place of the prostitutes, then he steps into the middle of the circle, he says he sees something that he wants, he says he is a stranger and he is seized by desire; he has come from a certain town and his reputation is unknown here, but when he heard the drumming and the dancing he came out to see; then he saw one whom he desired, he is spending his money, he wants her. Then the praise-singer calls out 'I am to tell the stranger we welcome him, we bid him welcome, we are rejoicing at his arrival. He is staying in the compound of such-a-one. He desires so-and-so, he rejoices to see her, he is spending his money because of her. See such-and-such money he has given her!' Then the prostitute tells the praise-singer what to say for her: 'He is a stranger who belongs to his own town, he the stranger was brought here by travelling, he the stranger has seen something which he desires; I am rejoicing at the coming of this stranger, I like him, I welcome him, I bid him welcome, I also am happy to see him.' If there is someone there who has desired her before, a man of the town, and the stranger is stealing her from him, he will get up hotly and say 'The lies of the stranger are at an end!' Then he gives her more money. 'You are lying, see what I will give her!' Then they start competing, if one gives a gown the other gives a gown too, if one gives her money the other gives more— she is much admired, she is desired. That is what they were doing here a few nights ago, it was over Zenabu in Jumau's compound (20) —you have seen her, a beautiful girl, she has come to seek a divorce in the district court. The Tobacco Malam was taking her out, then the Farming Malam took her, so the next time they were drumming the Tobacco Malam gave a gown and the Farming Malam gave money. There she was in Jumau's house, sitting on a chair among the things they had given her—forty shillings that night, apart from the gowns given to the drummers and the Tobacco Malam's wife's cloth which he gave to Zenabu. Madness—it's madness! There they are with their own wives at home, hidden away, then look at them wasting money on other women outside. It's been the nature of our menfolk since long ago. Even old men with white beards behave like that. Here and there there are upright men who don't do so, but there are old fornicators, men and women, there's an old woman in Sankira's house who still goes off to men—they take her out at night, they lie together, they don't give her any money; she prefers boys. Another one, who is dead now, used to call boys to her at night, she would shut the door, she would cook meat and rice and put oil into it, then she would give it to the boy, he would eat until he was satisfied and then they would lie down. Of course he will agree—it is a gift!

'Magajiya of the *bori*, Magajiya of the town—the house of worthless women where everyone comes!' The spirits come, Dangaladima, Sa'idu, Mairama, Sarkin Rafi—each women has her own who will possess her. We were girls, hawking food from house to house—'Bean-cakes! Bean-cakes! *Danwake! Kosai!*' Then we would set down our loads and watch. They even went to the entrance of Zarewa's compound, they were calling *bori* and he was throwing away his money, the day they held the marriage-feast for Tabulla; when she was married there were celebrations for two nights, we were her *kawaye*. The *imam* of the town and the *malams* would not come to that kind of thing, and there is no *bori* in their houses, it has nothing to do with them, but they do not forbid it. When I was married and could not go out, when I was in Malam Hasan's compound, our neighbour married Balaraba, a *bori*-dancer, and she used to be possessed. We drummed calabashes for her the day she joined him, today she arrived in the compound and tomorrow the *bori* was upon her. At Malam Maigari's home there was none of that, he was a *malam*. Balaraba at Giwa used to entertain us; on Friday or Sunday the women would come, and she would call the spirit when they wished it, but on some days not many of them would come. Balaraba knew nothing about medicine, she was only possessed by *bori*.

The town of the spirits is Jangare, they know their own town but we do not know it. When they are not mounting their mare they are there in their town, they do not keep wandering about the world. Then when they are called with their own drum-rhythm, they come at once. No one knows their town. They are away in their own town, when they hear their drumming call them they come. They like ceremonies and celebrations, they want to dance· They come, and people drum, they dance, they enjoy themselves and give gifts, men and women alike. The prostitutes, wherever they may be, dance in the open space of the compound. Married women cannot come out, they have no chance to do it. The spirits love people, indeed they do. They aren't the spirits of men dead, they are different spirits. They dismount and at once they return to their town. They mount in one place only, if you are drumming and calling a spirit and he does not come, that's because he is busy in another town. They are of the compound, no hurting, no harming, you share the ceremonies of the world and life with them. Those ones in Fagaci Ahmadu's compound were the ones of seeking rank and position; (21) he also gave gifts to Dangaladima the *bori* and the rest of them, they are of the same kind. A man knows the names of the spirits of his house. We haven't any in our compound, we are not possessed and we don't give them alms. Every *bori* adept kills them a chicken and a ram once every year on a Friday or a Sunday; they drink the blood and people eat the meat. It is not done at the feast, their festivals are different, but when the feast is over then they do it, indeed.

When we went to Gangara some time ago we saw some *bori*, there was a very good drummer and a woman was possessed by Dangaladima. She was all dressed in her best, there was drumming, everyone crowded round; there were twelve *bori*-dancers altogether. It was a feast in the butchers' compound. 'Allah, let us go to Biye in Zaria!', she was sitting and turning her head from side to side, they were singing splendidly. She was dressed up with her ornaments on, she was sitting there saying that some man should give her money. The generous Dangaladima gave it all away. Then another one was possessed by Bagobiri his slave, Bagobiri the slave of Dangaladima. She leapt up in the air and fell down, she leapt twelve times, Dangaladima sat looking on like a prince.

> *Bagobiri is a slave,*
> *But he is not a slave who is bound,*
> *He is not a slave who is beaten,*
> *He is not a slave who is abused,*

He is Dangaladima's slave.
See your master sitting there.
You are not like a horse,
You aren't a slave who is beaten,
But Dangaladima's slave.

Then there was dancing! Dangaladima likes his drummer, his slave, he takes off his gown and gives it to him. The one who was possessed by Bagobiri kept her hands crossed over on either shoulder like this, as slaves did; Dangaladima gave him presents, money and a gown. When the spirits had gone the things Dangaladima had given to Bagobiri belonged to Bagobiri's mare. When Bagobiri's mare met Dangaladima's mare, she would kneel to greet her. Then they sang another of Dangaladima's songs to him, the one that goes 'Give the women money'—give them lots and lots of gifts and they will desire men. Then they sang this song:

You women, lords of the town,
You women, lords of the town,
It's with the women we enjoy ourselves,
Aye, they're the lords of the town,
Women, they're the lords of the town! (22)
Take out your money and give to the drummers,
Take out your money and give to the singers,
> *Seek, call me, you're ignoring me,*
> *Sons of Ahamman, what's wrong with you?*
> *Daudu with the drummers,*
> *Ahamman what's wrong with you?*
> *One is pounding with another outside,*
> *Ahamman,*
> *One pounds with you, one makes* tuwo.
Take out your money and give to the drummers,
Take out your money and give to the singers.

He is the one with the pestle, he is snooze-in-the-hut, quietly he comes in and takes everything and gives it away. He is always seeking and seeking for something he can give away. Dangaladima Muhamman, the generous, the seeker after women. Isn't it the woman who rules? If there were none of us, where would the men be? Everyone likes Dangaladima, and his daughter Nana. When Bagobiri went away his mare took her hand like this and pulled out the finger-joints, slavery had finished. Then when Dangaladima had gone, his friend the Barber started up with his razor. He's Dangaladima's friend, the prostitutes' friend; they are all lovers of fine things. Even their mares love fine clothes. The reason the nobleman and the craftsman are friends is simply liking—mutual liking and the love of enjoyment, and spending of money.

> *The barber doesn't want a burning passion,*
> *He doesn't wish it to break him up.*

> *There is no king but Allah,*
> *It is fortune I am seeking from Allah.*

> *What has brought you to Bawa's bed?*
> *Love has brought me to Bawa's bed,*
> *Desire has brought me to Bawa's house.*

His name is Bawa too, like the Alkali. He's a profligate too! They're the ones who like to enjoy themselves with women. Then there is Sarkin Rafi, the chief of the stream, he often comes. We call him with the drum, regularly, like this: Sar-kin Ra-fi! he hears and he comes. Nana is his wife, but his paramour is Badakuwa, Nana and Badakuwa do not like one another; if Nana sees Badakuwa she beats her. Their mares don't like one another either. Sarkin Rafi goes about looking for her, his mistress. If Nana comes she goes looking for the adulteress to kill her.

Here in Giwa the spirits visit the compounds of secluded wives, but in Zarewa they only went to the prostitutes. In Old Giwa there was Magajiya's compound, the house of the prostitutes, she was appointed in the time of the old Fagaci, she was about my age. Her compound was inside the town close to a huge tree, near to our home by the ford. She was a *bori* adept, she used to initiate new *bori*-dancers. She was the head of all the prostitutes in Fagaci's district, she alone; every prostitute would come to her house, in the other towns you would only find those who come and stay for a night or so. She gave Fagaci some money and he appointed her Magajiya; he asked the prostitutes and they said they agreed. Then the prostitutes, men and women, were summoned, and they celebrated her appointment for seven nights. When he was going to appoint her Fagaci came to the entrance of his compound with his attendants and Magajiya came with her people, he called her and she and her women came and knelt down. He gave his *jakadiya* a beautiful new head-kerchief, the *jakadiya* took off Magajiya's old one and put on the new one. (23) She thanked him, then the women all applauded, and they went to her compound to drum and dance. Her work was to fine the men who didn't pay and to preside over the *bori*-dancing. After that old Magajiya died, Fagaci appointed the present one at Shika, and now there is also one at Kaya and one at Gangara. Here in Giwa now most of the prostitutes are in Sankira's house, there are 'Yaryaya, Kande, Amina, Nasara, Adama and Mai Sarkin Makada. In Cindo's house there are Habi and Kande, Gwamma and Caji, but Caji has gone to Shika now.

If there is any sort of gathering at Giwa, Magajiya comes from Shika with her prostitutes and there is *bori*-dancing. Then when Fagaci tours his district, when he gets to Kaya all the prostitutes assemble, and the young girls in their fine clothes, and they dance for him. When he arrives in Gangara the women of the town do the same—girls and prostitutes. They all come in their best clothes and ornaments and perfume and at night they dance for him. The prostitutes are in one place with their fiddlers, the unmarried girls are in another place with their drummer and his big drum. The prostitutes do *bori*-dancing. If he sees a nice one, won't he take her? He, the chief, the owner of the district? Of course he'll choose one. But only a prostitute, he would not take a young girl. Fagaci Ahmadu used to go on tour with his wife Gude, but if he saw a really beautiful prostitute he took her; when they had finished their affairs in the hut in the forecourt, he dismissed her and went inside the compound to Gude—she was better than any prostitute, she was very beautiful. Then he would have his affairs with her, so that she should not know there was anyone else, she wouldn't suspect he had taken another. If a man just lies down exhausted, his wife will reproach him, but if he touches her all is well. A man who likes his wife always lies with her, but one who doesn't particularly like his wife just goes to sleep. Some of them take prostitutes, then they go inside the house to their own wives too, either because they like their wife, or because they don't want a quarrel. They don't get weary.

The Hut in the Forecourt

You know Ibrahim the leather-worker? Well, one night a short time ago his wife was sitting at the door of her hut, she hadn't lit her fire; she heard a movement in the hut in the forecourt of the compound. She got up and went out, then the door of the hut was closed. Ibrahim's wife opened the door slowly, the leather-worker said 'There's no one here, go away'. She said 'I saw someone, I know she's here', then she peeped in, she grabbed at the woman but she was hiding behind Ibrahim. He got up and said 'Go away!' then his wife caught her and they struggled *kichi-kichi-kichi*, Ibrahim's wife was furious. The other woman fled. 'You! Leave her alone, leave her!' We heard it all, we laughed and laughed. The woman was one who had come in to the court to seek a divorce.

The women who come here to seek divorces in the district court are like that; (24) my Ladi took the head-kerchief off one of them in the hut in their forecourt; she had come there to commit adultery with Ladi's husband—Ladi caught them, indeed they were together. Aminu, Ladi's husband, got up and said 'Go out and visit your family, go out and visit your family!' She asked 'Isn't anyone going to escort me?' He said 'Go away'. Then she leaned over and snatched off the woman's head-kerchief, then she went off to visit her kinsfolk. When she returned she deposited the kerchief with Na Gangara's wives next door; Aminu said 'Give me that kerchief!' She refused. Aminu's adulteress was quite an old woman, she came to seek a divorce, she was lodging at a compound near to ours. She kept on saying that Ladi had pulled off her kerchief— everyone knew how! When she had got her divorce from her husband, she wandered about on her own for a while, then she went to Shika and got married there.

Married women can only go to other men when their husbands are away—like Tambudi and Sarkin Tandu in Zarewa; (25) he went away, then she hastily washed her body, she washed her face, she sent a message to her lover and he came to fetch her to the compound of his friend. Just as they were about to enter the hut by the door of the compound, she heard talking inside the hut. It was one of those huts with two rooms in it, you know the kind. When she heard voices she stopped—it was the voice of Sarkin Tandu and another woman! She heard them talking inside the hut, she went in and caught them, she seized her cloth and her kerchief, Sarkin Tandu rushed home and hid in shame. He didn't ask her what she had been doing there, she said 'I heard you, I heard you, today I caught you both!' He didn't know she was there with her lover. She had had three children by him, she didn't break off the marriage; she didn't take him before the Chief of Zarewa; there were her children, one of them his and the other two which she had brought with her from a previous marriage. She kept his secret for him.

You see how useful is the hut in the forecourt of the compound. A woman comes from one compound, a man comes from another, they do as they please in his friend's compound. (26)

There was Dandada, a young man—we lived in the same ward in Zarewa—his wife Abu slipped out into the town, and when he looked in her hut and didn't see her he also went into the town, he went to a certain compound, he peeped into the hut and saw her by the light of the lamp, with her lover. He said 'Get up and we will go home'. She was terrified. He pulled off the man's gown, he seized his blanket, he put them together and took the case to Sarkin Zarewa. It was her own young man whom she had wanted to marry, but she had been taken as a bride of alms to her husband; he knew she really wanted the other one. He took the man's gown to the chief. Sarki caused them to be sent for, they were brought to his entrance-hut for judgment; the man was bound, but the woman was not. The chief passed judgment and fined her lover thirty shillings, which he paid. Her husband whipped her, he beat her so that she was ill and couldn't get up. When she got up she went to break off the marriage, she said she didn't wish to live in that compound. Zarewa forbade her to marry her man, so she married Nasamai, the son of my Aunt Rabi; she became pregnant and miscarried, when she had miscarried she left Nasamai. Then she married the man she wanted and Zarewa did not prevent it; she had married another before she had married him. Then she became pregnant, she had a boy; when she had weaned him she had a girl—a most beautiful girl. She had three children with her lover, she is still there in his compound; she is happy with him, they are marrying off their children now. Her kin forced her to marry against her will, that was what caused all that; she has stayed with the man she wanted right up till now.

But whether women like their husbands or not, they will go to other men; give them a little money and they feel pleasant, or they want to deceive their husbands. The head wife in the compound of Abu, about whom I've just told you, was the one who slept with the father of her daughter's husband, Malam Sani; their compounds were opposite one another across the path. When we first heard that story we said 'No'. After that Malam Sani's three wives (he had about eleven children) came and caught him with his son's mother-in-law in the hut in their forecourt. The woman's daughter Lami heard their abuse, she was weeping, indeed she had something to be ashamed of, adultery between people whose children are married to one another is not a good thing. They both fled, Malam Sani's wives seized her cloth, but they did not take a complaint. They were secluded wives, also it was very shameful, the adulteress was the mother of the daughter married in their compound, she and Malam Sani were avoidance-relations. So they merely sold her cloth and divided up the money between themselves. They said they would all agree to abscond together, they would leave his compound, they had never seen such a thing, they were tired of Malam Sani. He talked and talked to them, he asked them to forgive him, Sallau his son whose mother-in-law was the woman concerned, and his elder brother, begged the wives to forgive their father, they said if they ran away everyone would hear about the matter. They promised that it would never occur again. Malam Sani used to give the mother of his son's wife money, she liked money and she also desired him. That is how it was. Where there is desire and greed for money and deceit, there is trouble.

Then there was a man called Madangari, they made a song about him and sung it behind his back.

> *Father of Alila, father of Ajuma,*
> *Madangari of Doka, you are Alila's father,*
> *You are Ajuma's father, you are also Ajuma's husband.* (27)

He married her off, she and her husband went westwards on a trading expedition. They returned. When they returned, father and daughter cleared a space on the bank of the stream amongst the sugar-cane, they fornicated. Someone saw him come out, then he saw her come out from amongst the sugar-cane, he went and told her husband. After he had told the husband she went out one day and the husband followed her. She went into the cane field and found her father, then they lay down—father and daughter. The husband came closer and saw them. He said he did not like it. Then he went home. The girl went to her father's home, and a little later her father came home too. Her husband said she could take her possessions away, he did not want her in his compound. She went and fetched her belongings and returned to her father's home.

Her mother was there in the compound, then they would go off to the bush, father and daughter, together. After some time a complaint was taken to Zarewa, (28) the story was all over the town. Zarewa sent for Madangari, he said to him 'If your daughter leaves her husband, is it you who are going to marry her?' Madangari was a wealthy man. He gave his daughter money and she went on a trading expedition. Zarewa said he would be sent to Kano City and put in the house of correction and bound and whipped; so Madangari brought Zarewa a gift of a hundred shillings to close his mouth, and nothing more was done. Everyone in the town stared at him and despised him, everyone in his compound knew about it. The girl's mother did not leave him. When the daughter returned from her trading expedition she used her money to buy medicine and charms and after four months a message came from her husband to say he was no longer angry; the *malams* had done their work and her husband's anger had cooled. Her father also left her alone because he was afraid of being bound and imprisoned. Then she was remarried and went back to her husband; the kinsfolk came to the feast, no one refused to come. Some people objected and some people sang songs, they sang songs about him and they sang songs about her. Her father had four children but she was the only one he desired, although she wasn't at all beautiful. That was a long time ago, before the Europeans came, when I was in Malam Maigari's compound. There aren't many people who behave like that, just one here and there. That case I know myself.

In a village near Gwibi there was an elder brother who desired his younger brother's wife—avoidance-relations, you see. When the younger brother was away from home the elder brother went into his wife's hut and took her; they were observed so they ran away and hid, they went out into the world and no one saw them. There was news that they were somewhere westwards, he said that she was his wife. After a time they got tired of each other and she left him and married someone else, he married someone else; they never returned home, shame drove them away.

There was a drummer too in a nearby village whose father gave money to the wife of his son, he called her and she went into his hut. Her husband looked for her and couldn't find her, so he sat down at the door of his father's hut. Later the door was opened and she came out quietly, it was late at night; he was sitting there and he saw her, then she saw a man outside the hut. Then he pounced on her and beat her (she got a dreadful beating), they struggled and fought. The man was his own father, he could do nothing about it. He drove his wife away, he said that he could not live with her, and in the morning he refused to go and greet his father, but apart from that there was nothing he could do. These things happened in our town, in Zarewa, but it is better here in Giwa; here there are only the women who come to get divorced, and the prostitutes.

A Nobleman's Female Messengers

When we moved here to New Giwa, Fagaci Muhammadu had only one *jakadiya*, Laraba, who had been with him when he held the office of Sarkin Ayyuka. Then he saw Kubendu, he persuaded her to break up her marriage so that she could become his *jakadiya*; her husband, who was one of Fagaci's clients, was upset by this and went away to Kaduna. Kubendu remained a *jakadiya* for two years, but after that Fagaci became tired of her and she went away. Then Kande came to seek a divorce from the judge at Giwa, and when Fagaci saw her he said he wanted her; he paid back the marriage-money to her husband for her, and she became his *jakadiya*. She remained with him for four years and then he turned her out, and married her off to Atamfa, his servant; Atamfa did not like her and she did not like Atamfa; he was one of Fagaci's retainers and had his hut in the forecourt of Fagaci's compound. Then Fagaci got Salamatu who is still there, and when she and Kande were both there together they did not like one another at all. When one came the other went—he had Salamatu for a time, then when he sent for Kande, Salamatu went off; later she returned and Kande went away. Kande was jealous even of Fagaci's wives, she didn't like anyone to be near him except herself, in her hut near the entrance of his compound. A *jakadiya* is different from a concubine, (29) you don't put her in a hut and keep her inside the compound as you do to a concubine, and a *jakadiya* doesn't take her turn with the cooking, either. The *jakadiya* comes to fetch her master if he is in the women's quarters and someone comes to see him; his men cannot come inside the compound where the women live, so she brings him the message. Then apart from his wives and various *jakadiyu*, there are the women who come seeking divorce in the court, and there are prostitutes—he has them all, whoever he likes. Ai, he doesn't get tired, he is a title-holder; that is their work. I hear Kande is breaking off her marriage at Funtua; that means she'll come back. Then there will be a fight, she and Salamatu don't like one another one little bit. You know that very nice hut at the door of his compound, where Salamatu lives now? That is Kande's hut, Salamatu used to be in the mud-roofed room. His real messenger is Laraba, she only works; she has been with him a long time.

CHAPTER XVI

MY QUARREL WITH MY BROTHER'S WIFE

My younger brother Kadiri had three wives when we came to New Giwa, Gwamma and two others. Gwamma was jealous of the other two and she went to a *malam* at Tatare to get medicine and charms to get rid of them. She put the medicine into Kadiri's food, but he knew nothing about it. Within three months he hated her co-wives, one, also called Gwamma, left him, and he turned out the other. Before this, he had said that he did not like the first Gwamma. Her one co-wife had two children by him, and the latest wife hadn't been there nine months when Gwamma got rid of her, yet earlier he had liked them both so much that he had begun to get tired of Gwamma. But when she got the medicine and made him very delicious food with the medicine concealed in it, it was she whom he desired. I used to hear him with each of them, when he went to the hut of one, I heard quarrelling; when he went to the hut of the other, I heard quarrelling; then he went to Gwamma's hut, and I heard laughter. He plagued them with grumbling until the second Gwamma went off to the judge and broke off the marriage. Then the wife with the children was left, she did not feel happy. He quarrelled with her, then he sent for her mother and said she was to take her away. He said he did not like her. When I heard I got angry, I liked her very much, in fact I liked them both. I abused him and told him off, but he wouldn't heed me. He gave notice to the judge and they were parted. She left her daughter with us, she is here with me now. The judge asked me, 'Do you love the child?' The child's mother's family said, 'No, they don't want her, give us our daughter'. Even Kadiri said he didn't want his daughter—you see the work of the magic. I said 'May Allah forgive you, *malam*, it is not so. I want the child, she grew up before my eyes. If you were to give me the king's palace I should not want it, but I do want this child'. He said 'May Allah give you His blessing, we will break up the marriage, we will give you your daughter'. She stayed in her father's house with me. Her mother entered on Iddah, when it was finished she married Sankira; she is here now. (1)

Gwamma sat down like this, she filled up the whole of the compound, she grew enormous; there was no one else besides her. The other Gwamma who left first of all, Kadiri would now like to remarry, but he cannot in case the Gwamma in his home should leave, and he desires her also. The other Gwamma is married and lives nearby; the two Gwammas do not like each other, they always quarrel and we keep them apart. But my daughter's mother is not quarrelsome. I should prefer the other Gwamma to come back, then both of them would fight and I should laugh. They would attack each other and I should say quietly, 'You must forgive one another and leave one another alone'. When the master of the house returned he would scold them both and I should listen. Then you would hear one say to him, 'You don't want me!' and the other say 'You don't like me!' and I should sit in my hut and listen.

I usually like this Gwamma but I was cross with her recently. For three months I was angry with her, I was annoyed and did not speak to her. The reason for it all was that my daughter went to market to sell groundnut cake for Gwamma, and she did not come back. At Azahar there was silence, she had not come home. Then I sent two people after her, but still she did not return. Then I got up myself and went and fetched her, she hadn't sold so much as one cake. I brought her back home. When Gwamma heard she was annoyed and she scolded the girl, there was the wind and the dust, there was two shillingsworth of groundnut cake and nobody would buy it. I went out, and when I came back I found my daughter crying, she said Gwamma had told her that if she was her mother she would give her a whipping, and she had been abusing her. Then Gwamma began to abuse me, she said it was I who had stopped the child from selling the groundnut cake. I was annoyed, it was no interest of mine to stop the child selling things. Then Gwamma made her husband Kadiri angry with me, and I wouldn't speak to either of them. She went to her own hamlet and borrowed Tata, the daughter of her elder brother, she brought Tata back with her and sent her to market every day. Then she said I had

stopped my daughter from going to market; I said I had not stopped her, we argued, and then I said I would eat their food no
longer. After that my brother Kadiri went to my *kawa*, the wife of
Sarkin Pawa the chief of the butchers (we are both old ladies and
we have become *kawaye*). Kadiri said he was weary of the abuse
and quarrelling in his home, he wanted my *kawa* to speak to me
and persuade me to eat their food and forget my anger. She said
'Very well', they put their heads together, and Kadiri got Gwamma
to buy things for stew—salt, locust-bean cakes, peppers, onions,
and the rest. My *kawa* said to me 'Your younger brother is tired of
abuse, forget the matter and cool down and you can all live peace-
fully together in the compound'. We talked it over, then I said
'Very well'. I went home, Gwamma had bought me the things for
soup, I accepted them and we settled it. Now we are there, the
three of us, like that.

I Marry my Present Husband

If Kadiri should bring back the second Gwamma, then I should
leave her hut, in which I am living at the moment, I should get
rid of the goats that are in my own hut and sell them, I should
return to my own hut. Then there would be quarrelling. If I got
tired of it I should go to the home of my children here in Giwa,
or I should go to the compound of my children in Zarewa—there
are plenty of them. Or I could go to the house of my husband
Ibrahim, I married him last year; ever since I finished my mourning for Malam Hasan he had been seeking me, they said to me
'Marry him, it is better than living alone'. Last year I said 'Very
well, I will', we performed the marriage, but I did not join him.
His wife went to visit her kin last dry season, she went to a naming-
feast, but she hasn't returned yet and he hasn't followed her. It is
eight months since she left. True she may never come back, but
the marriage is still there. He said to me 'Come and live in her
hut', but I refused, I am afraid she may come back and drive me
out. I said that if he wished me to come he should build a hut for
me and I would come in. He hasn't done it yet. In the mornings I
go and greet him and enquire how he has slept, and when I don't
go he comes to our compound and I meet him in the entrance-hut
and we greet one another. (2) A few days ago he said 'I hear you
are working with your European woman'. I said 'Yes, we are busy

with our work'. He said 'You didn't tell me? I, the master of the house?' So on market-day I gave him sixpence, I said 'Enjoy the market, buy kolanuts and meat and things for stew.' I said 'We are working'. He was very pleased.

I married Ibrahim last year. His grandfather was a Giwa man, he was well-off and he farmed. He kept on buying slaves and more slaves, then he looked around at the compounds in Giwa and saw that they were not well built. When Ibrahim's grandfather had become very rich indeed, he persuaded the townspeople to build their town properly. He collected men, free men joined with slaves, they called working-bees from hamlet to hamlet, from kin to kin, children and youths and compound heads; the drummers drummed while everyone worked and they built huts and rooms with mud roofs, square thatched huts, and two-storeyed huts, with roofs of mud-cement. (3) They built walls to the town and they built four gates, north, south, east and west. Before his time they were living at Old Giwa but there were no proper compounds, they built them of corn-stalks like the Bush Fulani huts! Ibrahim's grandfather did not get any official position, he was only a wealthy man. His son was given a turban, the King of Zaria made him Danfangi, (4) Chief of Giwa; Usuman was his name. After he had been chief for a time he was dismissed, his time was finished. (5) Then Danfangi Umaru was appointed, both were Sabawa men from the same hamlet in Giwa country. When he was dismissed Danfangi Yero was appointed, a Fulani from Turbe; he was the father of the present Danfangi. When the king dismissed Yero he went back to Kano, he was angry; all his kinsmen followed him. After he came to Zarewa he got the chieftainship of our town. I don't know why they were all dismissed—it was just their fate. The present Danfangi, Yero's son, often says 'We are your kin, we held the chieftainship of your town'. I always reply 'Mm'. When Danfangi Yero came to Zarewa we were children; they dismissed him first, then Sarkin Zarewa Habu; after him there was Hanciji—that was his swear-word, he came from away up north and he was always saying 'Hanciji!' In Zarewa the chieftainship was not hereditary, the King of Kano appointed whom he liked; perhaps it was because of wealth, or because the townspeople wanted him? I don't know the grounds for his choice. Here in Giwa it is inherited, from kinsman to kinsman. Then after Hanciji we had Danfangi Dangoshi; all of them, when they were turned out of Giwa they picked up their

family and went off to Zarewa. When they came people were glad
to see them and they were appointed—hadn't something pleasant
come? Over there they cooled off, then when they were put out of
office in Zarewa they came back to Giwa. First they were driven out
of Zaria, so they went to Kano and greeted the king, they greeted
him very well indeed, then he made them the chiefs of Zarewa.
Perhaps it wasn't really just as simple as that, but that is what was
said. Certainly there were one or two Fulani from Giwa who ruled
in Zarewa also.

You see there are a lot of us Kano people here in Giwa now; one
would come, then you would come to visit him, you would see a
place to farm, you would see kinsfolk, then you would join him. It
isn't because of a place to farm that people move, it is because of
kinsmen. Kinship is what takes a man to a new place. (6)

My Adopted Daughter's Marriage and her First Childbirth

When Malam Hasan the warder died, Malam Maigari sent to
ask me to come back to his compound, but I refused to go back;
I like Kadiri, my younger brother, and I wanted to live near him.
I have lived in his compound for five years now, I haven't been
away at all; I haven't been to Zarewa and I haven't been to
Gwibi. I look after my goats, I make a little money, I sell a little
firewood, I get a little money to buy marriage cloths for my
adopted children. I rear the goats, then when there are five I sell
one and buy a little cloth. I sell a goat for fifteen shillings but if
they are small they won't fetch more than seven or eight shillings.
Last year I sold one, this year I shan't sell any because there are
none big enough. Next year, if Allah preserves them alive, I shall
sell two and buy cloth. That is what I've inherited from my father
'Babantakwiya', though he wasn't keeping goats any more at the
time he died. I buy my daughters a few cloths and I give them a
little money; this cloth I'm wearing is Yelwa's, she lent it to me to
come to Zaria with you. (7)

When we had been here in New Giwa for a year, 'Yardada my
adopted daughter was courted by a retainer of the District Scribe's
who lived in his compound. She said she did not want him. She put
on her Friday best to go to market, and there another young man
told her he desired her. His elder brother came to greet me, I didn't

know who he was; he said the people of the Chief of Yelwa's compound greeted me; I said 'Thank you, we reply to their greeting'. He asked about 'Yardada, I said to him 'Isn't it the girl who should choose?' After a little, her young man gave her ten shillings. Then Hasana, 'Yardada's father's sister, went to the Chief Scribe's compound and told them to let her know how much they had given; they said fifty shillings. Then Hasana went to Sarkin Yelwa's compound and told them that the Scribe's retainer had given fifty shillings; Sarkin Yelwa's compound gave her the fifty shillings to return, Abba, the scribe's retainer, accepted it, and we were free to arrange the marriage with Sarkin Yelwa's compound. (8)

At the Greater Feast the bridegroom's elder brother brought her powder, perfumed oil and perfume, with four shillings. We accepted it and gave it to 'Yardada to divide amongst her *kawaye*. When the bridegroom gave her gifts of money, I used to take the money, if it was ten shillings I added four of my own, that made fourteen shillings, and I would buy her a head-kerchief. The gifts that a girl's suitor brings to the compound, you use to buy something for the girl; the 'market gifts' she keeps, and gives to the drummers when they are dancing at night. He brought another four shillings and I put one shilling to it and bought her a blouse. The feast passed and her own mother and I discussed it, then we said 'Very well; bring the gifts for the betrothal and for setting the day'. On a Sunday they brought the gifts, two calabashes of kolanuts, for the betrothal and for setting the day, one basket of guineacorn and one of millet, one of rice, salt, and salt for the grandparents, a shilling for the grandparents, four shillings for the mother's kin and four shillings for the father's kin. They came to our compound, with the drummers, but I said 'No', and I took them to Hasana, 'Yardada's father's sister, in Sankira's house. 'Yardada had never spent the night in Hasana's hut, she had slept with me in my hut ever since I took her from her mother's breast. But Hasana was her father's kin. When they came to set the day they said 'Where shall we go?' and I answered, 'To Sankira's compound'. Then they said 'What, that home of worthlessness, that disreputable compound—is the house of prostitutes the place where we are to seek a wife?' They refused to go. Fagaci and the judge and the *mufti* had all come, they were sitting on mats outside our compound and they also refused to go to the house of the disreputable Sankira. (9) Kadiri was her *wali*. The praise-singers called out what he said.

'We give her to you; go and get ready to take her in the month after next, on the twelfth day. Abba's luck is out, Mamman's luck is in; the one with a shilling shall have her, the one without a shilling can go over there!' That's what the praise-singer said, they act as spokesmen. 'Yardada had gone to Yakawadda market with the girls, we had sent them off.

When the ceremonies of betrothing the couple and setting the day for the marriage were complete (we do them both at once nowadays), (10) the girls and young men went off and the officials and elders went home. We, the kinsfolk, divided up the gifts. In the evening when everyone had dispersed, 'Yardada returned from market with the things I had sent her to buy.

Two months later on the tenth day of the month, 'Yardada went to Fagaci's compound with her *kawa*, who is now Waziri's wife, and a daughter of the pipe-players. They all hid somewhere in Fagaci's compound. I said to her *kawa* Gambo and her *yaya* Soda, 'If you have hidden her and you don't produce her tomorrow or the day after, what will become of the feast?' They said 'Where's the hiding-money?' I said 'Go and see the bridegroom, he'll give you a shilling and Talle will put on her henna'. Off they went to Talle, her joking relation in the blacksmith's compound—isn't 'Yardada a daughter of the Buzaye, the Sokoto people, so won't she joke with a blacksmith's daughter? Talle was a grown woman with children. (11) The *kawaye* went to Fagaci's compound to look for the bride, then the wailing began. I heard her wailing and my body began to tremble like this, I did not want to be parted from her. Fagaci was in his entrance-hut and the wailing annoyed him. 'Come come, 'Yardada,' he said, 'you're going to Yelwa's compound, the marriage compound, and you're crying? Cheer up, don't cry!' After she had had her first child and she came to Fagaci's compound with her child on her back to greet her friends, he said 'Is it you, 'Yardada, have you grown up like this? Where's the wedding weeping now?' Then she fled inside the compound! I sent her *kawaye* to the bridegroom to get the hiding-money, but when they returned they refused to bring the bride, they came to me looking for her, and I said she wasn't with me. 'The bridegroom has given us kolanuts,' they said; 'Right,' I said, 'then go and put the henna on her.' Then they went and indicated where she was, they went and stood outside Fagaci's compound, then Talle arrived and went into the compound and seized her and put the henna on her while 'Yardada cried and struggled, *kichi-kichi*. Talle ran away with 'Yardada after her, saying she was going to beat her. When Talle caught them in the hut, she and the girls were crying and shouting, throwing themselves on the ground and saying 'Alas, marriage has eaten up 'Yardada!' They all fell in a heap on top of her; the *kawaye* were weeping, if the tears wouldn't flow they put spit on their eyes instead! It was in the midst of this that Fagaci came into the compound and said 'Quieten them down and take them home'. Then my daughter and about fifty boys and girls all came to my hut. They were wailing and we, the elders in the compound, were also weeping for 'Yardada. Then the drummer came to the entrance of the compound with his drum, and when 'Yardada heard the deep drum she started to cry all over again.

At night, when she was quiet, I took her over to Hasana's compound. I said to her kinsfolk, 'Come, we will take her to her father's house'. Her kinswomen and lots of children all escorted her to Hasana's house. When we arrived outside the compound with our drumming, we found the entrance-hut full of men, there was no way through. We stopped at the front of the compound, there were the prostitutes and men, they were playing the fiddle. They moved out of the way and we all went in and sat down. I said to Hasana, 'Here is your daughter, I have brought you your daughter. To-morrow she will be taken to Tatare, to her *mawankiya's* compound.' Then Hasana replied, 'Oh no, you say I am her father's kin, but see your father gave her father a wife, and her father worked with your father for many many years; then, too, 'Yardada's father gave the girl to you to be your daughter. Take her home to your compound.' (12)

When I went home again the girls slept in our compound, they filled up my hut and they filled up Gwamma's hut too. The drummer drummed at the front of the compound, the children played and danced until they were tired, then they all lay down and went to sleep. 'Yardada was playing and dancing too. In the morning they got up, then her two chief *kawaye*, Joji and Audi (who is now Waziri's wife), both came with a huge following. I said 'Oh no, you can't all go', and I reduced their numbers, finally I sent them off with five girls each, to escort her to her *mawankiya's* compound at Tatare. Yelwa and A'i, both Adama's children like 'Yardada, were her two younger sisters but I stopped her *kanwar rana* from going, I said they really must cut down their numbers. The 'Slave of the bride' arrived then from the bridegroom's compound, (13) everyone chased her and beat her—she had a bad time! The girls picked up the gifts that had come from the bridegroom's compound, the 'millet for millet-paste in front of the horse' and the guineacorn, they took them all with them so that they could eat porridge in the *mawankiya's* compound. They rubbed the 'Bride's slave' with porridge—if she had been bad-tempered she would have got up and gone to wash it off, but as she wasn't she only wrestled with them.

'Yardada's *mawankiya* was Lare, the elder sister of her mother. Lare had borne eight children and the family had left Giwa and gone to live in a hamlet. When the bride's party arrived at *mawankiya's* compound in the hamlet, they divided out the guineacorn and pounded it and made porridge to eat. Then they got a drummer and they danced. At night they tied up 'Yardada's arms and legs in henna, while she struggled and tried to get hold of the henna and her chief *kawa* hung onto her legs. Next morning they started on the work of making porridge again. When everybody had eaten, they made the 'millet-balls in front of the horse'; the people of the hamlet all brought their gifts, 'reinforcements', as they say; they brought money, rice, calabashes and bowls, both neighbours and kinsfolk from round about. Then the girls picked up the loads and they all started back. *Mawankiya* took the bride to the compound of her father's sister Hasana.

That morning before noon the marriage was solemnized, when Fagaci and the judge and the other elders refused to enter Sankira's compound, the ceremony was held in our entrance-hut. Then later on, about La'asar (5.30) the girls returned to Giwa; they all went to 'Yardada's mother's compound, Adama's compound, and they sent to tell me she had arrived. The chief *kawa* hid the millet-paste 'before the horse', no one must eat it. You see in the old days we spent two nights in the bride's father's compound with our *kawaye* and two nights in the compound of *mawankiya*; nowdays they only spend one night in each.

Then Hasana brought a full bowl of grain and a chicken, I filled a bowl with dumplings and put a chicken on the top, Adama brought a huge bowl of porridge; we all went to the house where Lare the *mawankiya* was, and took her the 'porridge of arrival', we said to her 'Give it to your children'. The bridegroom's family sent her 'porridge for the day after tomorrow', so that she could feed her children and people. In the compound of her kinswoman Hakama they cooked her a huge pot of 'porridge of the sense of kinship'. There were a great many kinsfolk and girls there. From the bridegroom's compound came young men, boys and girls with ten bowls of millet-balls, ten full bowls of grain, ten chickens and a large bowl of milk; they took the *jere* food to Hasana's compound. We had sent to invite the women of the bride's father's kin and of her mother's kin and they were all there—we hadn't forgotten one; they all came to Hasana's compound. Then *mawankiya* arrived, she divided out the food equally between all the women, giving the children who had brought it their dues, one bowl of millet-paste and one of porridge. The kinswomen would look at their portion of porridge, they would say 'This is no good!' then the kinswomen of the bride's father said that *mawankiya* was one of the mother's kin, so of course she was giving them the best bits! They were teasing and joking, then *mawankiya* picked up her share for her family and went off home with it, and everyone else picked up their share and went home too. I took mine across to our compound—dumplings, milk, millet-balls, porridge, and a chicken; when I arrived in our compound, I spread it all out and proceeded to divide it up among everyone in the household.

Late at night the bridegroom's family sent to say we must bring *mawankiya* to wash the bride and give her to the bridegroom. They came with their drumming and sat down in front of our compound.

> *Give us the daughter of our town,*
> *She isn't the daughter of your town today,*
> *Give us the daughter, and rest,*
> *Give us the daughter of our town.*

We sent out a message to them, 'We shall not give you our daughter today, go away and dance and come back tomorrow'. The girls who were in our compound fetched two drummers and while we were inside our crowded huts *mawankiya* began to heat water in the middle of the compound. She called out to the bridegroom's party outside, 'Ai, the water isn't warm yet, go and dance and drum, when morning comes we'll give her to you!' Then it was time to wash the bride. There was drumming and dancing at the front of our compound and the bride was hiding in Hasana's house, her *kawaye* were hiding her. I said 'It's nearly dawn, Asubahi is near, go and bring the bride out'. Then the bridegroom's friends came, they were seeking the bride, we said 'We can't find her, her *kawaye* have hidden her'. The bridegroom's chief friend gave the bride's chief *kawa* a shilling and the groom's younger brother gave her sixpence, then the chief *kawa* and *mawankiya* went to Hasana's compound, then they turned the mortar upside down, the bride sat on it, they tied up her skirts and started with the soap. A *kawa* stood on each side of her and her grandmothers were in front, Hakama, and Maiwa, Hakama's younger sister, as no grandmother on her father's side was alive. She wailed all the time her grandmothers washed her. The girls were all round singing, they gave her two kolanuts. She was wailing because she was leaving the dancing and leaving the life of a girl. They sang 'Save my life, *hankaka*', they washed her with the soap and the girls were singing about the white-breasted crow. 'Yardada was crying quietly. When they sang 'When you hear our drumming you won't come' she burst out crying. They gave her her vest, she went and washed herself privately and came back again, then they gave her her lovely cloths, her marriage cloths and slippers and they covered her head and face with a cloth. I sat in my hut with Asabe and Lare, Adama's elder sisters, and Jumai and Ba'i, her younger sisters, and Adama herself, 'Yardada's real mother. Then *mawankiya* took her to the entrance-hut of Hasana's compound, the men of her father's kin and her mother's kin lectured her and blessed her marriage, then they said 'Take her to Baba's compound'. They brought her to our compound, to my hut where we were all sitting, her 'mothers'. I was crying and Adama was crying; we said 'You must be good, don't quarrel, settle down to your marriage'. We talked to her like that. Then I said 'Is the bridegroom's friend here?' They said 'Here's Dandada'. I knew them all well, our compounds were close together. They said 'But we haven't got a horse', then Dandada said 'No, but I'm the horse!' We put the bride into trousers and a man's big gown and we wound a white cloth on her head. The girls clung to her until Dandada gave them sixpence. He took her on his back and the girls hung onto him, but he got away; then they chased him and caught him again, until he gave them some more money to divide among themselves. We stayed behind in the compound. The girls and young men went off with the bride, the drummers with them; we heard them singing 'The big hunt was good, The big hunt got meat'. They all set out. We older women of the bride's kin followed a little way behind. The bridegroom's kinsfolk were waiting for them to come, they had their ears open, listening for the bride. (14)

When they arrived at Sarkin Yelwa's compound in Anguwan Shehu, they found the entrance-hut full of men—all the men in the hamlet are his kinsmen. They made way for the bride's party, saying 'See, the bride has come! Praise be to Allah, we give thanks!' They passed through the entrance and went in to the bride's hut. There the *kawaye* refused to enter the bride's hut and began to sing 'Bring water with a sixpence, Bring us water with a sixpence'. They tried to carry the bride off to the river, but Dandada hung onto her, and she couldn't run away. Then the bridegroom's younger sister brought the water and the sixpence. When it became light the owners of the compound gave them food, the 'porridge in front of the horse' with stew; they brought out the 'millet-paste in front of the horse' and mixed it with sour milk and ate it. They kept a little and put it in a bowl with water, then they covered the bowl and took it to the bridegroom's hut; he bought it for a shilling and the girls wouldn't let him look inside.

The bridegroom already had two wives so he did not hide. He went in and out from the huts of his wives to the entrance-hut of the compound, taking food to his friends, and returning inside the compound to speak to his wives. His two wives were celebrating with their own kinswomen and friends, all in their finest clothes and ornaments.

The next morning we, the older women, returned to Sarkin Yelwa's compound with the hairdresser, who dressed the bride's hair; her grandmothers washed her again all over and rubbed her body with perfumed oil. When that was done we all returned to our compound, and gathered up the dowry; there were a great many loads and a great many women to carry them. There were about two hundred metal and enamel bowls and plates, about twenty cloths, two sacks of rice, two sacks of guineacorn, one sack of *wasa-wasa*. (15) There were twenty-five bottles of oil—a tin and a half—a basket of locust-bean cakes and a basket of salt. We covered the wall of her hut with the plates and bowls, and the cloths filled up the hut! Everyone had brought a little, and when it was all put together it was a great deal. We remained in the bridegroom's compound all day arranging the dowry until the evening; the bride was there with the children, she was quite cheerful and had stopped weeping.

When the feast came round I gave 'Yardada locust-bean cakes, two bowls of salt, rice, grain, millet and a bottle of oil. Hasana, Adama and Lare each brought the same—we were her parents. Lawal and Asabe and Namata, her brothers, also brought her gifts for the feast, but ours were bigger since we are her parents. When we had collected our gifts together, the day before the feast, we took them to Sarkin Yelwa's compound and gave them to 'Yardada. Everyone rejoiced. We went one by one to her hut, each with our gift; she saw first one come in, then another—she was delighted. By then she was cooking, after only three weeks she had started to share in the cooking. She dipped into the food we had brought and gave some to the owners of the compound, she distributed some of it to everyone in the household. Her husband took nothing from his granary for two months. At the Greater Festival we brought her more gifts, but they were nothing like so much as the ones for the Lesser Festival. Then she became pregnant, and after that we made no further gifts.

When 'Yardada was seven months pregnant her husband went to the Forest Guard and got a permit to cut wood in the bush for her washing. I was her midwife, I was there at the birth and I took my grandchild and washed him and washed him; I washed 'Yardada thoroughly with hot water; I remained in her hut for forty days.

It was one day about noon that the people of Sarkin Yelwa's compound sent for me, they said her head was aching; I went over and found her lying on her bed. The kinswomen came, then late at night they got up and said 'May Allah preserve us', and went home. 'Yardada lay down on her bed, then in the middle of the night I saw she had got off the bed and was kneeling down; I said 'Are you all right?' she replied 'Yes, quite all right'. A little later I heard 'Ya-a-a-a-a!' I opened the door of the hut and called 'Kande, Rabi, Kwari—see, here's the child, a boy!'

When the child is coming, the mother lies on her bed, she turns from side to side. When she feels that he is about to be born she gets up and kneels down on the floor on all fours. If he does not come, she gets back onto her bed and lies down. If the pains go on too long, then you get leaves of *kalkashi* (16) and make them into a medicine for her to eat; it is like okra, but more oily.

'Yardada washed for five months and she became strong and healthy, she ate hot spices and drank hot drinks; everything must be hot so that the chill shall not seize her. If the chill seizes a mother, then her arms will swell up, her legs will swell up, and she will probably die. You give her delicious food with plenty of meat and spices, and you heat the bed—the cold can't get her. You put the baby into a big calabash of warm water and wash him morning and evening with soap so that he is nice, you put antimony round his eyes, and you carry him about on your back; he gets healthy and strong. I washed 'Yardada, I boiled the water and took her behind her hut and dipped leaves in the water and splashed her all over so that the water should enter her skin and make her feel good. I said 'Don't make a sound, see the people of the compound are listening'. Then she shut her mouth tightly while I washed her with the hot water. For the first seven days you must wash the vagina and round it with a soapy cloth so that it is quite clean. I said to 'Yardada 'Hold on, if you scream I will run away and leave you— see you have had an easy childbirth, there is your son to carry on your back'. She never screamed once, she was a very good girl. Some of them do, you know Ba'i in the judge's compound? Her screaming was dreadful, even the judge had to speak to her, he said she mustn't scream like that, she must endure it. There was some illness in her inside. When she had resisted the old ladies, Malama and Ladi, then the judge's retainers had to hold her while she was washed. Daughter of uselessness and worthlessness, bastard! (17) Every day we heard it. There she was, with men looking on her thus, we don't approve of their seeing women naked, but what was her family to do? On the naming-day when we went at La'asar (5.30) we heard screams, we went into the hut of her mother's co-wife; her mother was saying 'May Allah deprive you of His blessing!' When they had finished the forty days' washing twice a day, the judge said they must rest from her screams. For the next twenty days he sent to a man at Tsibiri, a hunter, who had medicine of herbs, and got medicine from the bush. It was wood, chips of *sanya* wood. The chips were put in a big cooking-pot and hot water was added; when it was cool Ba'i drank the water, she drank no other water for fourteen days. One day you made a decoction, then you dried that wood and used fresh the next day; on the following day you used the first wood again, and so on. On the fortieth day after the birth, since Ba'i was not going to wash for the proper five months, what remained of her firewood that had been cut to heat the water was taken out to the crossroads and burnt. Apart from this medicine which she drank, there was no other medicine, but the child is quite healthy and so is Ba'i.

MY QUARREL WITH MY BROTHER'S WIFE

I washed 'Yardada carefully, when I had boiled the water I put it in a big water-pot and then I washed her. You know the little boy with the flat face and the ears that stick out, the one I used to bring on my back when I came to see you at first—he's 'Yardada's son.

The Past and the Future

When 'Yardada and Yelwa were girls, sometimes they would sleep in my hut with all their friends, and at other times they would sleep in some other compound. When we were young, we used to fill up the hut of our grandmother, Anja, and we also used to sleep with our mothers, our own mother and her co-wife. The girls would say 'Come and sleep with us tonight in our hut!' We were about ten girls, with our young men, but our parents would not let us spend the night with the young men, they were in the hut in the forecourt of the compound, and the girls slept with the women inside the compound. Then when we were full grown, the man who desired us came with money, and we were married. Yelwa is not married yet; the boys don't come for her, she plays and sleeps with the young girls, her friends.

My elder sister Dije died after she had had four children in Zarewa, she died seven years ago, the year before my father died. Father was always smiling, and the children liked him—all Ibrahim Dara's children were pleasant smiling people. My brother Kadiri is farming, he has no other craft besides farming. When he harvests the guineacorn he puts it in his granary, then there are millet and groundnuts too; we eat until next year. He takes the cotton to the scales to be weighed and bought. This year he got two big loads of cotton and he·took them to the cotton market (18) to sell them, but I don't know what he got for them, he didn't tell me. Adama's son Lawal got forty shillings for his. My husband Ibrahim is picking his cotton now, he was just off to the farm when I went and said 'I have come to say good-bye, I am going to Zaria with my European woman because we haven't finished our work yet. If Allah wills it I shall be back in seven days.' He said 'Don't let us hear nothing from you'. I said 'Oh no, indeed I shall be back soon'. He said 'Come back safely, come back safely'. When I return home I shan't go into the bush to fetch wood for sale, my foot is sore. I shall do some spinning. If you spin for about five months and collect many spindles of thread, then you can sell it and get money for a cloth, about four or five shillings, or if thread is dear you may get seven shillings. I don't weave any more now, the big loom is hard work. Then if a feast comes along I shall sell a goat and buy things for the feast—that is the usefulness of keeping goats. Four years ago I married off 'Yardada, next year if Allah preserves us I will arrange Yelwa's marriage. Next year we shall send for Danbaba and Kande, my cross-cousins (their mother was my father's younger sister) and Tanko na Bawa and Malam Akilu Sarkin Tasha, Magajin Kasuwa and my husband Ibrahim and Malam Aminu— Kadiri and I will call all our friends and neighbours and discuss the matter. If we decide to give her as a bride of alms, we shall get the dowry together; if we decide to marry her for money, we shall discuss the matter of money. I should prefer to give her as alms, I haven't many children, so I should like to give her to a good *malam*, a student, but a young man, because maidens don't like old men; then we should give her as alms. If it is to be a marriage of alms I should be happy. (19) But if it should be a marriage for a little money, very well, I should agree too. When we have discussed it, I shall take Yelwa to my hut alone with me and ask her whom she wants. When she tells me, then we shall arrange the marriage, we will put her in her new hut. Late at night, with an old man in front and an old woman behind, we should take her to their compound. The man calls, 'Peace be upon you! Are the owners of the house asleep? . . .'

If we decide on a marriage of alms our kinsfolk will all help me. Kadiri agrees, he would like to give her as alms too, I have talked to him about it already. Next year she should be starting to get market gifts.

We shall consult Malam Aminu because his wife Ladi is the daughter of Gwamma's elder brother; Gwamma adopted her when she was weaned, she brought her to Kadiri's home and she married her off from there; we are her mothers. Malam Aminu is Fagaci Ahmadu's son. (20)

I shall be midwife several times this year; there are the wives of my *kanen rana* Shera, whom I call Danmori; there is Gude, Magajin Kasuwa's wife—I remember when she was born; there is Talle, the wife of Danbaba my cross-cousin. I don't act as midwife to outsiders, only to kinsfolk. No one says anything to me, but I know they will send for me the day the child is born; I just know how it is, so there is no need for them to ask me about it beforehand.

POSTSCRIPT

(translation)

Giwa, Zaria Province.

15 April 1951.

From Baba at Giwa.

Very many greetings to Mrs. M. G. Smith. After greetings, I received the news that you arrived at your home safely by aeroplane. This year I married off Yelwa to Yakubu at Sabon Birni. Ladi, the wife of Malam Aminu greets you. My husband Danauta also greets you. Kadiri greets you. I hope that you won't let work prevent you from answering me.

I am yours,

BABA GIWA

Written by Malam Abdu, a school teacher at Giwa, from Baba's dictation.

Giwa School,

Zaria Province.

3 June 1951.

Very many greetings to Mrs. Mary Smith. I hope you are all as well as we are here at Giwa. After greetings, I wish to inform you that Baba received your letter of the 14th of May 1951. She received it on the 18th of May 1951. I read her the news of your son Daniel's birth, also the news of his cot and sucking and great sleeping, and his lack of patience when hungry. She laughed a great deal. Also that he has a lot of hair on his head. She says he has got all that hair from his mother, his father has not got much hair on his head.

Baba became ill on the 28th of May 1951, she died on the 3rd of June 1951. She was 74 years old, that is to say she was born in 1877. Before she died she was saying 'I shall die without seeing my son Daniel'. I hope you will write down this story for him, so that he can read it one day when he grows up. I gave £1 2s. so that they could buy her a shroud. . . .

MALLAM ABDU,
Arabic Teacher,
Giwa School.

GLOSSARY OF HAUSA TERMS

Aunaka: Grain sent by a bridegroom to his bride after the marriage ceremony, but before she comes to live in his compound. She makes porridge from it (the *tuwon aunaka*) and sends it to the bridegroom's household. See p. 112 and note 3, Ch. 7, p. 271.

Bori: The spirit-possession cult, also the possessing spirits.

Cuge: A special food distributed after a death, and made from uncooked grain-flour (see p. 217).

Gandu: Joint family organized for farming. See Introduction, p. 22.

Jakadiya: A female messenger of a nobleman or official.

Jere: Tuwon jere, the food sent from the bridegroom's household to the bride's household on the day she is to come and live with him. *Jere*—lit. 'in a row'. See p. 114 and note 4, Ch. 7, p. 271.

Kawa pl. *kawaye:* A woman's female friend, used loosely for any friend, but more specifically for one with whom she has established a formal bond-friendship by exchange of gifts. *Kawaye* are of equal age and status.

Kanen rana: lit. 'younger brother of the day'. A woman's male bond-friend, considerably younger than herself. Men also have *kanen rana*.

Kanwar rana: lit. 'younger sister of the day'. A woman's female bond-friend, younger than herself.

Malam: A Koranic scholar (see note 27, Ch. 8, p. 274).

Mawankiya: lit. 'the washer'. The younger sister of a bride's mother, in whose compound part of the marriage ritual takes place.

Rinji, pl. *rinjoji, rumada:* The place where slaves lived; it might be in the forecourt of their master's compound, or a separate village settlement like Anguwan Karo.

BABA OF KARO

Tsarance: Institutionalized love-making between unmarried youths and girls. *Tsaranci*—sexual intercourse between them.

Wali: A woman's guardian and representative at the marriage ceremony. In Muslim law, women are minors.

Yaya, yayar rana: lit. 'elder sister of the day'. A woman's (or a man's) female bond-friend, older than herself and senior in status.

HAUSA TITLES

These are very numerous, but the following appear in the text:

Sarki: Chief; i.e. Sarkin Zarewa—Chief of Zarewa town; Sarkin Kano—Chief (king) of Kano; Sarkin Makada—Chief of Drummers; Sarkin Aljannu—Chief of the spirits.

Fagaci: A title which nowadays in Zaria emirate is held by the District Head of Giwa District.

Other titles: Ciroma, Dangaladima, Danmori, Galadima, Ma'aji, Madaki, Majidadi, Turaki.

Note: 'c' is always pronounced 'ch' as in 'church'. No attempt has been made in this record to indicate the different kinds of 'd', 'b' and 'k' which occur in Hausa.

NOTES

CHAPTER I

(1) 'Grandfathers': her own grandfather and his brothers. Similarly 'fathers' is used of her own father and his brothers, 'mothers' of her own mother and her sisters. Hausa use these classificatory terms when speaking generally about such relatives, but they specify 'my own father', 'my own mother', 'my mother's sister', etc. when necessary.

(2) Kukawa—capital of the Kanuri (Barebare) kingdom of Bornu, north-east of Kano emirate bordering on Lake Chad, the scene of much political unrest in the first half of the nineteenth century. *Galadima* and *Ciroma* were titles in use in Bornu in the nineteenth century. For information on this period in Bornu, see: H. Barth, *Travels and Discoveries in North and Central Africa*, chapters 29–30 etc.; H. Urvoy, *Histoire de l'Empire du Bornu* (Paris, 1949); O. and C. L. Temple, *Notes on the Tribes, Provinces and Emirates of Northern Nigeria* (Cape Town, 1922, 2nd edition); Sir H. Richmond Palmer, *The Bornu Sahara and Sudan* (1938).

(3) Baba was not clear about the seniority of her great-grandfathers, and whether Turaki or Ciroma was the elder.

(4) For *gandu*, see Introduction.

(5) Marriage of kinship (*auren zumunci*)—see Introduction. Marriages between the children of slaves of the same master, as illustrated in the text, also came under the heading of 'kinship marriages'. They would be preferred by the master to marriage with an outsider.

(6) Naming-ceremony. Slaves bought in the market were usually captive Gwari or other pagan tribesmen; their children, however, became Muslims at the naming-ceremony held on the seventh day after birth, and were brought up as Muslims even if their parents had not adopted the faith. It was the owner's religious duty to see to this.

(7) Porridge—*tuwo*—is the staple food of the Hausa of this area and is prepared from grain, usually guineacorn, and eaten with a spiced stew (*miya*) made from various ingredients. The snacks (*marmare*) prepared by women for sale in the market are not thought of as 'real food', which is porridge and stew.

(8) 'The child was freed'—but the status of slaves' children (*dimajai*, s. *dimajo*) was different from that of free persons. Like slaves, they remained in their owner's *rinji* and worked for him, and had to obtain his

257

permission to marry, though unlike slaves they could marry free Hausa women. They had no title to the land they farmed or the compound in which they lived, but they probably enjoyed greater rights over movable property, such as small stock, grain, cash, etc. Unlike slaves, *dimajai* were not liable to be sold. Hausa describe the position of the *dimajo* in the stereotyped analogy, 'If you buy a cock and a hen in the market and they have chickens, aren't the chickens yours?' The Hausa for slaves' children is *dimajai* or *cucanawa* (s. *bacucane*) but the term slave (*bawa*) is often used loosely for both classes of unfree persons.

(9) *Malams*—(h. *malam*, pl. *malamai*)—Koranic scholars and teachers. Their knowledge of Islamic texts or the Arabic language varies greatly, but as a class they are the traditional religious teachers and leaders, from whom the imams (official priests) or judges (*alkalai*, s. *alkali*) are drawn. On ceremonial occasions such as marriage, circumcision and funeral, any *malam* may recite the necessary Koranic verses, but gifts are made to all the *malams* present.

(10) *Iburu*—a cereal similar to upland rice. Millet and maize should probably be added to this list.

(11) Midday meal—Hausa wives usually provide this for themselves.

(12) Ceremonial exchange-gifts (*buki*)—women's ceremonies and the gifts they give one another are described in detail later, see pp. 191–2 *et al*.

(13) Assistance, or reinforcements (*gudummuwa*) is the term used for the gifts made by men on ceremonial occasions. The rules for these are different from those for women's gifts.

(14) Millet-balls (*fura*)—made from spiced millet- or guineacorn-flour, mashed up with sour milk or tamarind juice, are the favourite midday meal.

(15) *Bori* dancing—*Bori* is the Hausa name for the cult of spirit-possession described later (cf. p. 260), and introduction. See also J. Greenberg, *Influence of Islam on a Sudanese religion*; Tremearne, *Ban of the Bori*; Baba here makes the point that the men of her family, as Koranic scholars and teachers, were opposed to non-Islamic rituals such as *Bori*.

(16) *Mai Anguwa*—Ward head (a title).

(17) Grandparents are a person's joking relations.

(18) Cowrie-shells were the principal form of currency in Hausaland in the nineteenth century. They were exchanged at one hundred for a halfpenny in Zaria after the British conquest.

CHAPTER II

(1) Kurama are one of the tribes of eastern Zaria Province who traditionally practised a form of vaccination for smallpox. In 1950 they were still using these traditional techniques.

NOTES

(2) De Saint Croix dates the great rinderpest epidemic between 1887–91. (F. W. de Saint Croix, *The Fulani of Northern Nigeria* (Lagos, 1945), pp. 12–13.) This suggests that Baba was born between 1885–8. References to other events, however, make 1887–90 a more likely date.

(3) *Idda*—period of three months' celibacy necessary for a woman before a divorce from her husband becomes final, the object being to prevent paternity disputes. (See Ruxton, *Maliki Law*, p. 141.)

(4) *Sarki*—chief. Sarkin Gwibi—Chief of Gwibi (village).

(5) Whenever Baba's parents are mentioned by their names this was in reply to the question, 'Which one?' Under the rules of name-avoidance, Baba did not use the names of her parents or of her husbands unless it was necessary to do so.

(6) The praise-song quoted is that of a later Madaki of Zaria, Yero, the son of the emir Aliyu (1903–20). He was given the title in 1916. At the time Baba is speaking of, Kwassau, son of the emir Yero, was the Madaki, but his fiefs did not include Giwa town. Probably Baba remembered the tune and sang the words of a later Madaki's praise-song.

    Dodo is a thing to be feared, an evil spirit; the term is also applied to chiefs, Europeans, and other powerful persons.

(7) Pipe—*algaita*—a woodwind like an oboe which however produces a sound reminiscent of bagpipes. It is blown in honour of senior title-holders. A group of *algaita* players, as well as drummers, is attached to the title of Fagaci in Zaria and is mentioned later in the text, in connection with Baba's life at Giwa; *Dangaladiman Busa* is the title of one of these musicians.

(8) Marriage in which wives are confined to the husband's compound is known as *auren kulle*. See Introduction.

(9) *Iya*—term of address to one's mother and also one's great-grandmother (alternate generations).

CHAPTER III

(1) *Kawaye* (s. *Kawa*) are lifelong female bond-friends who engage in special exchanges of gifts on ceremonial occasions. For a fuller description, see later, especially pp. 191–2, 198–205, 140.

(2) *Aboki* is a man's male friend; his principal male bond-friend is his *babban aboki*. The relationship is as important for men as that of the *kawa* is for women, but the obligations are different, and a man usually has fewer bond-friends than a woman.

(8) Hausa praise-songs are often chanted by two or more praise-singers to an accompaniment on a large two-membraned drum (*ganga*) and a smaller drum shaped like an hour-glass (*kalangu*). Both are 'talking' drums—i.e. they produce sounds of different pitch which can be made to correspond to the tonal variations in spoken Hausa.

(4) *Gwari*—i.e. pagans, slaves. '*Yar kwaliya, dan kwaliya*, etc.—wrong genders, mistakes with implosive 'd', in general a play on the incorrect Hausa spoken by pagan slaves.

(5) *Jakada*—the fiefholder's agent, see Introduction, p. 30.

(6) There follows an incomplete account of the associations of young men and girls in the community of Zarewa town and its surrounding hamlets during Baba's childhood. The titles held by the leaders of the boys' association, as *Sarki, Madaki*, etc., with the exception of *Danmori*, are the usual titles found at all levels of the Hausa rank system. The custom of *kallankuwa* at the two annual festivals is not mentioned, nor is the usual authority of all titled members of the association over the 'commoners' (*talakawa*), which included the levying of small fines on the boys and coercion of the girls to become their partners in *tsarance* (see below). In some villages of rural Zaria where these associations no longer exist, the older people quote these practices as the grounds for their hostility to the youths' association and their refusal to permit their children to join it. Apparently Baba's parents did not entirely approve of it, either (p. 60). The allocation of titles to certain compounds and wards may be a local peculiarity. *Tsarance*—sleeping together, cuddling, etc., of unmarried youths and girls. *Tsaranci*—sexual intercourse between them.

(7) Mama—in pre-Fulani Habe states the chief always had an official 'mother', usually with the title *Iya*, the senior woman in the realm. She had certain important political functions.

(8) *Fataucin 'yammata*—not to be confused with *talla*, cf. p. 54 *et al.*, which is trading on commission within their own neighbourhood, on behalf of their seniors. These trading expeditions now described were to other towns or villages, the girls using their own capital and trading individually, after having mastered the techniques of bargaining at an early age, while peddling their mothers' wares. When they are married and secluded, Hausa women continue to trade through children, spending the profits on goods and services for themselves (cloth, hairdressing, perfume, etc.) and their daughters, in the formal exchanges of bond-friendship and kinship and at give-aways such as that described on p. 197.

(9) *Bori* dancers, lit. 'children of the *Bori*', the Hausa term for a cult of spirit-possession and for the spirits worshipped in this way. Other terms for these spirits are *iskoki, iblisi* and *aljannu*, the two latter having Arabic associations. In Hausa, possession is described reversibly as 'the spirit mounted her' or 'she mounted the spirit'. The adept or dancer is referred to as the 'mare'. To avoid confusion, however, the word 'possessed' is used in translation. The spirits worshipped in the cult have names, regular characteristics, and stand in well-known relationships to one another. The important spirits are believed to control certain illnesses and each has his appropriate type of sacrifice used to propitiate him (or her). Thus Dangaladima receives as sacrifice either a white sheep having

NOTES

one eye encircled with black, or a red cock with saddle-shaped markings in black and white. Spirits also have their individual praise-songs, which are used to call them to come and possess a dancer, special instruments being used to play the tunes. Each spirit is recognized by its distinctive behaviour and gestures as it takes possession of its medium. Its departure is marked by the latter's sneezing and recovering from the trance. Despite certain Arabic elements and associations, the *bori* cult which Baba describes among the Muslim Hausa shows clear connections with the *iskoki* cult of the Maguzawa (pagan Hausa) as described by Greenberg (op. cit.). The spirits in both are the same, their names, characteristic behaviour, praise-songs and powers are often unchanged, and the sacrifices prescribed for any particular *iska* are the same for both Muslim and pagan Hausa. However the difference is noteworthy: in the *bori* cult persons seek to be possessed by the spirits, whereas the pagans worship *iskoki* by sacrifices at set times and places, no attempts to secure possession being made. Among the pagan Hausa, also, the worship of *iskoki* is linked directly with the principal units of the social system, the patrilineal clans, whereas the *bori* cult among the Muslim Hausa is largely though not exclusively in the hands of initiated women of the *karuwa* group—most nearly translated 'prostitute', although this is not a complete translation (see Introduction, p. 25).

Bori among the Muslim Hausa can be regarded as a transformation of and adaptation to changed conditions of ancient pagan *iskoki* ritual, of which the contemporary Maguzawa customs may be taken as a sample. The custodians of the cult among the Muslims are the prostitutes, a class of women who deviate from the correct Muslim patterns of behaviour, but cannot be effectively controlled or eliminated from the body of the Faithful, from whom both these women and their clients are recruited. The functions of *bori* and the attitudes of the Muslim Hausa towards it are indicated by numerous references in Baba's story.

(10) *Magajiya*—a woman's title and in pre-Fulani days in Zaria a state title, with fiefs attached to it, usually held by the king's sister or daughter. In Fulani times, however, women ceased to hold state titles, and Magajiya is now a title conferred on the woman head of the prostitutes in any area, whether a village area or district. In the nineteenth century she was responsible for collecting the tax on *bori* dancers under her authority—4,000 cowries per dancer.

(11) Prostitutes—H. *karuwai*, s. *karuwa*—lit. a profligate person of either sex, but for fuller discussion see Introduction, p. 25. Baba's references to *karuwai* and their activities before the British pacification are interesting, in view of statements made by some Hausa recently in letters to the vernacular newspaper *Gaskiya ta fi Kwabo* that prostitution was unknown in Hausaland before 1900.

(12) 'Steal her own body'—*sace jikinta*, a vivid linguistic expression of the fact that at marriage a woman surrenders the rights over her body and its issue to her husband.

(13) '*Yandauda*, lit. sons of dirt, are male homosexuals who associate with prostitutes, often acting as their agents.

CHAPTER IV

(1) Note how the coming of the British is assimilated into the traditional order of things as something prophesied by the Koranic scholars, whose learning is not thereby belittled.

(2) Tejani were the Fulani followers of the Sarkin Tejani, a vassal of the Sultan of Fez, whose empire stretched from the Senegal eastwards to Aribinta and included Timbuktu, at the date, 1894, when the French defeated him and the Tejani fled to Sokoto, where the sultan gave their chief the country of Zamfara to rule. He died shortly afterwards and his younger brother then moved eastwards to Misau and was killed fighting for the sultan against the British at Burmi in July 1903. Presumably the westward flight of the Trejani occurred after this fight.

(3) Europeans are often referred to as Christians (*Nasara*), particularly by older people.

(4) This war of succession between the sons of two brothers of the ruling house of Kano took place in 1893–4. It was characterized by brutality, even between kinsmen, since the ruling family was divided between the two claimants, Tukur, son of the previous king Mohammed Bello, and Yusufu, son of Bello's brother Abdullahi. (See R. East, *Labarun Hausawa da makwabtansu* (Zaria, 1933), II, pp. 66–8.) Note Baba's error—Tukur was younger than Yusufu, but he was the ruler appointed by the Sultan of Sokoto.

(5) *Mai Sudan*—lit. 'the owner of the Sudan'—the Hausa term for Ibrahim Nagwamatse, the ruler of the state of Kontagora which his father Umaru Nagwamatse founded between 1864–75. The Kontagora dynasty are Torankawa Fulani, descended, like the rulers of Sokoto, from Shehu Usuman dan Fodio, the Fulani leader who founded the Fulani empire from 1804 onwards. In 1901 Ibrahim was driven from Kontagora by the British and in 1902 was raiding western Zaria and southern Katsina, though no record has been traced that he himself raided southern Kano; no doubt raiding parties from his camps in the border country of Katsina-Zaria were active over a considerable area. Of Mai-Sudan it is related that, when told that slave-raiding must cease, he asked, 'Can you stop a cat from mousing?'

(6) In fact Yusufu died in 1893, and Aliyu, his son, was ruling Kano in 1903, having won the civil war. After the capture of Mai-Sudan at Kaya, a small force under Colonel Morland invaded Kano emirate, having already moved into Zaria in response to a request from the king of Zaria for help against Mai-Sudan's raiders. The king of Kano refused to agree to Lugard's requests and Kano City was occupied by the British, who repulsed counter-attacks led by the vizier (*waziri*); Sokoto itself was invaded by another force, and the conquest of the Fulani empire was complete.

NOTES

(7) Lugard's 'Slavery Proclamation' "abolished the legal status of slavery, prohibited slave-dealing, and declared all children born after the 1st of April 1901 in the Protectorate of Northern Nigeria to be free. The Proclamation did not make the holding of slaves illegal, the abolition of the legal status merely preventing a master from recovering a runaway slave through the medium of the Courts." (Sir A. Burns, *History of Nigeria* (4th edition, London, 1948), p. 187.) The native interpretation of this Proclamation, and the expression of the new relation in kinship terms already in use between slaves and their masters, is recorded in the text, as also is the reduction of prosperity of persons who had previously relied on slaves for all their farm-labour. Cf. note 17, p. 273.

(8) Probably ten to eleven years old.

(9) Abuja is a small kingdom to the south of Zaria. At this time its people were actively engaged in slave-raiding and also in harassing the trade-routes to the Niger.

(10) Slavery—i.e. slave-raiding and dealing. Abubakar, Sarkin Katsina, made his submission in 1903 to the British, was deposed in 1904, and his successor was also deposed in 1906. Probably the 'Slavery Proclamation' did not become effective in Katsina before this date.

(11) Chronology obscure; if townsfolk started farming bush *c.* 1904, this would place Baba's first marriage in 1910. Probably, however, she is referring to the pacification, *c.* 1901, which made it safe to leave the town alone, and she has overestimated the time which elapsed between her mother's death and her own marriage.

(12) Hausa beds are raised platforms of clay, with a place hollowed out beneath where a fire can be made on cold nights.

(13) Cowries were converted at one hundred to a halfpenny, but the value varied seasonally and from place to place. Four hundred thousand at this rate would equal £8 16s., but the value of cowries at that time was probably higher than the later value used for conversion.

(14) An instance of the solidarity of the kinsfolk, and how they mobilized their resources. Bakori is a town north-east of Funtua in Katsina emirate, and hence under the jurisdiction of the emir. The account of procedure for recovering Muslim Hausa captured and sold into slavery is interesting.

(15) Cf. earlier chronology. The accounts of these events were given on different occasions, and arranged in chronological order later. These raids by Mai-Sudan's men may be dated 1901-2 with fair certainty.

(16) Kidnappers ('*yan kwanto*) were small groups of brigands whose practice was to ambush solitary persons and clear out of the area before the alarm spread, selling their captives in the slave-markets of neighbouring towns or states.

(17) Zaria and Kano people expressed the same attitudes to Katsina in 1950.

(18) Maska—a district of southern Katsina bordering on Zaria, whose chief town is also called Maska.

(19) In a compound where the wives are secluded, womenfolk and young boys may go in freely, for trade or social visits, but men are excluded.

(20) *Karemari*—an additional payment of one-tenth the agreed sum.

(21) The heavy payments for ransoms, their losses of slaves during the raids and by absconding, and the prohibition of slave-dealing which became effective soon after, brought to an end the prosperity of Dara's sons. This is indicated by the sale of horses to pay ransom, and Baba's brief reference to her father doing his own farm work, p. 67.

(22) *Laraba*—Wednesday—a name often given to girls born on that day; 'Baba' is, as she herself explained, the nearest the younger children of the family could get to 'Laraba', and she was known as Baba ever after. Her Koranic name was Hasetu.

(23) This is the end of Tsoho's prosperity. It had been based on slave-labour and had been wrecked by slave-raiders, Mohammedans like himself.

(24) The early rains in May and June are heralded by intense electrical storms, and many deaths are caused each year by lightning. The Great Feast (*Babbar Salla*)—*Id-el-Kabir*, the festival on the tenth day of Zul Hajji.

(25) Burials nowadays are on the outskirts of the settlements for sanitary reasons.

(26) Women wail at deaths and men must not do so.

(27) Chronology, cf. pp. 68 and 70.

(28) Lack of a wife is a sign of poverty and is undesirable, particularly when a man has nubile daughters in his compound.

(29) The owner of a slave had the right to end his marriage by simple repudiation. See Ruxton, *Maliki Law*, pp. 97–8. Two male slaves were equal to one female.

(30) Light skin-colour, referred to as 'red', ranks high in the Hausa criteria of beauty; many variations of colour, from black to a very light reddish-brown, are seen. In general, the less negroid features, approximating to the Fulani or Arab types, are admired.

(31) The custom of *bangwalle*, or returning to her parents' home before or after the birth of a first child, is discussed later. See p. 274.

(32) Inheritance—cf. Ruxton, op. cit., pp. 373–97.

(33) The bond between a man and his mother is of lifelong importance. Tsoho's move to Giwa to be near his mother is described later.

(34) Crafts were traditionally inherited occupations.

(35) Cross-cousins. In the cross-cousin joking relationships, the children of the brother are said to be slaves of the children of the sister, though

NOTES

this is often inverted. Parallel and cross-cousin marriage are preferred forms among the Hausa, both patrilateral and matrilateral cross-cousin marriage being frequent. Cross-cousins of the same sex are also joking relations. (Cf. Sir H. R. Palmer, *The Bornu Sahara and Sudan*, pp. 73–4.)

(36) *Sarkin Makada*—'Chief of drummers'—a craft title. Formerly tax was collected through the appointed heads of crafts in each community, and each craft had its own hierarchy of office-holders, with the usual range of titles—*Sarki, Madaki, Galadima*, and the rest. With the loss of tax-collecting function has gone much of the importance formerly attached to these craft titles.

(37) *Kaka*—Hausa for grandparent of either sex or line. *Baba*—with one intonation is 'father', with a different intonation 'father's sister'. *Goggo* is also used for 'father's sister'.

There was some confusion here, since these are Hausa, not Kanuri (Barebare) kinship terms. The plural of *Baba* (f.) is *Babani* but there is no plural for *Baba* (m.). *Yani* and *Abba*, however, are not Hausa terms.

(38) This reference dates Baba's mother's death in 1901–2, the years in which Mai-Sudan's men raided Wawaye and Karo (see pp. 68 and 70) and Dije was married.

(39) An account of marriage ceremonies is given later. The *Mawankiya* is a woman of the bride's mother's kin who supervises part of the ritual, in which grandmothers take part.

(40) A man 'jokes' with his wife's younger sisters, and a woman with her husband's younger brothers.

(41) Dije was recalled from her mother's kin, in order to be married to a son of her father's brother.

(42) Kadiri—Baba's younger half-brother. The relation of *ya* (elder sister) and *kane* (younger brother) is one of mutual affection among the Hausa. Baba was living in Kadiri's compound at the time this biography was dictated.

(43) Note the high rate of infant mortality.

(44) Cf. note 1, Ch. I, and note 42, Ch. IV.

(45) If Rabi's mother had a young child at this time, Rabi herself could hardly have been as old as the catalogue of her children on the previous page suggests. Probably some of these were born later; Baba was not always quite clear about the time-sequences of events in her large family.

(46) A woman's account of tax-collection in the old days. Note the vagueness—women are unfamiliar with the details of political affairs.

(47) Zarewa tax was probably higher then Baba estimates. The town chiefs used to retain a portion of the tax they collected, sending the bulk to the fiefholder, or in this case Sarkin Karaye (see map). The town chief probably made other levies as he required them. Kano paid tribute, not tax, to Sokoto.

BABA OF KARO

CHAPTER V

(1) This is a record of Baba's first marriage, generalized by her as an account of traditional procedure at that time. She mentions the main differences between first-marriage customs for free people and slaves, but assumes two conditions—that both parties were slaves of the same owner, and that both were Moslems. These conditions were generally present.

(2) Great Salla—*Id-el-Kabir*. Lesser Salla—*Id-el-Fitr*.

(3) The presence of praise-singers (*maroka*) and drummers (*makada*) is traditionally necessary at certain stages of the marriage ceremonial. It is a poor man indeed in Hausaland who lacks a praise-song (*kirari* or *taki*), a rhythm on the drums to which certain verses are sung, listing an individual's important or titled ancestors and praiseworthy characteristics. Like men, the spirits also have individual praise-songs (see p. 63 *et al.*).

(4) Sisters—real or classificatory, or their substitutes.

(5) Unfortunately it was not established by field-enquiries whether or not a girl's hands and feet are ever stained with henna before she is married, and the ritual significance of henna in this context is thus not as clear as it should be. In general, married women stain their hands and feet by covering them with a paste of dried ground henna-leaves, tied on with more leaves and old pieces of cloth, the whole being left overnight. When it is removed in the morning the skin is a reddish-brown colour and the nails are red. This is done before any festive occasions or visits to friends or relatives, and looks more attractive than it sounds.

(6) See Introduction marriage as a *rite de passage*. The bride's protests and wails are traditional, but she certainly has very mixed feelings about her forthcoming marriage and the end of her free life with the girls, especially if, as is often the case with a first marriage, she is not to wed the man of her own choice.

(7) The opposition of the generations in the marriage ceremony is illustrated by the account of the bride's flight and forcible capture by her grandmother. In the nineteenth century Maclennan based his theory of marriage by capture on similar incidents of marriage ritual in which the bridegroom's kin captured the bride, drawn from different cultures. (See Maclennan, *Primitive Marriage* (1891), *Studies in Ancient History*, etc.) Among the Hausa the bride's move to her husband's home is carried out in a manner which fits Maclennan's requirements for classification as a 'survival of primitive capture'. But no such interpretation can possibly apply to the bride's flight from her grandmother before the henna ritual. This behaviour of flight and recovery is clearly seen as marking stages in the *rite de passage* which marks the girl's transfer from the social category of minors (girls) to that of adulthood, or marriage, and similarly her transfer from the household and control of her parents to that of her husband. These two functions are socially inseparable,

though analytically distinct, and it is unthinkable to Hausa that a physically mature woman—i.e. one over about fourteen years of age—should be unmarried. The change in the bride's status is thus as important an element in the ritual as the transfer of her fertility by her parents to her husband.

(8) Turban—used also on other occasions to mark changes in social status.

(9) For this part of the ceremony the bride's head and face are completely covered by a large cloth thrown over her head, and she is led by the hand.

(10) *Cellerai-cerauki*—a game played with cowries. The bride's friends taunt her with her future change of status. This and other songs which Baba recalled are traditional and are always sung at the part of the ceremony indicated in the text.

(11) This is the only occasion known to me on which all Hausa males are stained with henna.

(12) Note that in the absence of a mother's younger sister, her elder sister deputized. Differences in the birth order of siblings are terminologically, ritually and institutionally important. *Mawankiya* supervises the washing, which is carried out by the bride's grandmothers in her compound.

(13) I.e. a slave woman's master and his kin are the maternal kinsfolk of her children. This important legal principle provides a basis for explanation of the differential importance of maternal and paternal kinsfolk among contemporary Hausa of different social levels and classes, and of different origin.

(14) This epigram expresses the permanent change in status, from that of a girl to that of a grown woman, which a Hausa girl undergoes at her first marriage. It certainly does not mean that the marriage itself is irrevocable, since divorce is easy. That the role of married woman is bound up with adoption of adult status by Hausa girls is neither fortuitous nor of purely academic interest, and two instances will illustrate the practical significance of this universal principle of Hausa sociology. Firstly, the Hausa distinguish between the pre-marital affairs of young girls with youths, who give them gifts of money (*toshi*), this institutionalized relationship being known as *tsaranci*, and prostitution (*karuwanci*) which can only be practised by women who have been married at least once, although the two institutions may show little conceptual difference to one accustomed to European culture. Only an adult woman can be a *karuwa* (prostitute), and the status of adult woman involves performance of the *rite de passage* of the first marriage. Informants related that in pre-British days, complete deadlock between a girl and her parents concerning the choice of a husband for her first marriage was very rare, but if it occurred was resolved by the girl's throwing herself down a well—the only instances of suicide which were encountered, despite continual enquiry.

A second illustration concerns the Education Department's programme of education for Hausa women. On at least one occasion, the senior Hausa girls (aged thirteen to fourteen) at the Girls' School at Kano (a boarding school) have run away and returned to their homes. Sociologically, the reason is obvious. Between the ages of thirteen and fourteen it is essential for Hausa girls to undergo the ritual of a first marriage, not for reasons of sexual desire, since Hausa girls have more chance of satisfying this before marriage than afterwards, but because their physical development indicates that they are approaching adulthood, and must therefore be married, since the concept of an unmarried adult woman is one which does not exist in Hausa culture—even blind or leper girls being married at least once. Omission or postponement of this rite makes the girls abnormal persons in terms of their culture in a way in which even prostitutes are not abnormal. The Hausa regard European spinsters with bewilderment and disapproval, and it is possible that this attitude also influenced the girls who absconded, fearing that they would be prevented from marrying and entering into proper adult status, in Hausa terms. Administrative pressure on the Hausa rulers and chiefs to secure the return to school of the runaway girls placed the native officials in an unenviable position, since only they were aware of the issues at stake on both sides.

(15) The legal and religious rite of marriage is performed on the morning of the marriage day before the bride goes to her husband's home, and is the same for a first or subsequent marriage. After the recitation of set Koranic verses by the *malams*, the *wali* or guardian of the woman confirms the marriage arrangements, and the bridegroom's representative hands to the bride's guardian the *sadaki*, which is in Muslim law the only payment legally necessary to establish a marriage. In Zaria 1950 it averaged 10s. for a first marriage and was given to the bride for her own use. In event of a woman divorcing her husband, the *sadaki* must always be returned to him. The spouses are never present at the legal rite, and their real fathers rarely so.

(16) *Aninai* were introduced as currency by the British but have now gone out of circulation. They were small coins of white metal with a hole through the centre, and were extensively used as ornaments.

(17) See also p. 248. The bride's dowry on her first marriage provides an inventory of the domestic equipment required by a Hausa wife, except for items connected with the processing of grain as food, a task she does not undertake for some months in her new home.

(18) *Katukawa*—reference not clear. May refer to the people ruled by Katuka, an official of Zaria state, whose district is inhabited by the Katab and Kaje tribes, among others.

(19) *Wali*—see notes 13 and 15, also Ch. V, and Ruxton op. cit., p. 90 and footnote.

(20) Marriage of alms—*auren sadaka*, cf. pp. 129, 153 *et al.*

NOTES

CHAPTER VI

(1) Hausa girls are usually married when thirteen or fourteen years old, rarely at fifteen. A girl's parents often try to arrange for her to marry one of her kinsmen, paternal or maternal, in the kind of marriage known as *auren zumunci*, as Baba's father did.

(2) Rabi took the place of Baba's mother after her own mother's death, and Baba often referred to her as 'my mother' in the real as well as the classificatory sense.

(3) Her father's people were primarily farmers, and in addition many of them were *mallams* (Koranic scholars).

(4) Blacksmiths and farmers—preferred marriage between occupational groups.

(5) A conflict of institutionalized relations was here involved; as joking-relations of the Fulani, it was proper for Baba's kin to give her to the Zarewa chiefs; but as *malams* and farmers there was an opposition of interest and occupational class between them and the town chief.

(6) *Danfangi*—the title of the village chief of Giwa in Zaria Province, where Baba was living when I knew her. The chiefs of Zarewa and Giwa are related.

(7) An account of the formal procedures of a first courtship and marriage follows. Compare with Baba's account of her adopted daughter 'Yar-dada's first marriage in 1947, on p. 241, and also with the accounts of marriage in E. W. Lane, *Manners and Customs of the Modern Egyptians* (London, 1837).
Note the practice of giving gifts to the girls, known as *toshi*. These are traditional, the amount and occasion of gift-giving being clearly specified. It is possible to formulate a general rule that in Hausa society there is no institutionalized relation between persons or groups which is formed without the formal exchange of economic goods or services as a necessary procedure (see Introduction). Note also that rejection of a gift implies refusal to enter into the institutionalized relation.

(8) One of Baba's rare generalizations, which is borne out by her own life-story and much other data, from pagan as well as Hausa groups, in Zaria Province.

(9) See earlier notes on seclusion of women—Duma, as a young kins-man, was allowed into the women's quarters. Baba's father, as his father's classificatory brother, was Duma's father in the classificatory sense.

(10) All the objects purchased or given are the ones traditionally required on this occasion. The bilaterality of Hausa kinship is expressed most strongly on all the occasions of family life, in the ritual and ceremonial exchanges which take place.

(11) My co-wife—*kishiyarta*, from *kishi*, jealousy—lit. 'my jealous one', 'my rival'. Used as a term of reference by wives but not of address, unless the two wives happen to be also joking relations, which occurs rarely.

(12) *Marka, Ciwake*—Hausa 'occasional' names, from events occurring, when or the time at which, a child was born.

(13) Charms—usually small leather bags containing Koranic texts with certain herbal or animal elements, they form the principal form of protective magic used by the Hausa; the making of them is an important activity of the *mallams*, or Koranic scholars. *Baduhu* and *layan zana* both make the wearer invisible and are usually used together as though to make the invisibility more complete. Divination is another function of *mallams*, as illustrated in this story.

(14) *Uwar Baba*—a teknonymous reference meaning 'the mother of Baba', the narrator. Rabi's precise relationship to Baba was that of father's sister (*goggo*), but after Baba's mother's death Rabi had taken the place of a mother to Baba, who was still a young girl.

(15) The Satiru incident, a Mahdist uprising, and the rebellion of the Emir of Hadejia against the British in 1906, marked the final stage in the British conquest of the North.

(16) Cf. pp. 56–65 sqq., 129, 217. Baba's genuine preference for living in towns is used as a rationalization of certain actions in which kinship factors are dominant, as appears later in this story. The distinction between town and village life is widespread and important in Hausa culture.

(17) Cf. note 14 above. Baba never used Rabi's name except in answer to a request for clarification; it has been used, however, in translation where it makes the sense clearer, as with other of her kin who came under the rules of name-avoidance.

(18) With Rabi to support her, Baba is able to resist the wishes of her father's kinsmen. The brothers cannot effectively control their sister, Rabi, and this division among her 'parents' prevents their taking effective action to keep Baba married to Duma. Note that the remarried widows of Ibrahim Dara are present at the meeting.

(19) Before the British reorganization of native courts, local chiefs had jurisdiction over civil suits including divorce. See Introduction.

(20) I.e. the rulers of our town. There were probably also other Fulani in Zarewa.

(21) A written statement of the date at which a divorcee commences *iddah* (see note 3, Chapter II above). The divorce is not final until the three months *iddah* has been completed.

(22) I.e. the compound of Rabi's son Nasamai, Baba's paternal cross-cousin, therefore her 'brother'.

(28) Only persons of the same sex and generation eat together.

NOTES

CHAPTER VII

(1) Rabi and Baba disagree on the choice of her next husband, after having jointly overcome the opposition of the kinsmen to her divorce from Duma. The disagreement between Baba and Rabi permits her father and his brothers to resume some control of Baba's affairs. Haleru is a maternal half-brother of Baba's father Tsoho, who has no authority to give her in marriage, and he refers her suitor to her father's brother, who follows the correct procedure for Hausa patrilineages, by taking them to Malam Buhari, the senior brother. Tsoho, Baba's own father, takes little part in the arrangements, his brother Ubangida acting as 'father' to his children in matters of marriage, while Tsoho does the same for Ubangida's children.

(2) A woman who has already been married, whether she is divorced or widowed, is a *bazawara*, in contradistinction to a maiden, a *buduruwa*.

(3) Since a week elapses between the marriage ceremony and the bride's going to live in her husband's compound (unlike a woman's first marriage), the husband sends her grain in discharge of his obligation to feed his new wife, and she sends back food in discharge of her obligation to cook for his compound.

(4) *Tuwon jere* anticipates the bride's arrival and willingness to fulfil her role as wife completely. The period of the *aunaka* is over, and the *jere* marks this fact and is distributed among the kin of the bride.

(5) Cf. Ch. VI, note 2, p. 269 and note 14, p. 270.

(6) Compare with p. 96 sqq. It is usual for adult Hausa women on ceremonial occasions of this type to practise *bori* (see note 9, Ch. III. Possibly the segregation of the women within the compound on these occasions provides favourable conditions; more importantly, the inability of Hausa women to participate adequately in the ceremonial and public life of Islam leaves a gap which is filled by the spirit-possession cult.

Malam Bawa the *Alkali* (judge), Dangaladima, Inna are all spirits. *Dangaladima* is a title usually held by a son of the king—hence the spirit causes its medium to behave like a prince.

(7) A list of the craft activities of a skilful Hausa woman. Baba had plenty of time for these as she had no children, and her husband had other wives to share in the household work.

CHAPTER VIII

(1) For arrangement of compounds, see p. 36 and Introduction. For *gandu*, see Introduction.

(2) *Turaka*—see Introduction. Whether he has a separate sleeping-hut or not, a husband with more than one wife must spend two nights with each in turn, and the wife with whom he is sleeping is responsible for cooking the household food. Thus a woman's dislike of having a rival

wife is to some extent offset by the fact that she has more time for her own crafts than if she were the only one.

(3) This passage provides a noteworthy example of extension of kinship terminology and the appropriate behaviour by the women of the household to a freed slave. An account of how he was freed follows on p. 122.

(4) See Introduction.

(5) Note division of labour between free and slave women. See Introduction, p. 22. A reported increase in wife-seclusion in rural areas in recent years may be linked with increased cash-crop farming and the higher incomes earned from it by Hausa men, since wife-seclusion requires that the husband make arrangements for the fetching of wood and water.

(6) Since he had moved from Karo to Zarewa and lost his slaves, Tsoho had lent out his extra farms and probably found difficulty in acquiring suitable land nearer to the town—Karo being four miles distant from Zarewa; he farmed what he could of his old land, but the availability of virgin farmland near Giwa was a necessary condition of his move, though not the efficient cause. Cf. p. 241.

(7) Clientage—see Introduction, p. 31.

(8) See p. 119.

(9) Baba's first adopted son. As she had not yet borne any children, this was a very considerate act of Malam Maigari's. This manumission probably occurred in 1909. Cf. Ch. IV, note 7, p. 263.

(10) Cf. p. 113.

(11) *Waina.*

(12) Drumming with sticks on upturned calabashes which float in larger calabashes filled with water is part of the traditional way in which Hausa women celebrate festive occasions. The practice is known as *amada* or *kidan ruwa*. A similar type of drumming is found among the Maya of Guatemala and Mexico.

(13) A fuller account of post-natal ablutions is given later, pp. 138 sqq. and pp. 249 sqq.

(14) See Introduction. For the Hausa, the post-natal ablutions are an absolute necessity, and the imagined consequences of non-observance are often contradictory. A similar custom is reported by Fortes from the Tallensi (*Web of Kinship among the Tallensi*, pp. 164, 166). Nevertheless, there are alternative rituals, see pp. 250 sqq.

(15) *Dauro*—eleusine millet. Note the prestige associated with skilful and active farming.

(16) '*Filani ba su da tausayi—raba da su!*' The typical attitude of Habe to their Fulani rulers, and to Fulani in general. On the arrival of the British in the Fulani states of Northern Nigeria, the Habe rejoiced and assisted the troops when they could. Cf. Burns, op. cit., pp. 176, 178, 179, and p. 67 of this text.

NOTES

(17) Cf. p. 67, and note 7, p. 263. Some idea of the effect of the Slavery Proclamation of 1900 is given in E. J. Arnett, *The Gazeteer of Zaria Province*, p. 32: 'Self-redemption and ransom of slaves registered by the native courts reached a total of 1,075 for the year [1911]. The previous nine years totalled 2,274 in all.' In 1914 the Protectorates of N. and S. Nigeria were amalgamated, and the House Rule Proclamation, which permitted domestic slavery in association with 'houses' among Yoruba and other southern peoples, was repealed. It may be to this that Baba refers when she says 'when slaves were freed by law', if her dating is to be followed. However, no law passed by Government required that slaves should be freed in Northern Nigeria; either Baba here expresses a popular misconception, or it is just a manner of speech.

(18) Circumcision is obligatory for all Muslim males. Hausa boys are circumcised at seven to nine years. Circumcision of a slave boy is an indication that he will be brought up as a Muslim—i.e. a Hausa.

(19) Kamuku—a tribe in Birnin Gwari (western Zaria Province) and Niger Province.

(20) Baba here expresses the Hausa interest and delight in bilateral kinship connections. The marriage in question is a kinship marriage between second cousins as well as being a marriage of alms.

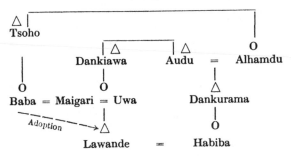

Diagram to illustrate note 20.

(21) Cf. pp. 76 (craft titles) and Introduction, p. 28. Butchers, though often comparatively prosperous, rank permanently lowest, as an occupational group, in the Hausa scale of occupational classes.

(22) For Dije's marriage, see p. 78. Compare the circumstances of Dije's divorce and remarriage with that of Baba (pp. 107 sqq). Whereas her parents were ineffective in Baba's case, they were united about Dije and able to control her later marriages. Compare also Baba's third marriage (p. 163). *Sadau* is a name given to an infant born after the divorced mother has returned to her husband because of the pregnancy.

(23) Probably it was at this period that Baba realized that she was unlikely to have children of her own, and sought compensation in the institutionalized practice of adopting other people's children.

(24) Long-distance expeditions, whether for trade (*fatauci*, see Introduction) or teaching are made in the dry season when there is no farm work to be done, and are referred to as *cin rani*—'eating up the dry season'. They were risky undertakings in pre-British days, as the story of Rabi showed. The following pages give an account of the expeditions of a Koranic teacher.

(25) A *liman* (Ar. *imam*) is the religious head of the Muslim community.

(26) It is a religious obligation to give away a tithe of grain and some of this *zakka* is usually given to scholars or teachers passing through the country. As the main grain harvest occurs at the start of the dry season, there is relative abundance of food then, and the travelling scholars enjoy great hospitality.

(27) Youths learn to recite the first sixty *sura* of the Koran parrot-fashion without understanding the Arabic. When able to recite this faultlessly, the student graduates (*sauka*), a sacrifice is made, and he is addressed thereafter as *Malam*. He then, if he continues his studies, commences to learn Arabic grammar and then proceeds to study and read the traditions of the Prophet (*hadith*), the law (*shari'a*) and the principal commentaries. The post-graduate studies *ilmi* (knowledge), the undergraduate studies the Book (*Al'kurani*). Malam Maigari taught the Koran to boy students during the day, and pursued *ilmi* at night with the elders of the community, both at home and on his dry-season expeditions. In the process of these discussions he probably learned as much as he taught, and this quest for religious knowledge is a motive leading *malams* to make these expeditions and older men to gather from the villages and hamlets to hear their teaching in the evenings.

(28) Cf. pp. 72, 81, 136, on safety of travel.

(29) For clientage, see Introduction, p. 31. Hasan had been a Koranic student of Malam Tsoho's, then he remained and farmed with him as a member of his household.

(30) For another instance of a wife divorcing her husband when he takes a second wife, see Ramatu herself, p. 136. Often the woman already wishes to leave her husband, and the rival's coming provides an institutionalized excuse for her to leave.

(31) *Malams* are often consulted in their capacity as diviners.

(32) Hausa distinguish between successful courtesans (*manya-manya karuwai*—very important prostitutes) or *karuwai zaune*—settled prostitutes, like Ramatu, and the less successful peripatetic class who tour rural towns and live in brothels.

CHAPTER IX

(1) This custom of *bangwalle* or returning home, before or after the first childbirth, is referred to in the Introduction. There are many variations as to the time at which the mother returns to her parents' home, how long she stays, etc., and in some cases she may not go at all—cf. p. 125.

NOTES

(2) Drinking the ink used in writing Koranic texts on a writing board is one of the standard techniques of Hausa protective magic and piety, and is usually performed at least once daily by pious adults during the annual fast of Ramadan. It is intended here to ensure that the child grows strong and healthy after weaning. He has, of course, been eating solid food for a long time before weaning, in addition to his mother's milk.

(3) These gifts link the two *rites de passage*—a woman's first marriage, and her first childbirth with its *bangwalle* or returning-home ritual. Parenthood is the fulfilment of marriage to the Hausa, but under a system permitting polygamous marriage, the husband may already be a parent by another wife, and it is therefore appropriate that the woman's kinsfolk should carry out the exchanges which centre about the daughter during the period of her first marriage and first childbirth, and serve as effective links between the two rituals. See Introduction, p. 25. Where the first birth does not take place in the compound of the first husband (cf. Ladidi, a widow, p. 125), *bangwalle* is not always performed. In a complex culture such as Hausa, many different, often competing and sometimes contradictory factors operate in different particular situations, with the result that considerable variation is found, even in critical ritual practices such as *bangwalle*.

(4) Songs of ridicule are generally levelled at sexual offences, such as premarital pregnancy and incest, and at inability to perform intercourse.

(5) The point of this tale is that intercourse occurred during the period of the post natal ablutions.

(6) 'Of the South Gate'—i.e. 'One born at the South Gate', name-avoidance between a woman and her eldest child. It is an index of the gravity of Musa's behaviour that his mother should speak to him about it directly instead of getting another relative to do so.

(7) Presumably Baba's treatment was intended to cause the child to pass all the 'pregnant milk' out of his system. The bull is symbolic of strength and sexual vigour.

CHAPTER X

(1) I.e. with a vaulted roof of clay instead of the more usual thatch, and in this case with an upper storey. These huts are a mark of prosperity and prestige.

(2) Notice the manipulation of kinship ties. See p. 175 for a parallel case.

(3) A book of Muslim songs.

(4) When one person is angry with another for some behaviour contradicting the norms of the kinship relation between them, the offended party breaks off the kinship relation for a longer or shorter period until the offender makes amends, or both are reconciled by other common kin. Sometimes, as in Dankiawa's case (p. 152) the repudiation may be permanent.

(5) The person who has built a hut owns its site, in Hausa land law, until the building collapses. See also p. 173 for an instance.

(6) For political titles, see Introduction.

(7) Maguzawa (s. Bamaguje)—the pagan Hausa, who live in their own communities in this area. They are regarded by the Muslims as specialists in non-Islamic medicine and magic.

(8) The season of the harmattan, the north wind which blows from the Sahara in the dry season. Epidemics of cerebro-spinal meningitis occur at this season annually, and these may be one reason why it is connected with madness. Hausa distinguish two types of madness, violence (mania) and muttering, which may be of a schizoid character. Both are explained in terms of spirits (*bori, iskoki, aljannu*).

(9) *Bamaguje*—sing. of Maguzawa, see note (7).

(10) This is an aspect of the general attitude of the older generation to Europeans (Christians).

(11) Note the respect given to energetic farmers; cf. p. 77.

(12) There is a link between boys who undergo circumcision together which often lasts into adult life.

(13) Cf. pp. 76, 102, and notes. Baba refers to Rabi as *goggo* (father's sister) and also as *uwa* (mother) because, as her father's sister, she is a classificatory mother to Baba, and also because after Baba's mother's death, Rabi became her own particular 'mother' among her senior kinswomen.

(14) See previous note.

CHAPTER XI

(1) A title generally associated with ward administration in rural communities.

(2) Mai-Sudan's raids—cf. p. 66 sqq.

(3) A man may have not more than four wives in Muslim law, hence if he already has this number he must dismiss one of his wives before marrying a new one.

(4) *Yari*—the traditional title of the warder of the prison of a chief. Giwa village is the headquarters of Giwa District; the District Head's title is *Fagaci*. When native Muslim judges (*alkalai*, sing. *alkali*) were appointed to the Districts by the British, local gaols were also provided for persons awaiting trial or serving short sentences, longer terms being served in Zaria city.

(5) Fagaci Muhammadu—the present District Head, Giwa. His predecessor's name was Ahmadu, but he held the same title of Fagaci. For descriptions of political system, see Introduction (p. 27). Under British rule, District Heads responsible to the Emir for the various districts in his emirate have taken the place of fiefholders. They are known by traditional titles.

NOTES

(6) *Aka girke ta*—lit. 'she was cooked'—i.e. initiated. After initiation, the novice is possessed in an orderly fashion by the spirits which formerly caused him to go into a trance at any time. Initiation into the *bori* cult lasts fourteen days, during which time all the *bori* initiates in the neighbourhood assemble, and sacrifices provided by the novice are made to all the spirits who appear by possessing their particular mediums in the assembly. The initiation rites are presided over by one of the leading local *bori* adepts, usually an older woman and often the Magajiya (cf. p. 63). A diagnosis is made of the particular spirits which are pursuing and calling the novice, from her behaviour when possessed. Thereafter the novice will make sacrifices to these spirits who are her regular patrons. As all the spirits who are pursuing one medium may not reveal themselves at once, however, it is sometimes necessary to perform a further initiation, as in Juma's case. *Girki* is thus not simply an initiation into an undifferentiated *bori* cult, but it is initiation into the particular cults of particular spirits.

(7) A very usual Hausa observation, possibly linked with the predominance of the Kadiriya sect of Islam in the area, which emphasizes predestination.

(8) We only have Baba's version of this tale. Compare the case of Kadiri's wives, pp. 237–8. For the history of another much-married lady, see Malam Hasan's twin sister Hasana, pp. 167–74.

(9) For marriage of alms (*auren sadaka*) see also pp. 99, 128–9, 151 sqq. Hasana's behaviour in repudiating her marriage to the Prophet's representative was serious and placed her father in an unenviable position. Meanwhile Hasana was living in Zaria City as a prostitute and her father refused to have anything more to do with her (next paragraph).

(10) 1926—work on the permanent way from Zaria to Kaura Namoda in Sokoto Province was undertaken. The line passes through Giwa District and village area. 'Company' (H. *kumfani*) here refers to the Public Works Department.

(11) Cf. p. 128–9.

(12) For land law affecting this, see Ch. X, note 5.

(13) The tale of Hasana is most instructive and repays careful study. Briefly, it records behaviour which directly reverses the norms of institutionalized kinship, marriage and clientage relations in Hausa society. It is a record of consistent deviance, and it is interesting to note that Hasana's mother died early, and she grew up in the compound with her brother, her father, and his wives, far from her mother's or her father's kinsfolk. But her interest is not exhausted merely by considering her as psychologically aberrant; Hausa culture provides various roles for psychologically aberrant persons—the *bori* cult, prostitution (*karuwanci*) '*yan dauda* (homosexuals), clientage, to name a few. The story of Hasana has a greater significance as a consistent and often deliberate rejection of

the structural axioms of the society, combined with a skilful manipulation of these axioms and norms to produce certain situations and achieve certain ends in direct opposition to those which are normally associated with the manipulated principles. It is as a record of deliberate reversal of the structural principles and relations of her society that Hasana's tale has such value for the student of that society. Her behaviour, in terms of Hausa social norms, is systematically atypical and appalling.

(14) 'Fetching the horse's grass'—the standard phrase used in describing a domestic client's duties, where his senior is an official: politically important persons (office-holders and their principal unofficial agents) have horses, as a rule, whereas ordinary commoners do not usually have them.

(15) Well-diggers—of the Public Works Department.

CHAPTER XII

(1) *Danfangi*—title of Giwa *village* (not district) chiefs. See pp. 106, 240 *et al.*

(2) During the years since her divorce from Maigari, on real grounds of childlessness, Baba has come to realize that she may never bear children of her own. She is therefore anxious to adopt children (see Introduction) as well as to have an amiable co-wife to share the household duties, so that she may have some time to devote to her crafts in order to earn money for her own personal use. Her friend Adama had given evidence of fertility and was pregnant at the time, and from her point of view the offer was no doubt attractive; marriage to an official implies prosperity and high status, and she was sure of a welcome for her infant, Audi, whose father had died before he was born, and of a pleasant home with her friend Baba as co-wife.

(3) Birnin Gwari—an independent state in western Zaria Province, bordering on Giwa District.

(4) Pipe-players: the *algaita*, an instrument resembling an oboe, but making a sound more like bagpipes, which is played for certain officials. The Zaria title of *Fagaci* has a group of pipe-players attached to it.

(5) *Magatakarda*—title of a chief's Scribe, in this case the clerk of the District office, trained in a Government school and employed by the Native Authority. In the course of their employment, such clerks may be moved fairly frequently from one district to another in the emirate.

(6) Retainers or clients (*barori*, s. *bara*)—see Introduction, p. 31.

NOTES

(7) *Tsarance*, see note 6 of Chapter III.

(8) Cf. p. 147 and note 4, Ch. IX. This song of ridicule is traditional.

(9) I.e. the man concerned had only one wife, and she was suckling her child and therefore could not have sexual intercourse with him. Fatika is a village in western Giwa, formerly the centre of a vassal-state of Zaria.

(10) Cf. 140, 142, 169, 175. An important obligation of kinship is to give childless relatives one's offspring to adopt.

(11) Cf. Ruxton, op. cit., p. 306–7. An individual's oath on the Koran is sufficient evidence of guilt or innocence; the sanction against perjury is madness and early death, as this story illustrates. There was, however, a man living in Giwa who was said to have perjured himself several years ago; knowledge of this was widespread, and there was little doubt that retribution would be his lot in due course.

(12) For clientage, see Introduction. *Tax*—either Hasan was exempt on grounds of age, or Fagaci paid a nominal tax on his behalf. This passage illustrates how the traditional personal bond between lord and client still operates, despite changes in their official administrative relations and duties. It also shows the way in which these modern administrative tasks are executed in the context of the clientage relation, to which they are assimilated.

Maintenance of prisoners—a charge on the N.A. Treasury, for which the District Head makes claims in respect of prisoners kept in the district gaol. Fagaci Ahmadu, according to Baba, sent food over from his own household, and when the maintenance money came, gave it to his Warder; this and similar references illustrate the ideal of *noblesse oblige* which applies in proportion to the rank of a man, and which was said to have been characteristic of Ahmadu Rufa'i.

Prices of grain quoted give an approximate date to this passage, 1932–4.

(13) I.e. the cattle-keeping nomad Fulani. Cf. de Saint Croix, op. cit., p. 17. 'It is supposed in the case of [Bush] Fulani that, if imprisoned, their fortune is dissipated for ever.' Settled Fulani officials are well aware of this dislike of imprisonment among their nomadic cousins, and sometimes exploit it.

(14) *Rikida* (metamorphosis, particularly associated with the hyena) is a power Hausa believe certain neighbouring pagan tribes can exercise at will. For Hausa and Fulani to achieve it, apparently magical assistance, in the shape of *malams*' charms, is necessary.

(15) Before 1918. As Madaki Yero was dismissed before his father, Aliyu, Emir of Zaria, was deposed by the British in 1920, he could not have gone mad because of his father's misfortunes while he was still D.H. Giwa. Baba's frequent inaccuracies about well-known political events are significant and express one aspect of the general ignorance among Hausa women concerning the details of the political system and

BABA OF KARO

its history. As legal minors, they are politically disenfranchized and ineligible for any offices other than *magatiya* and *jakadiya* (cf. p. 235). Political matters are thus almost entirely a male interest and activity. On types of madness, cf. p. 155, and note 8, p. 276.

The contrast here is with traditional treatment of deposed kings and important title-holders, who were either permitted to remain in their own countries, or thereafter resided at Wurno in Sokoto—that is, in Hausaland. In the nineteenth century depositions of officials, including kings, were frequent events.

(16) Ahmadu Rufa'i, formerly the Ma'ajin Zazzau (N. A. Treasurer, Zaria) was appointed the Fagacin Zazzau in 1918 on the dismissal of the Madaki Yero, and put in charge of Giwa district which the Madaki had ruled. Hence if Baba's statement that she came to live in Giwa when Ahmadu had been Fagaci for a year is correct, and is taken in conjunction with other critical dates (e.g. marriage at fourteen, first divorce at seventeen, second divorce at thirty-two), the year of Baba's birth would be 1885. More likely, however, her arrival in Giwa is dated *c.* 1922 when Ahmadu had held the title for four years, and this is simply another instance of the general imprecision of her knowledge of political history.

Aminu is the son of Fagaci Ahmadu by a concubine; he remained in Giwa after his father's death, and is an official messenger of the present District Head, Fagaci Muhammadu.

(17) A *mudu* (the standard bowl measure) weight approx. 2·6 lb. 40 *mudu*—approx. 100 lb. daily or 36,500 lb. per year; perhaps 30,000 lb. a year or 14 tons was the approximate grain intake of Fagaci's household. On retainers (*barori*), see Introduction, p. 31, on *gandu*, see pp. 22 and 119. It is interesting to compare Fagaci's domestic arrangements with those of Ibrahim Dara's *gandu*, pp. 41–2. The farms referred to are attached to the office (*sarauta*), and the right of use is inherited not by Ahmadu's children but by his successor in the title.

(18) Concubines were women of slave status, and hence the practice of concubinage in N. Nigeria steadily declined as a consequence of the abolition of the legal status of slaves in Lugard's 'Slavery Proclamation'. See Burns, op. cit., p. 49 and footnote.

(19) Each year after harvest the District Head, accompanied by his staff and retainers, makes a complete circuit of his district, visiting all the principal towns in turn. He does not usually take any of his wives with him. The custom was introduced by the British Administration, which abolished the traditional fiefholders residing in the capital of the state, and replaced them by District Heads resident in their areas. The new offices are linked to traditional titles and the old political system.

(20) The titled pipe-players and drummers are political clients attached permanently to the title on a hereditary basis. The titular *Zagis* (footmen) are similar. A *Zagi* walks beside his lord's horse, acts as a groom, and may perform other menial tasks (farm labour, etc.) associated with

NOTES

'domestic' clientage. The musicians attached to the title by ties of political clientage act as agents of their lord in certain matters, and do not perform any menial work for him. On Thursday nights (the eve of the Muslim sabbath) and on the various ceremonial occasions, they make music for him, drumming, piping, and singing his praise-song.

(21) A Hausa never appears in public with his wife. This taboo is paralleled by the taboo between spouses on the use of each other's name.

(22) Ahmadu was among the first Hausa to graduate through a European type school, learning the Roman script, arithmetic, and similar skills. The school referred to was probably the School for the sons of Chiefs started by Hans Vischer at Kano.

(23) Chronology: F. Ahmadu, D. H. Giwa, 1918–42; F. Muhammadu. D. H. Giwa, 1942– ? Biography written December 1949–January 1950, This gives Baba's arrival in Giwa 1922 and her birth c. 1890. See pp. 64, 68, 186, 253 et al.

(24) For further comparisons of Old and New Giwa, see pp. 218., also speculations about the reasons for the move. The District Notebook of Giwa for this period records severe guinea-worm in the area as well as a high incidence of sleeping-sickness. New Giwa is a village planned on a model layout with numerous wells sunk by the P.W.D. The shortage of water at the old village was so great that despite the Hausa preference for wife-seclusion, the wives fetched water daily from a stream three or four miles distant. The Administration had been trying for years to persuade the people of Giwa village to move to a more healthy place, but there was considerable opposition.

(25) The failure of Old Giwa market may have been linked with the 'depression' and the fall of prices for Hausa export products, or the partial depopulation of North Giwa District which took place to escape conscription for labour on the main road and railway to Sokoto, or to the greater accessibility of nearby competing markets situated on the new main road, or, as the District Notebook for the period suggests, possibly to exactions made by the D.H.s retainers in the Giwa market. More likely than not each of these factors contributed. The failure of the market, which preoccupied community and D.H. alike, was the occasion for a prolonged nativistic reaction, in which the spirits were exhorted to revive the market at public community ceremonies. The market is a traditional Hausa institution of great significance, and despite the long centuries of Islamic proselytization in Hausaland, the market derives its mystical charter and its economic vitality from the traditional pre-Islamic spirits. The following accounts of market ceremonies illustrate vividly the great importance Hausa attach to commerce, and the indigenous pre-Islamic character of the market as an institution.

(26) 'They' in this context are the spirits (bori, iskoki), who are referred to respectfully in this indirect fashion.

(27) See map. New Giwa is sited beside Anguwan Shehu on the main

Sokoto-Zaria road, and shares the flourishing old market there. Later Baba remarks that the present Fagaci does not provide the spirits with their dues, but in this context she says he gave them cloth and milk **as** requested.

(28) *Goge*—a large single-stringed instrument played with a bow, and used in calling the spirits, each with his praise-song.

(29) Abdulkarim, the third Fulani ruler and the founder of the Katsinawa dynasty of Zazzau, ruled from 1834–46 and died at the site of New Giwa. He is remembered in Zaria as an especially pious king, a sort of Edward the Confessor, and is often referred to as a *wali*, a man in special favour with Allah; prayers and sacrifices are made at his grave. His dying remark (real or attributed) was that later generations would see an important town spring up around his tomb. At that time Giwa district **was** mainly uninhabited bush, peopled by the leopard and the elephant (*giwa*) from which it takes its name. The present Fagaci, who has close ties with the Katsinawa descendants of Abdulkarim, related that while searching for the site for the new town, his horse suddenly stopped and refused to budge an inch. Fagaci said that to save himself embarrassment, since he could not get the beast to move, he announced that this would be the site of New Giwa, and dismounted. He says he knew nothing of Abdulkarim's prophecy at that time. Thus a mystical sanction for the move to the new site has been provided. Also cf. p. 208.

CHAPTER XIII

(1) See Introduction, and pp. 198 sqq.

(2) Another institutionalized relation, this time with the woman older and senior, and the man (*kanen rana*—lit. younger brother of the day) as junior.

(3) Antimony on the eyes—an essential part of the Hausa toilet; cf. p. 126.

Ramatu—M. Tsoho's wife whom he called home by his magical powers, see pp. 134–7.

(4) *Dogarai*—N.A. police (nowadays known as *dan doka*).

(5) For *tsaranci* cf. note 6 to Chapter III.

(6) *Danmori* is the titular name of the favourite of a chief or king. The parties in this relation express their bond formally by giving each other new and private names. The way in which this relationship between two persons of different sex and generation is assimilated to that of adoptive mother and child is striking. The difference is that the relation is formed voluntarily by both parties and is a private one, not involving the junior's change of residence. The inequality of the partners distinguishes it from the *kawa* and *aboki* relationships described above. The junior's spouses also share his inferior status in the relation.

(7) In the formal initiation of this relationship, the proper behaviour is

an exaggeration of that between mother and daughter rather than between elder and younger sister, although the terms used are those of the latter relationship. Initially, and later on all ceremonial occasions, the junior behaves obsequiously to her senior, who sometimes calls her her *baraniya*—a female client (*bara*); the exaggerated emphasis on inequality of status imitates the formal aspects of differences in rank and political authority of men linked by relations of clientage. The *yaya-kanwa* relation between two women has no political function, but it provides the senior with prestige and a sense of superior status, which is expressed by gifts to the *kanwar rana* ('younger sister') of much greater value than any gifts or services received in return.

(8) Men of superior rank never visit men of inferior rank in their homes except on important ritual occasions such as marriages or naming-ceremonies (see Introduction, p. 12).

(9) The *rana* relation is asymmetrical and its parties are not equals; by contrast, the relation of bond-friendship is symmetrical in all respects, and *kawaye* are equals. Hence a woman's *kanwar rana* is inferior in status to her *kawa*.

(10) Three principles of female bond-friendship (*kawa*) are illustrated in the following incident: firstly, that bond-friends should all be equals in status and approximately equal in age; secondly, as bond-friends are by definition equals, all bond-friends of the same person are equals in status; thirdly, there is a limit, not precisely defined, to the number of bond-friendships a woman may have, beyond which her value as a bond-friend declines in rough ratio to the increase in her *kawaye*. This incident has greater interest in another way; Baba is the warder's wife, Jika is the wife of an important nobleman, the ruler of the district, holding one of the senior titles of the state; yet the difference in rank between the husbands of the two women is completely irrelevant, and the inferior's wife publicly shames the superior's wife for impropriety of her *kawa* relationships. The significance of this principle—that the husband's rank in no way affects his wife's status (though of course difference in rank of husbands is noted, cf. p. 199)—lies partly in the exclusion of women from political life and authority, but also in the structural conditions of Hausa polygamous marriage. Within a household wives are ranked by order of marriage to their common husband, the one married to him longest being senior. It is therefore impossible for them all to share equally in his status, since they are not equal to one another. Further, the frequency of divorce would make for confusion if wives publicly shared their husbands' status, or if a woman's status outside the household depended on her ranking in order of marriage within it. For women, the following criteria alone have a status significance: generation of birth; marital status; ethnic origin (e.g. Fulani or Habe) and status of paternal or maternal ancestors; wealth. In these terms, a woman married to a commoner may be equal in status to a nobleman's wife.

(11) Ceremonies—i.e. *buki*, the exchanges between *kawaye* on ceremonial occasions.

(12) Note that children by concubines are recognized in the same way as those by wives (cf. Aminu, pp. 186 and 209). The silver bracelets and anklets are a traditional part of the gifts a nobleman makes to his daughter on her marriage; the silver was mainly obtained by melting down Maria Theresa thalers, used as currency in the trans-Saharan trade in the nineteenth century.

(13) Jika was probably too old to re-marry. Wealthy and important men often 'pensioned off' their older wives in this way in order to marry younger women.

(14) I.e. the firstborn-avoidance is extended to the *kawa* of the mother, cf. pp. 140 and 144.

(15) This is the only reference to this relation of bond-friendship between persons of different sexes but like age encountered in one and a half years field work in Zaria. Possibly the relation is important and frequent among children and is linked with *tsarance* between children not betrothed to one another, but either lapses after marriage or gives rise to a later marriage between the bond-friends.

(16) Cf. pp. 93–5, 195–6, 244–5.

(17) I.e. Haba was employed by the Native Authority as school-teacher in the elementary school at Old Giwa.

(18) *Majidadi*—a title given to a favourite of a chief, a kind of steward or chamberlain. *Ma'aji*—formerly an official of the king's household—means Treasurer. Women may give their *kawaye* new private names when establishing a bond-friendship; titles are most often used when both bond-friends are wives of N.A. officials.

(19) Compare a new bride's silence in her husband's compound until he has 'bought her mouth' with gifts. Cf. p. 95.

(20) On relations of women to chiefs, cf. pp. 68, 105, 193, 235. Kakangi is a village-area in Giwa district. As District Head Giwa, the Fagaci appoints the chiefs of the village-areas in the district.

CHAPTER XIV

(1) See Introduction.

(2) This tale was quite well known in Giwa, and the various versions collected from different persons agree in the main elements, and the outline, though of course there was variation in the details.

(3) The word *gida* (compound) is here translated 'house' because in addition to its usual meaning it also has the connotation of the genealogical structure in which a man and his descendants are located; although Hausa kinship is predominantly bilateral, descent traced patrilineally is very important among the nobility, primarily in relation to political

NOTES

matters of competition for or succession to office. We are told here that the spirit of Fagaci Ahmadu's house followed him to Giwa from his family compound in Zaria City. Space forbids a discussion of 'inherited spirits' among the Muslim Hausa, but cf. Greenberg, op. cit., p. 44, for the spirits worshipped by patriclans among the Maguzawa, the pagan Hausa, who are organized in dispersed exogamous patriclans.

(4) Baba makes several propositions about Muhammadu's appointment as Fagaci (she speaks as the wife of an old client of the late incumbent): (a) The spirit of Ahmadu's house so terrified his unrelated successor that he decided to build the new town and live there; (b) Ahmadu's son Aminu did not succeed his father because he failed to carry out his obligations to the spirits; (c) Aminu had a right by descent to succeed his father as Fagaci. The last proposition is of course purely a political argument; titles in Zaria fall roughly into two classes, those customarily held by persons of royal rank (members of one of the four dynasties eligible to rule the state), and those customarily held by those of other families, usually Fulani, who are clients of the king. The title of Fagaci is one of the latter class, and Ahmadu Rufa'i's father did not hold it. Ahmadu himself being appointed by the Emir Aliyu to succeed Madaki Yero as D.H. Giwa. Baba's use of the term 'son of the house' to describe Aminu is also misleading, since the actual compound in Giwa belonged to the title Fagaci, and Aminu's own family compound was in Zaria City. For titles as permanent corporations with property attached, see Introduction, p. 30, and text, p. 207, distinction between Ahmadu's personal property and that belonging to the title.

Muhammadu formerly held the title of Sarkin Ayyuka (Master of Works) and was head of the N.A. branch of the Public Works Department; his experience and qualifications, which include some skill at surveying, fitted him to play an effective part in building the new model town whose creation had been discussed for some years past.

Baba, like many others who told a similar story, attributes the move from Old Giwa to Fagaci Muhammadu's fear of the frightful apparitions he saw in the official residence; but whereas other informants ascribed these apparitions to charms and 'medicine' (i.e. magic) which Ahmadu had buried in the compound to drive away an unrelated successor, Baba interprets them in terms of 'the spirits'. Magic and spirits provide alternative principles of interpretation over a very wide range of Hausa activities, the third principle being provided by Islam in the form of 'fate' as the will of Allah.

(5) For another version of 'the move to New Giwa' cf. p. 190.

(6) The alms (*sadaka*) are mainly distributed at a death on the seventh and fortieth days after it. Kin and friends of the deceased and his family bring gifts which are distributed to the *malams* and visitors. Besides these gifts, the widows prepare uncooked sweetened grain-flour (*cuge*) which is distributed among those who brought gifts.

(7) I.e. Hasan was one of the clients attached to the title whom Fagaci

Muhammadu inherited on arrival; since he had retired from the work of Warder he had moved from the prison compound to another compound shared with two more clients.

(8) Baba lived for some time with her younger brother Kadiri before remarrying; her fourth husband Ibrahim was also known as Dantsoho or Danauta, presumably because he was the son of his parents' old age (see next section).

CHAPTER XV

(1) Cf. pp. 142 and 211 on the final alms.

(2) Cf. pp. 104 and 129.

(3) *Pitilli*—not traceable botanically.

(4) Destiny: cf. end of note 4, Ch. XIV, on the three different principles of explanation used by Hausa. The utility of the concept of fate, destiny (*rabo*) is twofold—it explains all cases in which manipulation of the principles of medicine (magic) and animism (spirits) fail, while at the same time it demonstrates the superior authority of Islam, in Kadiriya terms of predestined fate as the will of Allah.

(5) Bakori is a town over the border in the neighbouring emirate of Katsina, so it could hardly be the capital of Giwa district in Zaria emirate; another example of Baba's ignorance of political affairs. For other versions of the reason for the move to New Giwa, see p. 188–90, 207 *et al*. Baba's varying accounts of the reason for the move seemed to depend on the aspect of it which was uppermost in her mind at the time she was talking; all the reasons she gives were also mentioned by other people at Giwa, who like Baba herself did not seem to feel that any inconsistency was involved.

(6) Cf. p. 190.

(7) The names are those of well-known spirits in the *bori* cult. Each has its traditional shrine and resting-place in the community, before which sacrifices are made when necessary by its devotees. Inna (a term of address for 'mother') is a Fulani spirit who presides over markets. The information about the box in which she was fetched was Baba's conjecture in response to a question.

(8) The adherents of the different explanatory principles (spirits, medicine and the will of Allah) carry on the competition between these principles on the practical plane. As head of the state, the Emir of Zaria is also leader of the Faithful, and the champion of Islam in its struggle with non-Islamic magico-religious practice and belief. The *volte-face* of Fagaci Muhammdu is therefore attributed to fear of his overlord.

(9) Cf. invoking the spirits to improve the market at Old Giwa—pp. 188-189.

(10) Fillata in Kano emirate and Makarfi in Zaria are very thriving neighbouring markets.

NOTES

(11) Kantomati—Hausa name for a particular District Officer. The practice of nicknaming is extended to Europeans, whose real names are usually too unfamiliar to be easily remembered.

(12) Reference is to pp. 207–10, *Maifitilla* and the apparitions.

(13) On inherited spirits, cf. p. 208. A *bori* adept's spirits are 'inherited' by kinsfolk who are themselves *bori* adepts.

(14) The term *karuwa* here means 'profligate person' rather than prostitute, since Ba'i is still married; however, the term prostitute is appropriate since she practised as such on her visits to Giwa town.

(15) *Danfangi*—title of Village Head, Giwa; *Madakin Danfangi*—title of one of his officials. Village titles repeat the pattern of the state titles.

(16) *Sarkin Fadan Fagaci*—title of one of Fagaci's hierarchy of subordinates, *Sarkin Fada*, like *Madaki*, *Galadima*, etc., being one of the general stock of Hausa titles.

(17) This incident illustrates the clash of the different cosmological principles. The District Head upholds Islam and bans *bori* sessions; the spirits reply by possessing a woman in his presence and threatening calamities if the order is not revoked. As women cannot be punished at law for these *bori* practices, or disobedience to the D.H.'s orders, the D.H. cannot effectively prohibit or suppress *bori*. The incident was relished by the women in the town, particularly since the spirit concerned was one of the 'Europeans' who have appeared among the traditional *bori* spirits of recent years, and are presumably not subject to the Native Authority.

(18) The genealogical connections of the principal spirits are always precise, though sometimes stated differently. Cf. Greenberg, op. cit., p. 38. The Maguzawa of Kano say that Dangaladima is the son of Malam Alhaji by Sarauniya (Queen). Muslim Hausa of Zaria, where *Dangaladima* is one of the royal ranks, often say that he is the son of the King of the Spirits (*Sarkin aljannu*). Note how a firstborn in the world of spirits avoids his father, as he does in human society.

(19) The competitors in this instance are N.A. and company employees of equal status. Incidents of this type are a re-enaction of the give-away contests of childhood where the boys compete for the girls' favours and the drummers stimulate the competition. The boys are now grown men and the girl is a *karuwa* (prostitute), and to the old aim of securing her favours is added the desire to proclaim publicly their status by generosity. The generalized account which follows is both graphic and accurate. In Giwa was situated the district *alkali's* court, and to the prostitutes who visited the town were added wives seeking divorce who whiled away the time until their cases could be heard.

(20) Jumau—the most prominent of Fagaci Muhammadu's political agents (*fudawa*, sing. *bafada*). His praise-song is apt, but is only sung behind his back: *Jumau zaki,*   Jumau the lion,
      Tsuntsu mai-cin mutane.   Worm, devourer of men!

(21) Cf. pp. 207–10.

(22) The Hausa woman's statement of her position.

(23) Cf. earlier account of installation of Magajiya at Zarewa, p. 64.

(24) Cf. note 19, p. 287. Petitioners for divorce often had to wait a day or two while witnesses were sent for.

(25) Sarkin Tandu—craft title, chief of the makers of antimony pouches.

(26) See compound diagram, p. 36. The hut in the forecourt (*dakin kofar gida*) is also referred to as the *dakin kwartanci* (hut of adultery).

(27) On ridicule, cf. pp. 147, 179.

(28) Chiefs are often referred to by the names of the communities over which they rule—'Zarewa' is the Chief of Zarewa. In this case the matter was beyond his powers, so he threatened to send the man to Kano City for trial, but a 'gift for the mouth' (*toshin baki*) persuaded him to drop the matter.

(29) On another of Fagaci Muhammadu's *jakadiya*, see p. 147. On officials and women in general, cf. note 20, Chapter XIII.

CHAPTER XVI

(1) This wife of Kadiri's with the children, who later married Sankira the brothel-keeper, can only be· Hasana's daughter Lauretu, see pp. 171–4. Both accounts, given in equal good faith on different occasions, are of value, and they supplement one another in an account of what was evidently a complex situation. Gwamma, like most Hausa wives in polygamous marriages, was using medicine against her co-wives. Meanwhile Hasana, settled in Sankira's compound, was urging her daughter Lauretu to leave Kadiri and come and marry Sankira. At first Kadiri protested to the *alkali*, and both the *alkali* and Fagaci forbade Lauretu to marry Sankira if she divorced Kadiri. But during the final stages of the trial in court, Kadiri declared that he did not wish to keep Yelwa, his daughter by Lauretu. The child was Baba's by adoption and he was probably aware that the *alkali* would award Baba custody of her; Hausa fathers do not lightly repudiate their children, and perhaps Kadiri hoped by such an extreme course to move Lauretu to remain with him, · or the judge to forbid the divorce. Kadiri's declaration was patent evidence to Baba, as it would have been to most Hausa women, that he was out of his senses, an effect which she naturally attributed to magic, clearly the magic of the jealous co-wife, Gwamma.

(2) This type of marriage, in which the wife continues to support herself and lives apart from her husband, is only practised by older people and is known as *auren daukisandanka* (marriage of take-up-your-stick) or *auren takalmi* (marriage of shoes) because of the distance that the spouses must go to visit one another.

(3) The majority of huts in this part of Hausaland are round with a

thatched roof; those with two stories and vaulted clay roofs are a sign of the owner's prosperity. Some thatched huts are also made which are rectangular, and there are one-storey huts, both round and rectangular, with vaulted clay instead of thatched roofs.

(4) *Danfangi*—title of village chief, Giwa village. Eligibility for appointment to titles was not always based on descent. The overlord invests a new official with his office by giving him a turban at a public ceremony.

(5) 'His time was finished'—another reference to fate. Turbe is a town in Kano country.

(6) Cf. p. 120.

(7) The work with Baba was completed in Zaria City, see Introduction.

(8) *Bidan aure*, repayment of expenses by the successful suitor to an unsuccessful one, includes the traditional gifts (*toshi*) given to the girl. Compare the following account of 'Yardada's first marriage, 1947–8, with that of Baba's in *c.* 1903, pp. 85–99. Although Baba presides over the marriage-arrangements of her adopted daughter, she continually consults 'Yardada's mother, Adama, and, as is correct, endeavours to place Hasana, the girl's father's sister, formally in charge of the ceremonies as the only representative of her father's family within reach.

(9) Though Baba correctly tried to place the bride's paternal kin, in the person of Hasana, in charge of the ceremonies, public opinion was against her, as Hasana's home is a brothel and her character is unsuitable. The attendance of the District Head and Judge at both ceremonies is an example of the manner in which they participate in community affairs, and in this case is an act of courtesy to the bridegroom's father, the village chief of the neighbouring village-area. The *mufti* is the *alkali's* judicial assessor or assistant; there are usually two to each Court.

(10) Baba implies that the ceremonial stages of marriage are passed through more quickly today than would be proper fifty years ago, when she was young, but it is possible that the time differences may be traditional variations of practice between Kano and Zaria.

(11) Talle is chosen to act as 'grandmother' as she is a joking relation of 'Yardada's, as also are grandparents. This joking relationship is of the kind between ethnic and occupational groups, not between real kinsfolk.

(12) In refusing, Hasana summarizes succinctly the functional canon of effective kinship in a bilateral system, as contrasted with the formal canon of unilineal descent systems. To paraphrase, 'Tsoho gave Baba to Hasan in marriage, and Hasan worked as a "kinsman" of Tsoho's over many years. Hence Tsoho became like Hasan's father, and thus Baba is as much 'Yardada's father's sister as Hasana herself.'

(13) Cf. pp. 93–5, 195–6, 202—'bride's slave'.

(14) Baba is acting here as paternal kinswoman of 'Yardada, and her brother Kadiri is *wali*, hence their compound is the 'paternal' compound from which the bride is taken to her husband's home.

(15) *Wasa-wasa*—see p. 95.

(16) *Kalkashi*—a variety of beniseed.

(17) Improper behaviour in the context of critical ritual is felt to be unpardonable. This was the only outburst of this kind of feeling that my wife ever heard from Baba.

(18) In Northern Nigeria, cotton is bought by weight for export at official gazetted markets, one of which was sited at New Giwa, 1948–9.

(19) Cf. p. 253.

(20) This explains why Mallam Aminu is asked to the discussions—he is the husband of Kadiri's wife Gwamma's kinswoman.

INDEX

INDEX

Dancing, 57–8, 60, 61, 87–8, 90, 96–8, and *passim*
  bori, 63–5
Dandada, 232
Dandare, 75
Dandaudu, 64, 65
Dangaladima Busa, 52, 223
Dangoshi, Danfangi, 240
Danjuma, 65, 148
Dankamuku, 119, 120
Dankiawa, 129, 151, 152
Dankurama, 46, 129
Dankusuba, 40, 62
Danmahawaye, 68, 167, 189
Danmakarfi, 201
Danmasugida, 163, 164
Dansarki, 134
Dantanbai, 148–9
Dantsoho, Ibrahim (Danauta), 159, 213, 239–40, 251, 252
Danyaya, 43
Danzan, 131
Dara, Ibrahim, 37, 38–40, 43, 44, 102, 107, 111, 157, 251
Dawaka, 131
Death, and burial, 74–5, 127–8, 207–8, 211–13
Dederi, 131
Destiny, 34, 165, 218, 240
Dije, 47, 49, 50, 51, 71, 77–9, 128, 130–1, 157, 251
Divorce, 25, 26–7, 107–8, 170–1, 231, and *passim*
Dogo, 64, 116
Dogon Jakada, 165–8, 173
Doka, 61, 80
Domestic equipment and utensils, 53, 95, 104, 114–15, 124, 248
Dongara, 159
Dowries, (*see also* Gifts)
  childbirth, 144, 145, 146
  marriage, 95–6, 104, 112, 114–15, 124, 248
Drummers and their songs, 56–8, and *passim*
  at public ceremonies, 25, 60–2, 86, 88–91, 93, 96, 97, 140–1, 144, 168, 171, 186, 188, and *passim*
  Chief of, 74–6, 77
  compound of the, 76–7
  sound war warnings, 69–71
Drumming, as a traditional occupation (*see also* Drummers), 17, 25, 76
  on calabashes, 115, 122, 125, 140–1, 151, 152–3, 172, and *passim*
Dry Season, 131, 155
Duma, Baba's marriage to, 76, 78, 102–7

Dundubus, 189
Dutsenkura, 52
Dyers, 17, 42

Eating, 270
Economic activities, 15–21
Education, *see* Koranic teaching and schools
Enugu, 17
Europeans, arrival of British, 66–8, 136, 156, 185, 187
  spirits of the, 209, 219

Facial marking, *see* Family marking
Family marking, 37, 43, 139, 141
Farakasa, 75
Farmers, (*see also* Agriculture), 16–17, 37–40, 102–3, 127, 156–7, and *passim*
Farming, *see* Agriculture
Fatika, 47, 68, 179, 184, 186, 198, 218, 219
Fatsuma, Baba's mother, 51, 71, 74–5, 76–9
Fatsuma, Dangaladima Busa's mother, 223
Feats, 122, 146, 207, and *passim*
  special dances for, 97, 98
Female messengers (jakadiya), 18, 235–6
Festival, Salla, 57, 74, 85, 86, 104, 157–8, 242, 249
  New Year, 61
Fiddlers, (*see also* Stringed instruments), 189
Fillata, 61–2, 221
Fishing, 16, 17
Food, 16, 41–2, 45, 52–4, 55, 97
  betrothal and marriage ritual, 86–92, 99, 112–18, 124, and *passim*
  childbirth ritual, 126, 139–40, 142–3, 144, 145, 249–50, and *passim*
  festival, 61
Forest Guard (Jumau), 225
Fornication, 233, 234
Foster-mothers, 143–4, and *passim*
Fulani, 15, 21–2, 27, 28, 29–30, 66, 67, 108
  and marriage with the Habe, 24, 102–3, 146
  avoidance-relationship of, 26
  Cattle or Bush, 17, 19, 20, 47, 98, 119, 127, 183
  Settled, 60, 127–8, 142, 144, 146
Funtua, 163, 181, 182, 187, 204, 236

Galadimawa, 186

INDEX

INDEX

INDEX

Yelwa, 171, 178, 180, 217, 218, 241, 251, 252, 253
Yelwa, Sarkin, *see* under Sarkin
Yusufu, Malam, 43

Zaila, 56, 57, 100, 201
Zakari, Malam, 167–8
Zarewa, Baba and her family in, 37–40, 43, 44, 51–2, 56–7, 106–7
bori dancers and prostitutes in, 43, 63–5, 224–9
Chiefs of, 64, 69–70, 72–3, 102, 103,

108, 154–5, 185, 240–1
children's play-associations at, 58–61
market, 85
raids and war on, 46, 66–73
Zaria City, 38–9, 66–7, 75, 155, and *passim*
Zaria State, 15, 21–2, 29–30, 52, 68, 72, 136, 183
Kings of, 29, 165, 187, 189
Zenabu, 225–6
Zetanku, 46, 88, 91